D0807307

CHRIST IS
PASSING BY

Josemaría Escrivá

CHRIST IS PASSING BY

HOMILIES

SCEPTER
Princeton

This edition of *Christ is Passing By* is published in the United States by Scepter Publishers, 20 Nassau St., Princeton NJ 08542.

This is a translation of *Es Cristo Que Pasa* (1973, Madrid).

ISBN 0-933932-04-9

The cover is a painting by Ugolino di Nerio *The Ascent to Calvary* (National Gallery, London).

With ecclesiastical approval

CONTENTS

THE AUTHOR

Blessed Josemaría Escrivá was born in Barbastro, in northern Spain, on January 9, 1902. At the age of 15 or 16, he began to feel the first intimations that God was calling him and he decided to become a priest. He started his ecclesiastical studies in the Seminary of Logroño in 1918, and later, in 1920, in that of St Francis de Paula in Saragossa, where from 1922 he was a superior or tutor. In 1923 he began to study Civil Law in the University of Saragossa, with the permission of his ecclesiastical superiors. These studies did not interfere with his theological studies. He was ordained deacon on December 20, 1924 and became a priest on March 28, 1925.

He began his work as a priest in the village of Perdiguera, within the diocese of Saragossa, and afterwards in Saragossa itself. In the spring of 1927, with the permission of the Archbishop of Saragossa, he moved to the Spanish capital Madrid and there carried out abundant priestly work among all kinds of people, devoting attention also to the poor and destitute in the outlying districts of the city, and especially to the incurably sick and the dying in the hospitals. He worked as chaplain to the *Patronato de Enfermos* (Foundation for the Sick), a welfare organization run by the Apostolic Sisters of the Sacred Heart. He also taught at a university academy, and continued his studies for a doctorate in Civil Law, which at that time could only be obtained from the University of Madrid.

On October 2, 1928, God made him see clearly what up to then he had only inklings of; and Blessed Josemaría Escrivá founded Opus Dei (in English, the Work of God). Under God's continuing guidance, on February 14, 1930 he understood that he must open up the apostolic work of Opus Dei to women also. As a result, a new path was opening up in the Church, to promote, among people of all social classes, the search for holiness and the practice of the apostolate, through the sanctification of ordinary work, in the midst of the world and without changing one's state in life.

From October 2, 1928, the Founder of Opus Dei directed his energies to the mission God had entrusted to him, with great apostolic zeal for all souls. In 1934 he was appointed Rector of the *Patronato de Santa Isabel* (St Elizabeth Foundation). During the Spanish Civil War, at times putting his life at risk, he carried out his priestly ministry in Madrid and, subsequently, in the northern city of Burgos. Already in those years Blessed Josemaría Escrivá experienced harsh and sustained opposition, which he bore calmly and with a supernatural outlook.

On February 14, 1943 he founded the Priestly Society of the Holy Cross, which is inseparably united to Opus Dei and which, as well as opening up the possibility of ordaining lay members of Opus Dei to the priesthood and incardinating them for the service of the Work, would later on also enable priests who are incardinated in dioceses to share the spirituality and asceticism of Opus Dei, seeking holiness in the exercise of their ministerial duties, while remaining exclusively under their respective Ordinaries.

In 1946 he took up residence in Rome, which was to be his home for the rest of his life. From there, he stimulated and guided the development of Opus Dei throughout the world, using all his energies to give to the men and women of Opus Dei a solid formation in doctrine, ascetical spirit and apostolate. At the time of his death, Opus Dei had more than 60,000 members from 80 different nationalities.

Msgr. Escrivá was a Consultor to the Pontifical Commission for the authentic interpretation of the Code of Canon Law, and to the Sacred Congregation for Seminaries and Universities. He was a Domestic Prelate and an honorary Academician of the Pontifical Roman Academy of Theology. He was also the Chancellor of the Universities of Navarre (in Spain) and Piura (in Peru).

Blessed Josemaría Escrivá died on June 26, 1975. For years, he had been offering his life for the Church and for the Pope. He was buried in the Crypt of the church of Our Lady of Peace, in Rome. Msgr. Alvaro del Portillo (1914-1994), who for many years had been his closest collaborator, was unanimously elected to succeed him. The present Prelate of Opus Dei is Msgr. Javier Echevarria, who also worked for several decades with Blessed Josemaría Escrivá and with his first successor, Msgr. del Portillo. Opus Dei, which from its inception had had the approval of the diocesan authorities and from 1943, also the *appositio manuum* and subsequently the approval of the Holy See, was established as a Personal Prelature by his holiness Pope John Paul II on November 28, 1982: this was the canonical formula foreseen and desired by Blessed Josemaría Escrivá.

The reputation for holiness which the Founder of Opus Dei enjoyed in his lifetime has spread after his death to the far corners of the earth, as can be seen from countless spiritual and material favors attributed to his intercession; among them, a number of cures which are medically inexplicable. Many letters from all the continents, and among them those of 69 Cardinals and nearly 1300 Bishops (more than a third of the episcopate worldwide), were written requesting the Pope to open the Cause of Beatification and Canonization of Msgr. Escrivá. The Congregation for the Causes of Saints gave its *nihil obstat* for the opening of the Cause on January 30, 1981 and this was ratified by Pope John Paul II on February 5, 1981.

Between 1981 and 1986 two processes took place, one in Rome and the other in Madrid, to gather information on the life and virtues of Msgr. Escrivá. Following the results of these two processes and accepting the favorable opinions of the congress of theological consultors and the Commission of Cardinals and Bishops, members of the Congregation for the Causes of Saints, the Holy Father, on April 9, 1990, declared the heroicity of the virtues of Msgr. Escrivá, who thus received the title of Venerable. On July 6, 1991, the Pope commanded the publication of a Decree declaring the miraculous nature of a cure attributed to the intercession of the Venerable Josemaría Escrivá. This act completed the juridical stages for the beatification of the Founder of Opus Dei, which was celebrated in Rome on May 17, 1992, in a solemn ceremony presided over by his holiness Pope John Paul II in St Peter's Square. From May 21, 1992, the body of Blessed Josemaría rests in the altar of the Prelatic Church of Our Lady of Peace, in the central offices of the Prelature of Opus Dei. It is accompanied constantly by the prayers and thanksgiving of many people from all over the world who have been brought closer to God, attracted by the example and teachings of the founder of Opus Dei and by the devotion of those who turn to his intercession.

Among his published writings, apart from the theological and legal study *La Abadesa de las Huelgas*, there are books of spirituality which have been translated into numerous languages: *The Way, Holy Rosary, Christ is Passing By, Friends of God, The Way of the Cross, Loving the Church, Furrow, The Forge* (the last five titles have been published posthumously). Another book, which brings together press interviews, has the title *Conversations with Msgr. Escrivá.*

FOREWORD

In introducing this first volume of collected homilies by Blessed Josemaría Escrivá I recall, particularly, something he has said over and over again to all sorts of people, from all over the world: "I am a priest, and all I can talk about is God." The Founder of Opus Dei was ordained on March 28, 1925. "Chosen from among men and appointed to act on behalf of men" (Heb 5:1), for almost fifty years he has helped bring Christianity alive in the minds and hearts of many people.

He has given expression to the fruitfulness of Christian priesthood, which is really the action of grace, through tireless preaching. It is not surprising that he says that "preaching is the great passion of priests in Opus Dei." Since 1925 Blessed Escrivá has carried out an intense pastoral activity: first in country parishes, later in Madrid, particularly in the poorer districts and hospitals; then, in the thirties, throughout Spain; and he moved to Rome in 1946, with people from every corner of the world.

I first came to know him in 1935, and he has always been the same—talking about God, trying to bring people closer to God, through catechism classes, days of recollection, retreats, spiritual guidance and short, pithy letters which have brought peace to many souls. When towards the beginning 1936 he began to feel ill, the diagnosis was, quite simply, that he was worn out. Sometimes he preached for as many as ten hours a day. He preached to the clergy of almost every diocese in Spain. The bishops invited him very often to preach to their clergy, and he would go all over the country by train, in the wretched trains of the time, at his own expense for no other compensation than the loving obligation of speaking about God.

"I remember now, quite clearly," he wrote, "that when I was a young priest I used to be given, quite often, two firm rules for 'getting ahead': the first was not to work, not to take on much apostolic activity because that would only give rise to all kinds of envy and enemies. The second was not to write because what one writes, even if written with precision and clarity, is usually misinterpreted. I thank God that I never followed that advice, and I am happy I did not become a priest to 'get ahead'."

If Blessed Escrivá has ignored both pieces of advice, he has quite forgotten the first: not to work.

And only his work, his daily apostolic activity, has prevented him from writing more, in benefit of souls. He has written two widely published books of spirituality—*The Way* and *Holy Rosary*—and various legal and theological studies. But the bulk of his writings consists in letters, instructions, and commentaries addressed to the members of Opus Dei, dealing only with spiritual subjects. Resisting any kind of publicity, he has rarely given interviews, despite repeated requests from the press, radio, and television of many countries; those few he has granted have been published in a book entitled *Conversations with Monsignor Escrivá*. But nearly fifty years' preaching has produced a great deal of material as yet unpublished; a small part of this makes up the present volume. Although these homilies need no special introduction, it may be useful to draw attention to certain characteristics found throughout this volume.

The first is their theological depth. They do not of course form any sort of treatise or study of any specific theme; they were preached, spoken, to people of varied cultural and social backgrounds, with a gift of tongues which makes them readily intelligible. However, the thoughts they contain are knitted together by a careful, loving knowledge of the word of God.

Note, for example, how the author comments on the Gospel. He never simply brings it in for show or in a hackneyed way. Each verse has been meditated frequently and yields new aspects hidden, perhaps, for centuries. He is familiar with our Lord, with his mother Mary, with St Joseph, with the first twelve Apostles, with Martha, Mary and Lazarus, with Joseph of Arimathea and Nicodemus, with the disciples of Emmaus and the holy women. He has come to know them through unending conversation, by placing himself in the Gospel, becoming one more among participants of the scenes. It is not surprising therefore that some of Blessed Escrivá's commentaries coincide with those made more than fifteen centuries ago by the early Christian writers. His quotations from the Fathers of the Church seem quite at home in the text of these homilies, fully in the mainstream of the Church's tradition.

A second characteristic is the immediate connection the homilies establish between the gospel teaching and the life of the ordinary Christian. They never lose themselves, are never theoretical or abstract; they do contain theory, but it always dovetails with everyday experience. Blessed Escrivá is never addressing a group of theorists or people merely curious about Christian spirituality. He is talking to real people who either already have God's life in their soul or are ready to approach God in response to an inkling of his love. He is not speaking to a particular audience made up only of women or men or students or laborers or professional people. He talks to all of them at one and the same time, convinced as he is that if the word of God is preached with Christ's love in one's heart, it will always find its way into every soul. The Holy Spirit moves souls intimately in a way you cannot defect from outside; it is he who lets the seed fall on good ground and yield a hundredfold.

A third characteristic is the style. It is perhaps the least important. Blessed Escrivá has a simple, direct, and easy style which helps each person to look at God and draw definite resolutions for his everyday life.

The homilies in this volume encircle the liturgical year, from Advent to the feast of Christ the King, but they do have certain themes in common. Their core is a sense of divine filiation— a constant note in the author's preaching. He continually echoes St Paul's message: "For all who are led by the Spirit of God are sons of God. For you did not receive the spirit of slavery to fall back into fear, but you have received the spirit of sonship. When we cry 'Abba! Father!,' it is the Spirit himself bearing witness with our spirit that we are children of God, and if children, then heirs, heirs of God and fellow heirs with Christ, provided we suffer with him in order that we may also be glorified with him" (Rom 8:14-17).

This text speaks to us about the Blessed Trinity, which is another frequent theme in these homilies. It also reminds us that Jesus Christ is the way leading to the Father through the Holy Spirit. He is our brother, our friend—*the* Friend—our master and lord and king. The Christian life, then, means being continuously in touch with Christ in the context of our ordinary life, without abandoning our rightful place. How does this contact take place? Blessed Escrivá explains very concisely: "In the bread and in the word."

The bread is the Eucharist. The founder of Opus Dei considers the Mass to be the "center and source of the Christian life." It is not just another thing; it is a permanent supernatural fact which influences our whole day. Two of these homilies deal directly with this central mystery of the faith: "The Eucharist, Mystery of Faith and Love" and "On the Feast of Corpus Christi." The author tells us: "God has decided to stay in the tabernacle, to nourish us, strengthen us, make us divine, and give effectiveness to our work and efforts. Jesus is at one and the same time the sower, the seed, and the final result of the sowing: the bread of eternal life."

The "word" is prayer. God speaks and we listen to him; God listens and we speak to him. Our prayer should be constant, like the beating of our heart, like the breathing of a soul in love. Blessed Escrivá explains: "So, when a Christian sets out on this way of continuous relationship with the Lord—and it is a way open to everyone, not a path for certain privileged people—his interior life grows; it becomes secure and firm; and he keeps up this fight, both lovable and demanding, by doing the will of God in everything."

We are invited to see man as a keeper of divine treasures. He really and truly receives Christ—his body, blood, soul, and divinity; he is the temple of the Holy Spirit; in him dwells the Blessed Trinity. But we carry these treasures in "earthen vessels" (2 Cor 4:7). And so, in a kind of constant background music, the author reminds us to be humble. Humility is not a sad, depressing virtue. We should have true humility, which consists in a knowledge of our human littleness alongside the infinite greatness of God *and* an awareness that God delights in his creatures and wants them to become Godlike.

Ordinary life, with its joys and sorrows, with its laughter and problems, takes on a new dimension: "height, and with it, perspective, weight, and volume" (*The Way*, 279). As the founder of Opus Dei put it in a homily addressed to some forty thousand people in 1967: "I assure you, my children, that when a Christian carries out with love the most insignificant daily action, that action overflows with the transcendence of God. That is why I have told you repeatedly and hammered away time and again at the idea that the Christian vocation consists in making heroic verse out of the prose of each day."

These homilies are full of that connection between the most ordinary—and therefore most human—of interests and the transcendence of God. Very calmly, without any controversy, they avoid the schizophrenic idea of holiness as an unstable balance between a "normal life" and a "spiritual life." At the same time the author resists any temptation to "spiritualize" human things by dismissing their complexity; what Blessed Escrivá calls the "risk of freedom" is preserved: "Heaven and earth seem to merge, my children, on the horizon. But where they really meet is in your hearts, when you sanctify your everyday lives."

"Sanctifying your everyday lives": with human and Christian integrity, with supernatural outlook. If all our life is prayer, that is, contact with God, in the bread and in the word, then we can understand how our work, the everyday activity which takes up most of our day, is also a continuous prayer. Work which is sanctified is a sanctifying thing in itself and gives us an opportunity to cooperate in the sanctification of others, with the help of God's grace.

Ordinary Christian life, consisting in work which is prayer and prayer which is work, becomes apostolate. Personal contact with God—"face to face, without any anonymity"—not only does not prevent us from caring about others; it is like a spring of water that cannot but overflow, for the good of all men. Blessed Escrivá tells us: "Some people try to build peace in the world without welcoming God's love into their own hearts. How could they possibly achieve peace in that way? Christ's peace is the peace of Christ's kingdom, and our Lord's kingdom has to be based on a desire for holiness, a humble readiness to receive grace, an effort to establish justice, a divine outpouring of love."

These are some of the main ideas running through the homilies published in this volume, but in an introduction something more must be said. Certain qualities of the author's preaching are difficult, to grasp in a printed text: his humanity, his captivating sincerity, the way he gives himself to those listening, his constant reminder that we should be making our own personal prayer to God, "shouting silently." His warm realism, neither naive nor studied. A very uncommon common sense. Good humor which cannot contain itself, an infectious joy which belongs to a son of God.

Very many people have personally experienced Blessed Escrivá's preaching. Although he is not keen on publicity, he is always ready to reply to those who ask him about God. During a visit to France, Spain, and Portugal in 1972, he spoke to over one hundred and fifty thousand people, in groups of varying size. In 1970 in Mexico he met some forty thousand people, from Mexico, Canada, the United States and many Latin American countries. And in Rome many thousands of people from near and far have heard him say: "All honest human work, be it intellectual or manual, should be done with the greatest perfection possible... Human work done in this manner, no matter how humble or insignificant it may seem, helps to shape the world in a Christian way. The world's divine dimension is made more visible, and our human labor is thus incorporated into the marvelous work of creation and redemption. It is raised to the order of grace. It is sanctified and becomes God's work, *operatio Dei, opus Dei.*"

Those who read these homilies, remembering their author as a priest who speaks only about God, will readily grasp other features of Blessed Escrivá pastoral work: his clear awareness of being simply an instrument in our Lord's hands; his supernatural conviction that personal weaknesses and shortcomings—which, he reminds us, we will always have—must not keep us from Christ. Rather they are a stimulus to get closer to him. In a still unpublished homily he says: "In no sense do I put up with our Lord; it is he who puts up with me and helps me and encourages me and waits for me." And then, turning to his listeners: "How could I fail to understand your failings, when I am full of them myself?"

Another constant in all these homilies is a love for personal freedom. He says: "Freedom is very close to my heart... The spirit of Opus Dei, which I have tried to practice and to teach for more than thirty-five years, has made me understand and love personal freedom. When God our Lord gives men his grace, when he calls us by a specific vocation, it is as if he were stretching out his hand to us, in a fatherly way, a strong hand, full of love, because he seeks us out individually, as his own sons and daughters, knowing our weakness. Our Lord expects us to make an effort and show that we are free."

If God respects our personal freedom, how could we fail to respect the freedom of others, particularly in those very wide areas which admit of a pluralism of opinion and action? Elsewhere the author has written: "There are no dogmas in temporal affairs. To try to set up absolute truths in matters where the individual has to try to see things from his own point of view, in terms of his own interest, his cultural preference, and his own experience: this insults the dignity of man. Any attempt to lay down dogmas in the temporal sphere leads, inevitably, to coercing the conscience of others, to a failure to respect one's neighbor."

I hope it will not be long before a second volume of homilies appears. It will give us another opportunity to consider the ever present redemption in the words of a man convinced that "in the spiritual life there is no new era to come. Everything is already there: in Christ who died and rose again, who lives and stays with us always. But we have to join him through faith, letting his life show forth in ours to such an extent that each Christian is not simply *alter Christus*: another Christ, but is *ipse Christus*: Christ himself."

Alvaro del Portillo
Rome, January 9, 1973

THE CHRISTIAN VOCATION*

The liturgical year is beginning, and the **1** introit of the Mass invites us to consider something closely related to the beginning of our Christian life: the vocation we have all received. "Make me to know your ways, O Lord; teach me your paths."[1] We ask the Lord to guide us, to show us his footprints, so we can set out to attain the fullness of his commandments, which is charity.[2]

In considering the circumstances surrounding your decision to make every effort to live your faith, I imagine that you, like me, will

*A homily given on December 2, 1951, the first Sunday in Advent.

[1] Ps 24:4: *Vias tuas, Domine, demonstra mihi, et semitas tuas edoce me.*

[2] Cf. Mt 22:37; Mk 12:30; Lk 10:27.

thank our Lord. I know too that, without falling
into false humility, this thankfulness will leave
you even more convinced that you have
merited nothing of this on your own. Usually
we learn to invoke God as a young child from
our Christian parents. Later, teachers, friends,
and acquaintances have helped us in many
ways not to lose sight of our Lord.

Open your own heart to Jesus and tell him
your story. I don't want to generalize. But one
day perhaps an ordinary Christian, just like
you, opened your eyes to horizons both deep
and new, yet as old as the Gospel. He suggested
to you the prospect of following Christ earnestly, seriously, of becoming an apostle of
apostles. Perhaps you lost your balance then
and didn't recover it. Your complacency wasn't
quite replaced by true peace until you freely
said "yes" to God, because you wanted to,
which is the most supernatural of reasons. And
in its wake came a strong, constant joy, which
disappears only when you abandon him.

I don't like to speak of someone being
singled out to be part of a privileged elect. But
it is Christ who speaks, who chooses. It is the
language of holy Scripture: "He chose us in him
before the foundation of the world, that we

should be holy," St Paul tells us.[3] I know that such thoughts don't fill you with pride nor lead you to think yourself better than other men. That choice, the root of our vocation, should be the basis of our humility. Do we build monuments to an artist's paintbrush? Granted the brush had a part in creating masterpieces, but we give credit only to the painter. We Christians are nothing more than instruments in the hands of the creator of the world, of the redeemer of all men.

THE APOSTLES WERE ORDINARY MEN

I'm greatly encouraged whenever I consider a written precedent for what we have been talking about. We find it, step by step, in the Gospel's account of the vocation of the first twelve. Let's meditate on it slowly, asking those holy witnesses of our Lord to help us follow Christ as they did.

The first Apostles, for whom I have great affection and devotion, were nothing to boast

[3] Eph 1:4: *Elegit nos in ipso ante mundi constitutionem ut essemus sancti.*

about, humanly speaking. With the exception
of Matthew, who probably earned a comfortable living which he left behind at the behest
of Jesus, the Apostles were mere fishermen.
They eked out a meager existence, fishing all
night to keep food on the table.

But social status is unimportant. They
weren't educated; they weren't even very
bright, if we judge from their reaction to
supernatural things. Finding even the most
elementary examples and comparisons beyond
their reach, they would turn to the Master and
ask: "Explain the parable to us."[4] When Jesus
uses the image of the "leaven" of the Pharisees,
they think that he's reproaching them for not
having purchased bread.[5]

They were poor; they were ignorant. They
weren't very simple or open. But they were
even ambitious. Frequently they argued over
who would be the greatest when—according to
their understanding—Christ would definitely
restore the kingdom of Israel. Amid the intimacy of the last supper, during that sublime
moment when Jesus is about to immolate

---

[4] Mt 13:36: *Domine, edissere nobis parabolam.*
[5] Cf. Mt 16:6-7.

himself for all of humanity, we find them arguing heatedly.[6]

Faith? They had little. Jesus Christ himself points this out.[7] They had seen the dead raised, all kinds of sicknesses cured, bread and fish multiplied, storms calmed, devils cast out. Chosen as the head, St Peter is the only one who reacts quickly: "You are the Christ, the Son of the living God."[8] But it is a faith beset by limitations, which led Peter to reproach Jesus Christ for his desire to suffer and die for the redemption of men. And Jesus had to upbraid him: "Get behind me, Satan! You are a hindrance to me; for you are not on the side of God, but of men."[9]

"Peter was too human in his thinking," St John Chrysostom comments, "and therefore he reasons that those things (Christ's passion and death) were unworthy of him, something deplorable. Consequently, Jesus reprimands him and says: No, suffering is not beneath me; you only think so because your mind is limited

---

[6] Cf. Lk 22:24-27.
[7] Cf. Mt 14:31; 16:8; 17:19; 21:21.
[8] Mt 16:16.
[9] Mt 16:23.

to human thoughts."[10] And did these men of little faith at least stand out in their love for Christ? Undoubtedly, they loved him, at least in word. At times they were swept away by enthusiasm: "Let us also go, that we may die with him."[11] But at the moment of truth, they all fled, except for John who truly loved with deeds. Only this adolescent, youngest of the Apostles, can be found next to the cross. The others didn't find within themselves that love as strong as death.[12]

These were the disciples called by our Lord. Such stuff is what Christ chose. And they remain just like that until they are filled with the Holy Spirit and thus become pillars of the Church.[13] They are ordinary men, complete with defects and shortcomings, more eager to say than to do. Nevertheless, Jesus calls them to be fishers of men,[14] co-redeemers, dispensers of the grace of God.

3   Something similar has happened to us. With little effort we could find among our family,

---

[10] In Matthaeum homiliae 54, 4 (PG 58, 537).
[11] Jn 11:16.
[12] Song 8:6.
[13] Cf. Gal 2:9.
[14] Mt 4:19.

friends and acquaintances—not to mention the crowds of the world—so many worthier persons that Christ could have called. Yes, persons who are simpler and wiser, more influential and important, more grateful and generous.

In thinking along these lines, I feel embarrassed. But I also realize that human logic cannot possibly explain the world of grace. God usually seeks out deficient instruments so that the work can more clearly be seen to be his. It is with trembling that St Paul recalls his vocation: "And last of all, as by one born out of due time, he was seen also by me. For I am the least of the apostles, and am not worthy to be called an apostle, because I persecuted the Church of God."[15] Thus writes Saul of Tarsus, whose personality and drive fill history with awe.

As I said before, we have merited nothing. Before God called us, there was nothing more than personal wretchedness. Let us realize that the lights shining in our soul (faith), the love wherewith we love (charity), and the desire sustaining us (hope) are all free gifts from God. Were we not to grow in humility, we would

---

[15] 1 Cor 15:8-9.

soon lose sight of the reason for our having
been chosen by God: personal sanctity.

If we are humble, we can understand all the
marvel of our divine vocation. The hand of
Christ has snatched us from a wheat field; the
sower squeezes the handful of wheat in his
wounded palm. The blood of Christ bathes the
seed, soaking it. Then the Lord tosses the wheat
to the winds, so that in dying it becomes life
and in sinking into the ground it multiplies
itself.

NOW IS THE HOUR FOR US TO RISE

4   The epistle of today's Mass reminds us that
we are to acknowledge this responsibility of
apostles with new spirit, with desires, fully
awake. "It is now the hour for us to rise from
sleep, because now our salvation is nearer than
when we came to believe. The night is far
advanced; the day is at hand. Let us therefore
lay aside the works of darkness, and put on the
armor of light."[16]

You might tell me that it isn't easy, and you
are right. The enemies of man—the enemies of

[16] Rom 13:11-12.

his sanctity—try to deny him this new life, this putting on of the spirit of Christ. I can find no better summary of the obstacles to Christian fidelity than that of St John. "Because all that is in the world is the lust of the flesh, and the lust of the eyes, and the pride of life."[17]

Lust of the flesh is not limited to the dis- 5 ordered tendencies of our senses in general, nor to the sexual drive, which ought to be directed and is not bad in itself, since it is a noble human reality that can be sanctified. Note, therefore, that I never speak of impurity, but of purity, because Christ is speaking to all of us when he says: "Blessed are the clean of heart, for they shall see God."[18] By divine vocation, some are called to live this purity in marriage. Others, foregoing all human love, are called to respond solely and passionately to God's love. Far from being slaves to sensuality, both the married and the unmarried are to be masters of their bodies and hearts in order to give themselves unstintingly to others.

Whenever I talk about the virtue of purity, I usually qualify it by calling it *holy* purity.

[17] 1 Jn 2:16: *Concupiscentia carnis, concupiscentia oculorum et superbia vitae.*
[18] Mt 5:8.

Christian purity, holy purity, is not the same as priding oneself on feeling "pure", uncontaminated. We must realize we have feet of clay,[19] although the grace of God rescues us day by day from the dangers of the enemy. Those who write or preach almost exclusively on this topic are deforming Christianity, in my view, for they forget other virtues so important to the Christian and also to our life in society.

Holy purity is not the only nor the principal Christian virtue. It is, however, essential if we are to persevere in the daily effort of our sanctification. If it is not lived, there can be no apostolic dedication. Purity is a consequence of the love that prompts us to commit to Christ our soul and body, our faculties and senses. It is not something negative; it is a joyful affirmation.

Earlier I said that lust of the flesh is not limited to disordered sensuality. It also means softness, laziness bent on the easiest, most pleasurable way, any apparent shortcut, even at the expense of infidelity to God.

To abdicate in this way is equivalent to letting oneself fall completely under the impe-

---

[19] Dan 2:33.

rious sway of the law of sin, about which St Paul warned us: "When I wish to do good I discover this law, namely, that evil is at hand for me. For I am delighted with the law of God according to the inner man, but I see another law in my members, warring against the law of my mind and making me prisoner to the law of sin... Unhappy man that I am! Who will deliver me from the body of this death?"[20] But listen to the answer of the Apostle: "The grace of God through Jesus Christ our Lord."[21] We can and ought to fight always to overcome the lust of the flesh, because, if we are humble, we will always be granted the grace of our Lord.

St John tells us that the other enemy is the 6 lust of the eyes, a deep-seated avariciousness that leads us to appreciate only what we can touch. Such eyes are glued to earthly things and, consequently, they are blind to supernatural realities. We can, then, use this expression of sacred Scripture to indicate that disordered desire for material things, as well as that deformation which views everything around

---

[20] Rom 7:21-24.
[21] Rom 7:25.

us—other people, the circumstances of our life and of our age—with just human vision.

Then the eyes of our soul grow dull. Reason proclaims itself sufficient to understand everything, without the aid of God. This is a subtle temptation, which hides behind the power of our intellect, given by our Father God to man so that he might know and love him freely. Seduced by this temptation, the human mind appoints itself the center of the universe, being thrilled with the prospect that "you shall be like gods."[22] So filled with love for itself, it turns its back on the love of God.

In this way does our existence fall prey unconditionally to the third enemy: pride of life. It's not merely a question of passing thoughts of vanity or self-love, it's a state of general conceit. Let's not deceive ourselves, for this is the worst of all evils, the root of every false step. The fight against pride has to be a constant battle, to such an extent that someone once said that pride only disappears twenty-four hours after each of us has died. It is the arrogance of the Pharisee whom God cannot transform because he finds in him the obstacle

[22] Gen 3:5.

of self-sufficiency. It is the haughtiness which leads to despising other men, to lording it over them, to mistreating them. For "when pride comes, then comes disgrace."[23]

THE MERCY OF GOD

Today marks the beginning of Advent. And 7 it is good for us to consider the wiles of these enemies of the soul: the disorder of sensuality and easy-going superficiality, the folly of reason that rejects God, the cavalier presumption that snuffs out love for both God and creatures. All these obstacles are real enough, and they can indeed cause us a great deal of trouble. For these very reasons the liturgy invites us to implore divine mercy: "To you, O Lord, I lift up my soul. O my God, in you I trust, let me not be put to shame; let not my enemies exult over me"[24] as we prayed in the introit. And in the offertory we shall go back to the same idea: "Let none that wait for you be put to shame."

[23] Prov 11:2.
[24] Ps 24:1-3.

Now that the time of our salvation is approaching, it is consoling to hear from the lips of St Paul that "when the goodness and kindness of God our Savior appeared, he saved us, not by the works of justice which we have done, but according to his mercy."[25]

If you leaf through the holy Scripture, you will discover constant references to the mercy of God. Mercy fills the earth.[26] It extends to all his children,[27] and is "all around us."[28] It "watches over me."[29] It "extends to the heavens"[30] to help us, and has been continually "confirmed".[31] God in taking care of us as a loving father looks on us in his mercy[32]—a mercy that is "tender,"[33] welcome as "rainclouds."[34]

The life of Jesus Christ is a summary and compendium of the story of divine mercy: "Blessed are the merciful, for they shall obtain mercy."[35] And on another occasion our Lord said: "Be merciful, therefore, even as your

25 Tit 3:4-5.   31 Ps 116:2.
26 Ps 32:5.   32 Ps 24:7.
27 Sir 18:12.   33 Ps 108:21.
28 Ps 31:10.   34 Sir 35:26.
29 Ps 58:11.   35 Mt 5:7.
30 Ps 35:8.

Father is merciful."[36] Many other scenes of the Gospel have also made a deep impact on us, such as his forgiveness of the adulterous woman, the parable of the prodigal son, that of the lost sheep, that of the pardoned debtor, the resurrection of the son of the widow at Naim.[37] How many reasons based on justice could Christ have found to work this great wonder! The only son of that poor widow had died, he who gave meaning to her life, he who could help her in her old age. But Jesus didn't perform the miracle out of justice, but out of compassion, because his heart was moved by human suffering.

What security should be ours in considering the mercy of the Lord! "He has but to cry for redress, and I, the ever merciful, will listen to him."[38] It is an invitation, a promise that he will not fail to fulfill. "Let us therefore draw near with confidence to the throne of grace, that we may obtain mercy and find grace to help in time of need."[39] The enemies of our sanctification will be rendered powerless if the mercy of God

---

[36] Lk 6:36.
[37] Lk 7:11-17.
[38] Ex 22:27.
[39] Heb 4:16.

goes before us. And if through our own fault
and human weakness we should fall, the Lord
comes to our aid and raises us up. "You had
learned to avoid negligence, to flee from arrogance, to grow in piety, not to be a prisoner
of worldly matters, to prefer the eternal to the
passing. But since human weakness cannot
maintain a steady pace in such a slippery
world, the good doctor has prescribed remedies
for not getting lost and the merciful judge has
not led you to despair of pardon."[40]

RESPONDING TO GOD

8   It is under the "umbrella" of God's mercy
that Christian existence should develop. Ever
mindful of that, the Christian should strive to
behave as a child of God. And what are the
principal means to ensure that our vocation
takes root? Today let me point out two of them,
which are like living supports of Christian
conduct: interior life and doctrinal formation,
the deep knowledge of our faith.

---

[40] St Ambrose, *Expositio Evangelii secundum Lucam*, 7 (PL
15, 1540).

First of all, interior life. How few really understand this! If they hear about the interior life, they imagine some dark church. For more than a quarter of a century I have been saying that such isn't the case. I talk about the interior life of ordinary Christians who habitually find themselves in the hubbub of the city, in the light of day, in the street, at work, with their families or simply relaxing; they are centered on Jesus all day long. And what is this except a life of continuous prayer? Isn't it true that you have seen the need to become a soul of prayer, to reach an intimacy with God that leads to divinization? Such is the Christian faith as always understood by souls of prayer— "A man becomes God," writes Clement of Alexandria, "because he loves whatever God loves."[41]

At first it will be more difficult. You must make an effort to seek out the Lord, to thank him for his fatherly and practical concern for us. Although it is not a question of sentiment, little by little the love of God makes itself felt like a rustle in the soul. It is Christ who pursues us lovingly: "Behold, I stand at the door and

---

[41] *Paedagogus*, 3, 1, 1, 5 (PG 8, 556).

knock."[42] How is your life of prayer going? At times don't you feel during the day the impulse to speak more at length with him? Don't you then whisper to him that you will tell him all about it later, in a heart-to-heart conversation?

In the periods expressly reserved for this rendezvous with our Lord, the heart is broadened, the will is strengthened, the mind, helped by grace, fills the world of human reality with supernatural content. The results come in the form of clear, practical resolutions to improve your conduct, to deal more charitably with all men, to spare no efforts—like good athletes—in this Christian struggle of love and peace.

Prayer then becomes continuous, like the beating of our heart, like our pulse. Without this presence of God, there is no contemplative life. And without contemplative life, our working for Christ is worth very little, for vain is the builder's toil if the house is not of the Lord's building.[43]

[42] Rev 3:20.
[43] Cf. Ps 126:1.

THE SEASONING OF MORTIFICATION

In order to reach sanctity, an ordinary 9
Christian—who is not a religious—has no
reason to abandon the world, since that is
precisely where he is to find Christ. He needs
no external signs, such as a habit or insignias.
All the signs of his dedication are internal: a
constant presence of God and a spirit of
mortification. As a matter of fact, only one thing
is necessary, because mortification is nothing
more than prayer of the senses.

The Christian vocation is one of sacrifice,
penance, expiation. We must make reparation
for our sins—for the many times we turned our
face aside so as to avoid the gaze of God—and
all the sins of mankind. We must try to imitate
Christ, "always carrying about in our body the
dying of Christ," his abnegation, his suffering
on the cross, "so that the life also of Jesus may
be made manifest in our bodies."[44] Our way is
one of immolation and, in this denial, we find
gaudium cum pace, both joy and peace.

We do not look upon the world with a
frown. Some biographers of saints have in the

[44] 2 Cor 4:10.

past been interested only in highlighting extraordinary things in the lives of God's servants, from even their earliest days in the cradle. They have, unintentionally perhaps, done a disservice to Christian truth. They even said of some of them that as babies they did not cry, nor drink their mother's milk on Fridays, out of a spirit of penance. You and I came into this world crying our heads off, and we most assuredly drank our milk in total disregard for fasts and ember days.

Now, we have learned to discover, with the help of God, in the succession of apparently similar days, a time for true penance, and in these moments we resolve to improve our life. This is the way to ready ourselves for the grace and inspirations of the Holy Spirit in our soul. And with that grace, I repeat, comes *gaudium cum pace*:[45] joy, peace and perseverance in our struggle.

Mortification is the seasoning of our life. And the best mortification is that which over-

---

[45] "Gaudium cum pace, emendationem vitae, spatium verae poenitentiae, gratiam et consolationem Sancti Spiritus, perseverantiam in bonis operibus, tribuat nobis omnipotens et misericors Dominus. Amen." (*Breviarium Romanum*, preparatory prayer for holy Mass).

comes the lust of the flesh, the lust of the eyes, and the pride of life in little things throughout the day. Ours should be mortifications that do not mortify others, and which give us more finesse, more understanding, and more openness in our dealings with everybody. You are not mortified, if you are touchy; if your every thought is for yourself; if you humiliate others; if you don't know how to give up what is unnecessary and, at times, what is necessary; if you become gloomy because things don't turn out the way you had hoped. On the other hand, you can be sure you are mortified, if you know how to make yourself "all things to all men, in order to save all."[46]

BELIEF AND REASON

A life of prayer and penance, together with an awareness of our divine filiation, transforms us into Christians whose piety is truly deep. We become little children at the feet of God. Piety is the virtue of children. And if the child is to take refuge in the arms of his father, he must be, and know that he is, small, needy. I have

[46] 1 Cor 9:22.

often meditated on this life of spiritual childhood, which is not incompatible with fortitude,
because it demands a strong will, proven
maturity, an open and firm character.

We are to be pious, then, as pious as children, but not ignorant. Insofar as possible, each
of us should study the faith seriously, rigor-
ously—all of which means theology. Ours
should be the piety of children and the sure
doctrine of theologians.

Our desire to advance in theological knowledge, in sound, firm *Christian doctrine* is
sparked, above all, by the will to know and love
God. It likewise stems from the concern of a
faithful soul to attain the deepest meaning of
the world, seen as coming from the hands of
God. Every now and then, monotonously
sounding like a broken record, some people try
to resurrect a supposed incompatibility between faith and science, between human
knowledge and divine revelation. But such
incompatibility could only arise—and then only
apparently—from a misunderstanding of the
elements of the problem.

If the world has come from God, if he has
created man in his image and likeness[47] and

[47] Gen 1:26.

given him a spark of divine light, the task of our intellect should be to uncover the divine meaning imbedded in all things by their nature, even if this can be attained only by dint of hard work. And with the light of faith, we also can perceive their supernatural purpose, resulting from the elevation of the natural order to the higher order of grace. We can never be afraid of developing human knowledge, because all intellectual effort, if it is serious, is aimed at truth. And Christ has said, "I am the truth."[48]

The Christian must have a hunger to know. Everything, from the most abstract knowledge to manual techniques, can and should lead to God. For there is no human undertaking which cannot be sanctified, which cannot be an opportunity to sanctify ourselves and to cooperate with God in the sanctification of the people with whom we work. The light of the followers of Jesus Christ should not be hidden in the depths of some valley, but should be placed on the mountain peak, so that "they may see your good works and give glory to your Father in heaven."[49]

[48] Jn 14:6: *Ego sum veritas.*
[49] Mt 5:16.

To work in this way is to pray. To study thus is likewise prayer. Research done with this spirit is prayer too. We are always doing the same thing, for everything can be prayer, all activity can and should lead us to God, nourish our intimate dealings with him, from morning to night. Any honorable work can be prayer and all prayerful work is apostolate. In this way the soul develops a unity of life, which is both simple and strong.

ADVENT IS A TIME FOR HOPE

11 I don't wish to go on any longer on this first Sunday of Advent, when we begin to count the days separating us from the birth of the Savior. We have considered the reality of our Christian vocation: how our Lord has entrusted us with the mission of attracting other souls to sanctity, encouraging them to get close to him, to feel united to the Church, to extend the kingdom of God to all hearts. Jesus wants to see us dedicated, faithful, responsive. He wants us to love him. It is his desire that we be holy, very much his own.

You see within yourselves, on the one hand, pride, sensuality, boredom, and selfishness; on the other, love, commitment, mercy, humility, sacrifice, joy. You have to choose. You have been called to a life of faith, hope and charity. You cannot seek lesser goals, condemning yourself to a life of mediocre isolation.

Some time ago I saw an eagle shut up in an iron cage. It was dirty, and half its feathers were missing. In its claws was a piece of carrion. I then thought what would happen to me were I to renounce my vocation from God. I felt sorry for that lonely, fettered bird, born to soar the heavens and gaze at the sun. We too can scale the "humble heights" of love for God, of service to all men. However, in order to do this, we must make sure that our souls have no nooks or crannies into which the light of Jesus Christ cannot shine. And then Christ will be in your mind, on your lips, in your heart, stamped on your deeds. All of your life will be full of God—in its sentiments, its works, its thoughts and its words.

"Look up, and lift up your heads, because your redemption is at hand,"[50] we have just read in the Gospel. This time of Advent is a time for hope. These great horizons of our

[50] Lk 21:28.

Christian vocation, this unity of life built on the presence of God our Father, can and ought to be a daily reality.

Ask our Lady, along with me, to make it come true. Try to imagine how she spent these months, waiting for her Son to be born. And our Lady, Holy Mary, will make of you *alter Christus, ipse Christus*: another Christ, Christ himself!

CHRIST TRIUMPHS
THROUGH HUMILITY*

"This day shall light shine upon us; for the [12] Lord is born to us."[1] This is the great announcement which moves Christians today. Through them it is addressed to all mankind. God is here. This truth should fill our lives, and every Christmas should be for us a new and special meeting with God, when we allow his light and grace to enter deep into our soul.

We stop in front of Mary, Joseph, and the Child, looking at the Son of God who has taken on our flesh. I remember now a visit I made—for a very special reason—to the holy house of Loreto, Italy, on August 15, 1951. I said Mass there. I wanted to say it calmly and reverently, but I hadn't counted on the crowd's fervor. I

* A homily given on December 24, 1963.
[1] Is 9:2 (introit of second Mass of Christmas Day): *Lux fulgebit hodie super nos, quia natus est Dominus.*

had forgotten that the faith of the people of the region and their love for the Madonna meant there would be a huge crowd for the feast of the Assumption.

Their piety was not always entirely correct in its expression, at least from the point of view of the Church's liturgical regulations. When I would kiss the altar in accordance with the rubrics, three or four local women would accompany me. It was distracting, but certainly moving. I also noticed that above the altar in that holy house, which tradition says was the home of Jesus, Mary, and Joseph, these words were written: "Here the Word was made flesh." Here, on a bit of the earth on which we live, in a house built by men, God dwelt.

PERFECT GOD AND PERFECT MAN

13   The Son of God became man, and he is *perfectus Deus, perfectus homo*: "perfect God and perfect man."[2] There is something in this mystery which should stir Christians. I was and am moved. I should like to go back to Loreto.

---

[2] Athanasian Creed.

I go there now in thought and desire, to relive those years of Jesus' childhood and consider once more those words: "Here the Word was made flesh."

Iesus Christus, Deus homo: Jesus Christ, God-man. This is one of "the mighty works of God,"[3] which we should reflect upon and thank him for. He has come to bring "peace on earth to men of good will,"[4] to all men who want to unite their wills to the holy will of God—not just the rich, not just the poor, but everyone: all the brethren. We are all brothers in Jesus, children of God, brothers of Christ. His Mother is our mother.

There is only one race in the world: the race of the children of God. We should all speak the same language, taught us by our Father in heaven—the language Jesus spoke to his Father. It is the language of heart and mind, which you are using now, in your prayer—the language of contemplation, used by men who are spiritual, because they realize they are children of God. This language is expressed in a thousand motions of our will, in the clear insights of our

[3] Acts 2:11.
[4] Lk 2:14.

minds, in the affections of our heart, in our commitment to lead a virtuous life, in goodness, happiness, and peace.

You must look at the Child in the manger. He is our Love. Look at him, realizing that the whole thing is a mystery. We need to accept this mystery on faith and use our faith to explore it very deeply. To do this, we must have the humble attitude of a Christian soul. Let us not try to reduce the greatness of God to our own poor ideas and human explanations. Let us try to understand that this mystery, for all its darkness, is a light to guide men's lives.

As St John Chrysostom said: "We see that Jesus has come from us, from our human substance, and has been born of a virgin mother; but we don't know how this wonder came about. Let us not waste our energies trying to understand it; rather, accept humbly what God has revealed to us. Don't try to probe what God has kept hidden."[5] If we have this reverence, we will be able to understand and to love. The mystery will be a splendid lesson for us, much more convincing than any human reasoning.

[5] *In Matthaeum homiliae*, 4, 3 (PG 57, 43).

WHY JESUS CAME TO LIVE WITH US

Whenever I preach beside the crib, I try to   14
see Christ our Lord as a child wrapped in
swaddling clothes lying on straw in a manger.
Even though he is only a child, unable to speak,
I see him as a master and a teacher. I need to
look at him in this way, because I must learn
from him. And to learn from him, you must
try to know his life—reading the Gospel and
meditating on the scenes of the new testament—in order to understand the divine
meaning of his life on earth.

In our own life we must reproduce Christ's
life. We need to come to know him by reading
and meditating on Scripture, and by praying,
as we are doing now in front of the crib. We
must learn the lessons which Jesus teaches us,
even when he is just a newly born child, from
the very moment he opens his eyes on this
blessed land of men.

The fact that Jesus grew up and lived just
like us shows us that human existence and all
the ordinary activity of men have a divine
meaning. No matter how much we may have
reflected on all this, whenever we think about
it, we should always marvel at the thirty years

of obscurity which made up the greater part of
Jesus' life among men. He lived in obscurity,
but, for us, that period is full of light. It illuminates our days and fills them with meaning,
for we are ordinary Christians who lead an
ordinary life, just like millions of other people
all over the world.

That was the way Jesus lived for thirty years,
as "the son of the carpenter."[6] There followed
three years of public life, spent among the
crowds. People were surprised: "Who is this?"
they asked. "Where has he learned these
things?" For he was just like them: he had
shared the life of ordinary people. He was "the
carpenter, the son of Mary."[7] And he was God;
he was achieving the redemption of mankind
and "drawing all things to himself."[8]

15   As with other events in his life, we should
never contemplate Jesus' hidden years without
feeling moved. We should realize that they are
in themselves a call to shake off our selfishness
and easy-going ways. Our Lord knows our
limitations, our individualism and our ambition. He knows it is difficult for us to forget

[6] Mt 13:55: *filius fabri.*
[7] Mk 6:3: *faber, filius Mariae.*
[8] Jn 12:32.

ourselves and give ourselves to others. He knows very well what it feels like not to find love and to discover that those who say they follow him only do so in a halfhearted way. Just think of those striking scenes, described to us by the evangelists, in which we see the Apostles full of worldly ambitions and merely human plans. Yet Jesus has chosen them; he keeps them close to him and entrusts them with the mission he has received from his Father.

He has called us too and asks us, as he asked James and John: "Are you ready to drink the cup"—that cup which means giving yourself fully to the will of the Father—"which I am going to drink?" *Possumus!*: "Yes! We are ready!"[9] is the reply of John and James. Are you and I really ready to carry out, in everything, the will of our Father God? Have we given our Lord our whole heart, or are we attached to ourselves and our interests and comfort and self-love? Is there anything in our lives out of keeping with our Christianity, something which makes us unwilling to mend our ways? Today we are given a chance to set things straight.

[9] Mt 20:22: *Potestis bibere calicem quem ego bibiturus sum? Possumus!*

But first of all, we must be convinced that Jesus is putting these questions to us personally. He is the one who asks them, not I. I wouldn't dare even put them to myself. I am praying aloud, and each of you, silently, is admitting to our Lord: "Lord, how useless I am, what a coward I have been! How many mistakes I've made, over and over again." And we can go further and say: "It's good, Lord, you have kept me up with your hand; for, left to myself, I am capable of the most disgraceful things. Don't let me go; keep on treating me as a little child. I want to be strong and brave and manly. But you must help me. I am a clumsy creature. Take me by the hand, Lord, and make sure your Mother is also by my side to guard me. And so, *possumus!* We can; we will be able to have you as our model."

It is not presumptuous for us to say *possumus*. Jesus Christ teaches us this divine way and wants us to follow it, for he has made it human and accessible to our weakness. That is why he lowered himself so. "Here is the reason why he brought himself so low, taking the nature of a slave; he, the Lord, who as God was equal to the Father; he lowered himself in majesty and power—but not in goodness or mercy."[10]

The goodness of God wants to make the way easy for us. Let us not reject Jesus' invitation; let's not say "no" to him, turning a deaf ear to his voice. There is no excuse, we can no longer think we aren't able. He has shown us by his example. "Therefore, I ask you with all my heart, brothers, not to let this precious example go unheeded: rather, follow him and renew your soul in the spirit."[11]

HE WENT ABOUT DOING GOOD

Do you see how necessary it is to know Jesus 16 and lovingly observe his life? I have often gone to look for a definition or a biography of Jesus in Scripture. And I have found it written by the Holy Spirit: "He went about doing good."[12] Every single day of Jesus Christ's life on earth, from his birth until his death, can be summed up like that: he filled them all doing good. And in another place Scripture says, "He has done

---

[10] St Bernard, *Sermo in die nativitatis*, 1, 1-2 (PL 183, 115).

[11] St Bernard, *ibid.*, 1, 1.

[12] Acts 10:38: *Pertransiit benefaciendo*.

all things well,"[13] he finished everything well, he did nothing that wasn't good.

What about you and me, then? Let's take a look to see if we have to put anything right. I certainly can find plenty to improve. I know that by myself I am incapable of doing good. And, since Jesus has said that without him we can do nothing,[14] let us, you and me, go to our Lord and ask for his help, through his Mother, in one of those intimate conversations natural to souls who love God. I will say no more, for it's up to each of you to speak to him personally, about your own needs. Do it interiorly, without the noise of words, now—while I for my part apply these counsels to my own sorry state.

17   What did Christ do to pour out so much good, and only good, wherever he went? The Gospels give us the answer with another biography of Jesus: "He was obedient to them."[15] We must especially value obedience in the current environment of disobedience, rebellion, and disunity.

---

[13] Mk 7:37: *bene omnia fecit.*
[14] Cf. Jn 15:5.
[15] Lk 2:51: *erat subditus illis.*

Freedom is very close to my heart—that is precisely why I so love the Christian virtue of obedience. We should all realize that we are children of God; we should want to fulfill the will of our Father. We should do things as God wants them done, *because we feel like it*, which is the most supernatural of reasons.

The spirit of Opus Dei, which I have tried to practice and to teach for more than thirty-five years now, has made me understand and love personal freedom. When God our Lord gives us his grace, when he calls us by a specific vocation, it is as if he were stretching out his hand to us, in a fatherly way. A strong hand, full of love, because he seeks us out individually, as his own sons and daughters, knowing our weakness. The Lord expects us to make the effort to take his hand, his helping hand. He asks us to make an effort and show we are free. To be able to do this, we must be humble and realize we are little children of God. We must love the blessed obedience with which we respond to God's marvelous fatherhood.

We should let our Lord get involved in our lives, admitting him confidently, removing from his way any obstacles or complications. We tend to be on the defensive, to be attached to our selfishness. We always want to be top dog, even if it's only to be on top of our wretchedness. That is why we must go to Jesus, so that he will make us truly free. Only then will we be able to serve God and all men. This is the only way to realize the truth of St Paul's words: "But now that you have been set free from sin and have become slaves of God, the return you get is sanctification and its end, eternal life. For the wages of sin is death, but the free gift of God is eternal life in Christ Jesus our Lord."[16]

Let us be forewarned, then, for we will always tend to be selfish, and this temptation can occur in many ways. God wants us to show our faith when we obey, for he doesn't express his will with drums and trumpets. Sometimes he suggests his wishes in a whisper, deep in our conscience; and we must listen carefully to recognize his voice and be faithful.

He often speaks to us through other people. But when we see their defects or doubt whether they are well-informed—whether they have grasped all the aspects of the problem—we feel inclined to disobey. All this may have a divine

---

[16] Rom 6:22-23.

meaning, for God does not impose a blind
obedience on us. He wants us to obey intelli-
gently, and we have to feel responsible for
helping others with the intelligence we do have.
But let's be sincere with ourselves: let's examine, in every case, whether it is love for the truth
which moves us or selfishness and attachment
to our own judgment. When our ideas separate
us from other people, when they weaken our
communion, our unity with our brothers, it is
a sure sign that we are not doing what God
wants.

Let's not forget: we need humility if we are
to obey. Look again at the example Christ gives
us: he obeys Joseph and Mary. God has come
to the world to obey, and to obey creatures.
Admittedly they are two very perfect creatures:
Holy Mary, our mother, greater than whom
God alone; and that most chaste man Joseph.
But they are only creatures, and yet Jesus, who
is God, obeyed them. We have to love God so
as to love his will and desire to respond to his
calls. They come to us through the ordinary
duties in our lives: duties of state, profession,
work, family, social life, our own and other
people's difficulties, friendship, eagerness to do
what is right and just.

18   Every time Christmas comes around, I love to look at representations of the child Jesus. Statues and pictures which show a God who lowered himself remind me that God is calling us. The Almighty wants us to know that he is defenseless, that he needs men's help. From the cradle at Bethlehem, Christ tells you and me that he needs us. He urges us to live a Christian life to the full—a life of self-sacrifice, work, and joy.

We will never have genuine joy if we do not really try to imitate Jesus. Like him we must be humble. I repeat: do you see where God's greatness is hidden? In a manger, in swaddling clothes, in a stable. The redemptive power of our lives can only work through humility. We must stop thinking about ourselves and feel the responsibility to help others.

It can sometimes happen that even well-intentioned people create personal problems—really serious worries—which have no objective basis whatsoever. These problems arise in persons whose lack of self-knowledge leads to pride and a desire to be the center of attention, to be favored by everyone. They want to appear always in a good light, to be personally secure. They are not content simply to do good and disappear. And so, many who could enjoy a wonderful peace of soul and great happiness become, through pride and presumption, unhappy and unfruitful. Christ was humble of heart.[17] Throughout his life he looked for no special consideration or privilege. He began by spending nine months in his Mother's womb, like the rest of men, following the natural course of events. He knew that mankind needed him greatly. He was longing to come into the world to save all souls, but he took his time. He came in due course, just as every other child is born. From conception to birth, no one—except our Lady, St Joseph and St Elizabeth—realized the marvelous truth that God was coming to live among men.

There is a great simplicity also about his birth. Our Lord comes without any fanfare. No one knows about him. On earth only Mary and Joseph share in the divine adventure. And then the shepherds who received the message from the angels. And later on, the wise men from the East. They were the only witnesses of this transcendental event which unites heaven and earth, God and man.

---

[17] Cf. Mt 11:29.

How can our hearts be so hard that we can get used to these scenes? God humbled himself to allow us to get near him, so that we could give our love in exchange for his, so that our freedom might bow, not only at the sight of his power, but also before the wonder of his humility.

The greatness of this Child who is God! His Father is the God who has made heaven and earth and there he is, in a manger, "because there was no room at the inn"[18]—there was nowhere else for the Lord of all creation.

HE DID THE WILL OF GOD HIS FATHER

19   I am not at all stretching the truth when I tell you that Jesus is still looking for a resting-place in our hearts. We have to ask him to forgive our personal blindness and ingratitude. We must ask him to give us the grace never to close the door of our soul on him again.

Our Lord does not disguise the fact that his wholehearted obedience to God's will calls for renunciation and self-sacrifice. Love does not

---

[18] Lk 2:7: *quia non erat eis locus in diversorio.*

claim rights, it seeks to serve. Jesus has led the way. How did he obey? "Unto death, death on a cross."[19] You have to get out of yourself; you have to complicate your life, losing it for love of God and souls. "So you wanted to live a quiet life. But God wanted otherwise. Two wills exist: your will should be corrected to become identified with God's will: you must not bend God's will to suit yours."[20]

It has made me very happy to see so many souls spend their lives—like you, Lord, "even unto death"—fulfilling what God was asking of them. They have dedicated all their yearnings and their professional work to the service of the Church, for the good of all men.

Let us learn to obey, let us learn to serve. There is no better leadership than wanting to give yourself freely, to be useful to others. When we feel pride swell up within us, making us think we are supermen, the time has come to say "no". Our only triumph will be the triumph of humility. In this way we will identify ourselves with Christ on the cross—not

---

[19] Phil 2:8: *usque ad mortem, mortem autem crucis.*

[20] St Augustine, *Enarrationes in psalmos*, Ps 31:2, 26 (PL 36, 274).

unwillingly or restlessly or sullenly, but joyfully. For the joy which comes from forgetting ourselves is the best proof of love.

20   Let me go back again to the openness and simplicity of Jesus' life, which I have brought to your attention so many times. His hidden years are not without significance, nor were they simply a preparation for the years which were to come after—those of his public life. Since 1928 I have understood clearly that God wants our Lord's whole life to be an example for Christians. I saw this with special reference to his hidden life, the years he spent working side by side with ordinary men. Our Lord wants many people to ratify their vocation during years of quiet, unspectacular living. Obeying God's will always means leaving our selfishness behind, but there is no reason why it should entail cutting ourselves off from the normal life of ordinary men who share the same status, work and social position as we.

I dream—and the dream has come true—of multitudes of God's children, sanctifying themselves as ordinary citizens, sharing the ambitions and endeavors of their colleagues and friends. I want to shout to them about this divine truth: if you are there in the middle of ordinary life, it doesn't mean Christ has forgotten about you or hasn't called you. He has invited you to stay among the activities and concerns of the world. He wants you to know that your human vocation, your profession, your talents, are not omitted from his divine plans. He has sanctified them and made them a most acceptable offering to his Father.

To remind a Christian that his life is meaningless unless he obeys God's will does not mean separating him from other men. On the contrary, the commandment God gives us is to love others as he has loved us,[21] which in most cases means living alongside the rest of men and being their equals, giving ourselves to the service of our Lord in the world so as to make everyone know better the love of God, telling them that *the divine paths of the world have been opened up*.

God has not just said that he loves us. He has proved it with facts. Let's not forget that Jesus Christ became man in order to teach us to live as children of God. Do you remember the introduction to the Acts of the Apostles,

[21] Cf. Jn 13:34-35.

where St Luke says: "I have spoken of all the most significant things Jesus did and taught"[22]? He came to teach us, but he taught us by doing things. In teaching us, he was the model, being our teacher and setting us an example with his conduct.

Now, in front of the infant Jesus, we can continue our personal examination of conscience. Are we ready to try to make our life a model and an example to our brothers, the rest of men, our equals? Are we ready to be other Christs? It's not enough to *say* that we are. I am asking you now—as I ask myself: Can it be said also of you, you who have been called to be another Christ, that you have come to do and to teach, to do things as a son of God would? Are you attentive to the Father's will, so as to be able to encourage everyone else to share the good, noble, divine, and human values of the redemption? Are you living the life of Christ, in your everyday life in the middle of the world?

Doing God's work is not just a pretty phrase. It is an invitation to spend ourselves for Love's

---

[22] Acts 1:1: *Primum quidem sermonem feci de omnibus, o Theophile, quae coepit Iesus facere et docere.*

sake. We have to die to ourselves and be born again to a new life. Jesus Christ obeyed in this way, even unto death on a cross; that is why God exalted him.[23] If we obey God's will, the cross will mean our own resurrection and exaltation. Christ's life will be fulfilled step by step in our own lives. It will be said of us that we have tried to be good children of God who went about doing good in spite of our weakness and personal shortcomings, no matter how many.

And when death comes as it undoubtedly will, we will greet it with joy, as I have seen so many people greet it in the ordinary circumstances of their life. With joy: for if we have imitated Christ in doing good—in obeying and carrying the cross in spite of our personal deficiencies—we will rise like Christ: "for he has truly risen."[24]

Jesus, who became a child, overcame death. Just think of it. Through his annihilation, through his simplicity and obedience, by divinizing the everyday, common life of men, the Son of God conquered.

---

[23] Phil 2:8-9: *Propter quod et Deus exaltavit illum.*
[24] Lk 24:34: *Surrexit Dominus vere.*

That is the triumph of Jesus Christ. He has raised us to his level, the level of the children of God, by coming down to our level, the level of the children of men.

MARRIAGE: A CHRISTIAN VOCATION*

At Christmas our thoughts turn to the different events and circumstances surrounding the birth of the Son of God. As we contemplate the stable in Bethlehem or the home of the holy family in Nazareth, Mary, Joseph, and the child Jesus occupy a special place in our hearts. What does the simple, admirable life of the holy family tell us? What can we learn from it?

I would like particularly to comment on one of the many considerations that we might make on this theme. As we read in holy Scripture, the birth of Jesus means the beginning of the fullness of time.[1] It was the moment God chose to show the extent of his love for men, by giving

---

*A homily given during Christmas 1970.
[1] Gal 4:4.

us his own Son. And God's will is fulfilled in
the simplest, most ordinary of circumstances: a
woman who gives birth, a family, a home. The
power of God and his splendor come to us
through a human reality to which they are
joined. Since that moment Christians have
known that, with God's grace, they can and
should sanctify everything that is good in their
human lives. There is no human situation, no
matter how trivial and ordinary it may seem,
which cannot be a meeting-place with Christ
and a step forward on our journey toward the
kingdom of heaven.

It is only natural that the Church rejoices as
it contemplates the modest home of Jesus,
Mary, and Joseph. We read in the hymn from
matins on the feast of the Holy Family: "It is
pleasing to recall the lowly house at Nazareth
and its slender resources, it is pleasing to tell
again in song Jesus' hidden life. Jesus grows up
in hidden seclusion, to be trained in Joseph's
lowly trade. The loving Mother sits beside her
dear Son, the good wife by her husband,
content if her loving attention can ease and
comfort them in their weariness."

When I think of Christian homes, I like to
imagine them as being full of the light and joy

that were in the home of the holy family. The message of Christmas is heard in all its forcefulness: "Glory to God in the highest, and on earth peace to men of good will."[2] "And may the peace of Christ triumph in your hearts," writes the Apostle.[3] It is a peace that comes from knowing that our Father God loves us, and that we are made one with Christ. It results from being under the protection of the Virgin, our Lady, and assisted by St Joseph. This is the great light that illuminates our lives. In the midst of difficulties and of our own personal failings, it encourages us to keep up our effort. Every Christian home should be a place of peace and serenity. In spite of the small frustrations of daily life, an atmosphere of profound and sincere affection should reign there together with a deep-rooted calm, which is the result of authentic faith that is put into practice.

For a Christian marriage is not just a social 23 institution, much less a mere remedy for human weakness. It is a real supernatural calling. A great sacrament, in Christ and in the Church, says St Paul.[4] At the same time, it is a perma-

---

[2] Lk 2:14.
[3] Col 3:15.
[4] Eph 5:32.

nent contract between a man and a woman. Whether we like it or not, the sacrament of matrimony, instituted by Christ, cannot be dissolved. It is a permanent contract that sanctifies in cooperation with Jesus Christ. He fills the souls of husband and wife and invites them to follow him. He transforms their whole married life into an occasion for God's presence on earth.

Husband and wife are called to sanctify their married life and to sanctify themselves in it. It would be a serious mistake if they were to exclude family life from their spiritual development. The marriage union, the care and education of children, the effort to provide for the needs of the family as well as for its security and development, the relationships with other persons who make up the community, all these are among the ordinary human situations that Christian couples are called upon to sanctify.

They will achieve this aim by exercising the virtues of faith and hope, facing serenely all the great and small problems which confront any family, and persevering in the love and enthusiasm with which they fulfill their duties. In this way they practice the virtue of charity in all things. They learn to smile and forget about themselves in order to pay attention to others. Husband and wife will listen to each other and to their children, showing them that they are really loved and understood. They will forget about the unimportant little frictions that self-ishness could magnify out of proportion. They will do lovingly all the small acts of service that make up their daily life together.

The aim is this: to sanctify family life, while creating at the same time a true family atmos-phere. Many Christian virtues are necessary in order to sanctify each day of one's life. First, the theological virtues, and then all the others: prudence, loyalty, sincerity, humility, industri-ousness, cheerfulness.... But when we talk about marriage and married life, we must begin by speaking clearly about the mutual love of husband and wife.

THE SANCTITY OF HUMAN LOVE

Their pure and noble love is a sacred thing.   24 As a priest, I bless it with all my heart. Christian tradition has often seen in Christ's presence at the wedding feast in Cana a proof of the value God places on marriage. "Our Savior went to the wedding feast," writes St Cyril of Alexandria, "to make holy the origins of human life."[5]

Marriage is a sacrament that makes one flesh of two bodies. Theology expresses this fact in a striking way when it teaches us that the matter of the sacrament is the bodies of husband and wife. Our Lord sanctifies and blesses the mutual love of husband and wife. He foresees, not only a union of souls, but a union of bodies as well. No Christian, whether or not he is called to the married state, has a right to underestimate the value of marriage.

We have been created by God and endowed with an intelligence which is like a spark of the divine intellect. Together with our free will, another gift of God, it allows us to know and to love. And God has also placed in our body the power to generate, which is a participation in his own creative power. He has wanted to use love to bring new human beings into the world and to increase the body of the Church. Thus, sex is not a shameful thing; it is a divine gift, ordained to life, to love, to fruitfulness.

This is the context in which we must see the Christian doctrine on sex. Our faith does not

---

[5] *In Ioannem commentarius*, 2, 1 (PG 73, 223).

ignore anything on this earth that is beautiful, noble, and authentically human. It simply teaches us that the rule of our life should not be the selfish pursuit of pleasure, because only sacrifice and self-denial lead to true love. God already loves us; and now he invites us to love him and others with the truthfulness and authenticity with which he loves. It is the paradox expressed in St Matthew's Gospel: "He who seeks to keep his life will lose it; and he who loses his life for my sake will find it."[6]

People who are constantly concerned with themselves, who act above all for their own satisfaction, endanger their eternal salvation and cannot avoid being unhappy even in this life. Only if a person forgets himself and gives himself to God and to others, in marriage as well as in any other aspect of life, can he be happy on this earth, with a happiness that is a preparation for, and a foretaste of, the joy of heaven.

As long as we walk on this earth, suffering will always be the touchstone of love. If we were to describe what occurs in the married state, we could say that there are two sides to

6 Mt 10:39.

the coin. On the one hand, there is the joy of
knowing that one is loved, the desire and
enthusiasm involved in starting a family and
taking care of it, the love of husband and wife,
the happiness of seeing the children grow up.
On the other hand, there are also sorrows and
difficulties—the passing of time that consumes
the body and threatens the character with the
temptation to bitterness, the seemingly monotonous succession of days that are apparently
always the same.

We would have a poor idea of marriage and
of human affection if we were to think that love
and joy come to an end when faced with such
difficulties. It is precisely then that our true
sentiments come to the surface. Then the
tenderness of a person's gift of himself takes
root and shows itself in a true and profound
affection that is stronger than death.[7]

25   When love is authentic it demands faithfulness and rectitude in all marital relations. St
Thomas Aquinas comments[8] that God has
joined to the exercise of the different functions
of human life a pleasure or satisfaction, which

[7] Song 8:6.
[8] S. Th., I-II, q. 31 et II-II, q. 141.

is, therefore, something good. But if man, inverting the proper order of things, seeks satisfaction as an aim in itself, in contempt of the good to which it is joined and which is its aim, he perverts its true nature and converts it into a sin, or an occasion of sin.

Chastity is not merely continence, but a decisive affirmation on the part of the will in love. It is a virtue that keeps love young in any state in life. There is a kind of chastity that is proper to those who begin to feel the awakening of physical maturity, and a kind of chastity that corresponds to those who are preparing for marriage; there is a chastity for those whom God calls to celibacy, and a chastity for those who have been chosen by him to live in the married state.

I cannot avoid calling to mind the strong and clear counsel given to Tobias by the angel Raphael before the young man's marriage to Sarah: "Then the angel Raphael said to him: 'Hear me, and I will show you who are those over whom the devil can prevail. For they who enter into matrimony in such a manner as to shut out God from themselves and from their mind, and to give themselves to their lust, as the horse and the mule which have not understanding, are those over whom the devil has power'."[9]

Human love—pure, sincere, and joyful—cannot subsist in marriage without the virtue of chastity, which leads a couple to respect the mystery of sex and ordain it to faithfulness and personal dedication. I have never talked about impurity, and I have always avoided falling into a distasteful and meaningless casuistry. But I have very often spoken, and will continue to speak about chastity, purity, and the joyful affirmation of love.

With regard to chastity in married life, I can assure all married couples that they need not be afraid of showing affection for each other. On the contrary, this inclination is at the root of their family life. What our Lord expects from them is that they should respect each other and that they should be loyal to each other; that they should act with refinement, naturalness, and modesty. I must also tell them that the dignity of their conjugal relations is a result of the love that is expressed in them. And there will be love if those relations are open to fruitfulness, to bringing children into the world.

[9] Tob 6:16-17.

To stop up the sources of life is a crime against the gifts that God has granted to mankind. It proves that a person is moved by selfishness, not love. Everything becomes clouded, because husband and wife begin to look at each other as accomplices, and the dissensions that are produced, if this state is allowed to continue, are almost always impossible to heal.

When there is chastity in the love of married persons, their marital life is authentic; husband and wife are true to themselves, they understand each other and develop the union between them. When the divine gift of sex is perverted, their intimacy is destroyed, and they can no longer look openly at each other.

A married couple should build their life together on the foundation of a sincere and pure affection for each other, and on the joy that comes from having brought into the world the children God has enabled them to have. They should be capable of renouncing their personal comfort; and they should put their trust in the providence of God. To have a large family— if such is the will of God—is a guarantee of happiness and of effectiveness, in spite of everything that the mistaken proponents of a

life based on selfish pleasure may say to the
contrary.

26   Don't forget that it is impossible for husband
and wife to avoid at least some arguments. But
never quarrel in front of your children; you
would make them suffer, and they would take
sides in the argument, contributing unwittingly
to the lack of unity between you. But quarrels,
so long as they don't happen often, are also a
proof of love, and they are almost a need. The
occasion of a quarrel—not its motive—is often
the tiredness of the husband, worn out by his
work, or the fatigue, not to say boredom, of the
wife who has had to struggle with the children,
with domestic chores, or with her own character, which might be lacking in fortitude. Though
women can be stronger than men, if they set
their mind to it.

Avoid pride. It is the greatest enemy of your
married life. In your little quarrels, neither of
you is right. Whoever is the calmer should say
a word or two to ward off bad temper for a
while. Then, later on, when you are alone with
each other, go ahead and argue it out—soon
afterwards you will make peace anyway.

Wives, you should ask yourselves whether
you are not forgetting a little about your

appearance. Remember all the sayings about women having to take care to look pretty. Your duty is, and will always be, to take as good care of your appearance as you did before you were married—and it is a duty of justice, because you belong to your husband. And husbands should not forget that they belong to their wives, and that as long as they live they have the obligation to show the same affection as a young man who has just fallen in love. It would be a bad sign if you smile ironically as you hear this; it would mean that your love has turned into cold indifference.

BRIGHT AND CHEERFUL HOMES

We cannot talk about marriage without 27 referring to the family, which is the result and continuation of what is begun with marriage. A family includes not only husband and wife, but also the children, and, in different degrees, the grandparents, other relatives, and even the domestic help in those households that have it. All these persons should in some way share in the warmth of the home and family.

Of course, there are couples to whom our Lord does not grant any children. If this

happens, it is a sign that he is asking them to go on loving each other with the same affection and to put their efforts, if they can, into serving and working for the good of other souls. But the normal thing for a couple is to have children, who must always be their first concern.

Being a father or a mother is not simply a matter of bringing children into the world. The capacity for generation, which is a share in the creative power of God, is meant to have a continuation. Parents are called to cooperate with the Holy Spirit in the development of their children into men and women who will be authentic Christians.

The parents are the first persons responsible for the education of their children, in human as well as in spiritual matters. They should be conscious of the extent of their responsibility. To fulfill it, they need prudence, understanding, a capacity to love, and a concern for giving good example. Imposing things by force, in an authoritarian manner, is not the right way to teach. The ideal attitude of parents lies more in becoming their children's friends—friends who will be willing to share their anxieties, who will listen to their problems, who will help them in an effective and agreeable way.

Parents should find time to spend with their children, to talk with them. They are the most important thing—more important than business or work or rest. In their conversations, parents should make an effort to listen, to pay attention, to understand, to recognize the fact that their children are sometimes partly right—or even completely right—in some of their rebellious attitudes. At the same time, they should help their children to direct their efforts and to carry out their projects properly, teaching them to consider things and to reason them out. It is not a matter of imposing a line of conduct, but rather of showing the human and supernatural motives for it. In a word, parents have to respect their children's freedom, because there is no real education without personal responsibility, and there is no responsibility without freedom.

Parents teach their children mainly through 28 their own conduct. What a son or daughter looks for in a father or mother is not only a certain amount of knowledge or some more or less effective advice, but primarily something more important: a proof of the value and meaning of life, shown through the life of a specific person, and confirmed in the different situations and circumstances that occur over a period of time.

If I were to give advice to parents, I would tell them, above all, let your children see that you are trying to live in accordance with your faith. Don't let yourselves be deceived: they see everything, from their earliest years, and they judge everything. Let them see that God is not only on your lips, but also in your deeds; that you are trying to be loyal and sincere, and that you love each other and you really love them too.

This is how you will best contribute to making your children become true Christians, men and women of integrity, capable of facing all life's situations with an open spirit, of serving their fellowmen, and helping to solve the problems of mankind, of carrying the testimony of Christ to the society of which they will be a part.

29   Listen to your children. Give them your time, even the time that you have reserved for yourselves. Show them your confidence; believe whatever they tell you, even if sometimes they try to deceive you. Don't be afraid when they rebel, because, at their age, you yourselves were more or less rebellious. Go to meet them half-

way and pray for them. If you act in this Christian manner, they will come to you with simplicity, instead of trying to satisfy their legitimate curiosity by taking it to some rough or vulgar friend. Your confidence, your friendly dealings with your children, will receive an answer in their sincerity in dealing with you. Then, even if there are quarrels and lack of understanding, they will never amount to much; and this is what peace in the family and a truly Christian life mean.

"How can I describe," says a Christian writer of the early centuries, "the joy of a marriage united by the Church, strengthened by the dedication of husband and wife, sealed with a blessing, proclaimed by the angels, and accepted by God the Father?... Husband and wife are as brother and sister, servants of each other, and nothing separates them, either in the flesh or in the spirit. For they are truly two in one flesh, and were there is one flesh there should be one spirit... Contemplating such a family, Christ rejoices and sends his peace. Where there are two together, he is also present; and where he is present, there can be no evil."[10]

---

[10] Tertullian, *Ad uxorem*, 1, 2, 9 (PL 1, 1302).

30   We have tried to mention and comment on some of the characteristics of a family that reflects the light of Christ. As I mentioned before, theirs is a home full of light and cheerfulness. The unity between the parents is transmitted to their children, to the whole family, and to everyone who is involved in their life. In this way, every truly Christian family reproduces in some way the mystery of the Church, chosen by God and sent to be the guide of the world.

To every Christian, whatever his state in life—priest or layman, married or single—we can apply fully the words of the Apostle, which we read precisely on the feast of the Holy Family: "...chosen by God, holy and beloved."[11] This is what we all are, each one in his place and position in the world, despite our errors and in the midst of the struggle to conquer them: men and women chosen by God to give witness to Christ and to bring all those who surround us the joy of knowing that we are God's children.

It is very important that the idea of marriage as a real call from God never be absent, either

[11] Col 3:12.

from the pulpit and the religion class or from the conscience of those whom God wishes to follow this way. Couples should be convinced that they are really and truly called to take part in the fulfillment of God's plan for the salvation of all men.

For this reason, there is perhaps no better model for a Christian couple than that of the Christian families of apostolic times: the centurion Cornelius, who obeyed the will of God and in whose home the Church was made accessible to the gentiles;[12] Aquila and Priscilla, who spread Christianity in Corinth and Ephesus, and who cooperated in the apostolate of St Paul;[13] Tabitha, who out of charity attended to the needs of the Christians in Joppe.[14] And so many other homes and families of Jews and Gentiles, Greeks and Romans, in which the preaching of our Lord's first disciples began to bear fruit. Families who lived in union with Christ and who made him known to others. Small Christian communities which were centers for the spreading of the Gospel and its

[12] Acts 10.24-48.
[13] Acts 18:1-26.
[14] Acts 9:36.

message. Families no different from other families of those times, but living with a new spirit, which spread to all those who were in contact with them. This is what the first Christians were, and this is what we have to be: sowers of peace and joy, the peace and joy that Jesus has brought to us.

THE EPIPHANY
OF OUR LORD*

Not too long ago I saw a marble bas-relief 31
representing the adoration of the child Jesus by
the Magi. The central figures were surrounded
by four angels, each one bearing a symbol: a
crown, an orb surmounted by the cross, a
sword and a scepter. The artist had chosen
symbols with which we are all familiar to
illustrate the event we commemorate today.
Some wise men whom tradition describes as
kings come to pay homage to a child, after
having been to Jerusalem to ask, "Where is he
that is born king of the Jews?"[1]

Moved by this question, I too now contemplate Jesus "lying in a manger,"[2] in a place fit

*A homily given on January 6, 1956, the feast of the Epiph-
any.
[1] Mt 2:2.
[2] Lk 2:12.

only for animals. Lord, where is your kingship, your crown, your sword, your scepter? They are his by right, but he does not want them. He reigns wrapped in swaddling clothes. Our king is unadorned. He comes to us as a defenseless little child. Can we help but recall the words of the Apostle: "He emptied himself, taking the nature of a slave"?[3]

Our Lord became man to teach us the Father's will. And this he is already doing as he lies there in the manger. Jesus Christ is seeking us—with a call which is a vocation to sanctity—so that we may carry out the redemption with him. Let us reflect on this first lesson of his. We are to co-redeem, by striving to triumph not over our neighbor, but over ourselves. Like Christ we need to empty ourselves, to consider ourselves as the servants of others, and so to bring them to God.

Where is the king? Could it be that Jesus wants to reign above all in men's hearts, in your heart? That is why he has become a child, for who can help loving a little baby? Where then is the king? Where is the Christ whom the Holy Spirit wants to fashion in our souls? He cannot

[3] Phil 2:7.

be present in the pride that separates us from God, nor in the lack of charity which cuts us off from others. Christ cannot be there. In that loveless state man is left alone.

As you kneel at the feet of the child Jesus on the day of his Epiphany and see him a king bearing none of the outward signs of royalty, you can tell him: "Lord, take away my pride; crush my self-love, my desire to affirm myself, and impose myself on others. Make the foundation of my personality my identification with you."

THE WAY OF FAITH

We want to identify ourselves with Christ. 32 It is not an easy goal. But it is not difficult either, if we live as our Lord has taught us to live, if we have recourse to his word every day, if we fill our lives with the sacramental reality, the Eucharist, which he has given us for our nourishment. Then the Christian's path proves to be viable. God has called us clearly and unmistakably. Like the Magi we have discovered a star: a light and a guide in the sky of our soul.

"We have seen his star in the East and have come to worship him."[4] We have had the same experience. We too noticed a new light shining in our soul and growing increasingly brighter. It was a desire to live a fully Christian life, a keenness to take God seriously. If each one of you were to tell aloud the intimate details of how his vocation made itself felt, the rest of us would conclude immediately that it was all God's doing. Let us give thanks to God the Father, God the Son, God the Holy Spirit, and to Holy Mary, through whom all blessings from heaven come to us, for this gift which, along with our faith, is the greatest the Lord can bestow on any of his creatures. It is a clear desire to attain the fullness of charity, the conviction that sanctity is not only possible but necessary in the midst of our social and professional tasks.

Look how gently the Lord invites us. His words have human warmth; they are the words of a person in love: "I have called you by your name. You are mine."[5] God, who is beauty and greatness and wisdom, declares that we are his,

4 Mt 2:2.
5 Is 43:1.

that we have been chosen as the object of his infinite love. We need a strong life of faith to appreciate the wonder his providence has entrusted to us. A faith like that of the Magi, a conviction that neither the desert, nor the storms, nor the quiet of the oases will keep us from reaching our destination in the eternal Bethlehem: our definitive life with God.

A life of faith is a life of sacrifice. Our Christian vocation does not take us away from our place in the world, but it requires us to cast aside anything that would get in the way of God's will. The light that has just begun to shine is only the beginning. We have to follow it if we want it to shine as a star, and then like the sun. St John Chrysostom writes: "While the Magi were in Persia, they saw only a star. But when they left their homes behind, they saw the Sun of justice. We can say that they would not have continued to see the star if they had remained in their own country. Let us then hasten too; and even if everyone stands in our way, let us run to that child's home."[6]

---

[6] *In Matthaeum homiliae*, 6, 5 (PG 57, 78).

FIRMNESS IN YOUR VOCATION

"'We have seen his star in the East, and have come to adore him.' When Herod the king heard this, he was troubled and all Jerusalem with him."[7] This scene is still repeated today. Faced with the greatness of God or with a person who has made up his mind—with a decision both deeply human and profoundly Christian—to live up to the demands of his faith, there are people who find it strange and in their surprise they even get scandalized. It seems they are unable to countenance a way of life which does not fit into their limited earthly horizons. They smirk at the generous actions of those who have heard God's call. They are frightened by such dedication, and in some cases that appear frankly pathological, they do all in their power to thwart the holy determination of those who with complete freedom have given themselves to God.

On some occasions I have witnessed what could be called a general mobilization against those committed to dedicating their whole lives

[7] Mt 2:2-3.

to the service of God and souls. Some people think that our Lord ought to ask their permission before choosing others for his service. Apparently they believe man is not free to say an unequivocal yes or no to this proposal of Love. To people who think that way, the supernatural life of each soul is something secondary. They do believe it has to be reckoned with, but only after petty comforts and human selfishness have been accommodated. If this were the case, what would be left of Christianity? Are the loving but demanding words of Jesus only to be heard? Or are they rather to be heard and put into practice? Did he not say, "Be perfect as your heavenly Father is perfect"?[8]

Our Lord asks all men to come out to meet him, to become saints. He calls not only the Magi, the wise and powerful. Before that he had sent, not a star, but one of his angels to the shepherds in Bethlehem.[9] Rich or poor, wise or less so, all of us have to foster in our hearts a humble disposition that will allow us to listen to the word of God.

[8] Mt 5:48.
[9] Cf. Lk 2:9.

Take the case of Herod. He ranked among the powerful of this world and had the opportunity of availing himself of the help of the learned. "And assembling all the chief priests and scribes of the people, he inquired of them where the Christ was to be born."[10] His power and knowledge do not lead him to recognize God. In his hardened heart, power and knowledge are instruments for evil. His futile desire is to annihilate God, and he has only contempt for the lives of innocent children.

Let us turn again to the Gospel. "They told him, In Bethlehem of Judah; for so it is written by the prophet: 'And you, O Bethlehem in the land of Judah, are by no means the least among the rulers of Judah; for from you shall come a ruler who will govern my people Israel'."[11] We should not overlook these expressions of God's mercy. He who was to redeem the world is born in an insignificant little village. And the reason is, as Scripture tells us again and again, that God is not a respecter of persons.[12] When he invites a soul to live a life fully in accordance

---

[10] Mt 2:4.
[11] Mt 2:5-6.
[12] Cf. 2 Chron 19:7; Rom 2:11; Eph 6:9; Col 3:25; etc.

with the faith, he does not set store by merits of fortune, nobility, blood or learning. God's call precedes all merits. "The star which they had seen in the East went before them, till it came to rest where the child was."[13]

Vocation comes first. God loves us before we even know how to go toward him, and he places in us the love with which we can respond to his call. God's fatherly goodness comes out to meet us.[14] Our Lord is not only just. He is much more: he is merciful. He does not wait for us to go to him. He takes the initiative, with the unmistakable signs of paternal affection.

A GOOD SHEPHERD AND A GOOD GUIDE

If vocation comes first, if the star shines 34 ahead to start us along the path of God's love, it is illogical that we should begin to doubt if it chances to disappear from view. It might happen at certain moments in our interior life— and we are nearly always to blame—that the

[13] Mt 2:9.
[14] Ps 78:8.

star disappears, just as it did to the wise kings on their journey. We have already realized the divine splendor of our vocation, and we are convinced about its definitive character, but perhaps the dust we stir up as we walk—our miseries—forms an opaque cloud that cuts off the light from above.

What should we do if this happens? Follow the example of those wise men and ask. Herod made use of knowledge to act unjustly. The Magi use it to do good. But we Christians have no need to go to Herod nor to the wise men of this world. Christ has given his Church sureness in doctrine and a flow of grace in the sacraments. He has arranged things so that there will always be people to guide and lead us, to remind us constantly of our way. There is an infinite treasure of knowledge available to us: the word of God kept safe by the Church, the grace of Christ administered in the sacraments and also the witness and example of those who live by our side and have known how to build with their good lives a road of faithfulness to God.

Allow me to give you a piece of advice. If ever you lose the clear light, always turn to the good shepherd. And who is the good shepherd?

"He who enters by the door" of faithfulness to the Church's doctrine and does not act like the hireling "who sees the wolf coming and leaves the sheep and flees"; whereupon "the wolf snatches them and scatters them."[15] Reflect on these divine words, which are not said in vain, and on the insistence of Christ who so affectionately speaks of shepherds and sheep, of sheepfold and flock, as a practical proof of our soul's need for good guidance.

"If there be no bad shepherds," says St Augustine speaking about the good shepherd, "he would not have described the hireling, who sees the wolf and flees. He seeks his own glory, not Christ's glory. He does not dare to rebuke sinners with freedom of spirit. The wolf catches a sheep by the neck, the devil induces a man to commit adultery. And you are silent and do not rebuke. Then you are a hireling because you have seen the wolf and have fled. Perhaps you might say: 'No, I'm here, I haven't fled.' I answer: 'You have fled because you have been silent, and you have been silent because you were afraid'."[16]

---

[15] Cf. Jn 10:1-21.
[16] *In Ioannis Evangelium tractatus*, 46, 8 (PL 35, 1732).

The holiness of Christ's Spouse has always been shown—as it can be seen today—by the abundance of good shepherds. But our Christian faith, which teaches us to be simple, does not bid us to be simple-minded. There are hirelings who keep silent, and there are hirelings who speak with words which are not those of Christ. That is why, if the Lord allows us to be left in the dark even in little things, if we feel that our faith is not firm, we should go to the good shepherd. He enters by the door as of right. He gives his life for others and wants to be in word and behavior a soul in love. He may be a sinner too, but he trusts always in Christ's forgiveness and mercy.

If your conscience tells you that you have committed a fault—even though it does not appear to be serious or if you are in doubt—go to the sacrament of penance. Go to the priest who looks after you, who knows how to demand of you a steady faith, refinement of soul, and true Christian fortitude. The Church allows the greatest freedom for confessing to any priest, provided he has the proper faculties; but a conscientious Christian will go—with complete freedom—to the priest he knows is a good shepherd, who can help him to look up

again and see once more, on high, the Lord's
star.

GOLD, INCENSE AND MYRRH

Such was their sentiment that the Gospel 35
almost repeats itself: "When they saw the star
again they rejoiced with exceeding great joy."[17]
Why were they so happy? Because those who
never doubted receive proof from the Lord that
the star had not disappeared. They had ceased
to contemplate it visibly, but they had kept it
always in their soul. Such is the Christian's
vocation. If we do not lose faith, if we keep our
hope in Jesus Christ who will be with us "until
the consummation of the world,"[18] then the star
reappears. And with this fresh proof that our
vocation is real, we are conscious of a greater
joy which increases our faith, hope, and love.

"Going into the house they saw the child
with Mary, his Mother, and they fell down and
worshipped him."[19] We also kneel down before

[17] Mt 2:10: *Videntes autem stellam gavisi sunt gaudio magno
valde.*
[18] Mt 28:20.
[19] Mt 2:11.

Jesus, God hidden in humanity. We tell him once more that we do not want to turn our backs on his divine call, that we shall never separate ourselves from him, that we shall remove from our path all that may be an obstacle to our fidelity and that we sincerely wish to be docile to his inspirations. You, in your own heart, and I in mine—because I am praying intimately with deep silent cries—are telling the child Jesus that we desire to fulfill our duties as well as the servants of the parable, so that we too may hear the response: "Well done, good and faithful servant."[20]

"Then opening their treasures, they offered him gifts, of gold, frankincense, and myrrh."[21] Let us pause here a while to understand this passage of the holy Gospel. How is it possible that we, who are nothing and worth nothing, can make an offering to God? We read in the Scriptures: "Every good endowment and every perfect gift is from above".[22] Man does not even manage to discover fully the depth and beauty of the Lord's gifts. "If you knew the gift of

---

[20] Mt 25:23.
[21] Mt 2:11.
[22] Jas 1:17.

THE EPIPHANY OF OUR LORD

THE EPIPHANY OF OUR LORD   83

God!"[23] Jesus exclaims to the Samaritan woman.
Jesus Christ has taught us to expect everything
from the Father and to seek first of all the
kingdom of God and his justice, and everything
else will be given to us in addition, for he
knows well what we need.[24]

In the economy of salvation our Father looks
after each soul with loving care: "Each has his
own special gift from God, one of one kind and
one of another."[25] It would, therefore, seem
useless to be concerned about presenting to the
Lord something that he has no need of. As
debtors who have nothing with which to pay,[26]
our gifts would be like those of the old law that
are no longer acceptable to God: "Sacrifices and
oblations and holocausts for sin you have not
desired: neither are they pleasing to you."[27]

But the Lord knows full well that giving is
a vital need for those in love, and he himself
points out what he desires from us. He does
not care for riches, nor for the fruits or the
beasts of the earth, nor for the sea or the air,

---

[23] Jn 4:10.
[24] Cf. Mt 6:32-33.
[25] 1 Cor 7:7.
[26] Cf. Mt 18:25.
[27] Heb 10:8.

because they all belong to him. He wants something intimate, which we have to give him freely: "My son, give me your heart."[28] Do you see? God is not satisfied with sharing. He wants it all. It's not our things he wants. It is ourselves. It is only when we give ourselves that we can offer other gifts to our Lord.

Let us give him gold. The precious gold we receive when in spirit we are detached from money and material goods. Let us not forget that these things are good, for they come from God. But the Lord has laid down that we should use them without allowing our hearts to become attached to them, putting them to good use for the benefit of all mankind.

Earthly goods are not bad, but they are debased when man sets them up as idols, when he adores them. They are ennobled when they are converted into instruments for good, for just and charitable Christian undertakings. We cannot seek after material goods as if they were a treasure. Our treasure is here, in a manger. Our treasure is Christ and all our love and desire must be centered on him, "for where our treasure is, there will our hearts be also."[29]

[28] Prov 23:26.
[29] Mt 6:21.

We offer frankincense that rises up to the 36
Lord: our desire to live a noble life which gives
off the "aroma of Christ."[30] To impregnate our
words and actions with his aroma is to sow
understanding and friendship. We should
accompany others so that no one is left, or can
feel, abandoned. Our charity has to be affectionate, full of human warmth.

That is what Jesus Christ teaches us.
Mankind awaited the coming of the Savior for
centuries. The prophets had announced his
coming in a thousand ways. Even in the farthest
corners of the earth, where a great part of God's
revelation to men was perhaps lost through sin
or ignorance, the longing for God, the desire
to be redeemed, had been kept alive.

When the fullness of time comes, no philo-
sophical genius, no Plato or Socrates appears to
fulfill the mission of redemption. Nor does a
powerful conqueror, another Alexander, take
over the earth. Instead a child is born in
Bethlehem. He it is who is to redeem the world.
But before he speaks he loves with deeds. It is
no magic formula he brings, because he knows
that the salvation he offers must pass through

---

[30] 2 Cor 2:15: *bonus odor Christi.*

human hearts. What does he first do? He laughs and cries and sleeps defenseless, as a baby, though he is God incarnate. And he does this so that we may fall in love with him, so that we may learn to take him in our arms.

We realize once again that this is what Christianity is all about. If a Christian does not love with deeds, he has failed as a Christian, besides failing as a person. You cannot think of others as if they were digits, or rungs on a ladder on which you can rise, or a multitude to be harangued or humiliated, praised or despised, according to circumstances. Be mindful of what others are—and first of all those who are at your side: children of God, with all the dignity that marvelous title entails.

We have to behave as God's children toward all God's sons and daughters. Our love has to be a dedicated love, practiced everyday, and made up of a thousand little details of understanding, hidden sacrifice, and unnoticed self-giving. This is the "aroma of Christ" that made those who lived among our first brothers in the faith exclaim: See how they love one another!

The ideal is not out of reach. A Christian is no Tartarin of Tarascon, a literary character bent on hunting lions in the corridors of his home, where they were not to be found. I always speak about real daily life, about the sanctification of work, of family bonds, of friendships. If we aren't Christian in these things, where will we be Christian? The pleasant smell of incense comes from some small, hidden grains of incense placed upon the burning charcoal. Likewise is the "aroma of Christ" noticed among men—not in a sudden burst of flame, but in the constant red-hot embers of virtues such as justice, loyalty, faithfulness, understanding, generosity, and cheerfulness.

Together with the Magi we also offer myrrh, 37 the spirit of sacrifice that can never be lacking in a Christian life. Myrrh reminds us of the passion of our Lord. On the cross he is offered wine mingled with myrrh.[31] And it was with myrrh that his body was anointed for burial.[32] But do not think that to meditate on the need for sacrifice and mortification means to add a note of sadness to this joyful feast we celebrate today.

[31] Cf. Mk 15:23.
[32] Cf. Jn 19:39.

Mortification is not pessimism or bitterness. Mortification is useless without charity. That is why we must seek mortifications which, while helping us develop a proper dominion over the things of this earth, do not mortify those who live with us. A Christian has no warrant to act as torturer, nor should he allow himself to be treated as a feeble wretch. A Christian is a man who knows how to love with deeds and to prove his love on the touchstone of suffering.

But, I must remind you, mortification does not usually consist in great renunciations, for situations requiring great self-denial seldom occur. Mortification is made up of small conquests, such as smiling at those who annoy us, denying the body some superfluous fancy, getting accustomed to listening to others, making full use of the time God allots us... and so many other details. We find it in the apparently trifling problems, difficulties, and worries which arise in the course of each day without our looking for them.

HOLY MARY, STAR OF THE EAST

38   I will finish repeating some words from today's Gospel: "Going into the house they saw

the child with Mary, his Mother." Our Lady is always by her Son. The Magi are not received by a king on a high throne, but by a child in the arms of his Mother. Let us ask the Mother of God, who is our Mother, to prepare for us the way that leads to the fullness of love. *Cor Mariae dulcissimum, iter para tutum*: "Most Sweet Heart of Mary, prepare a safe way!" Her sweet heart knows the surest path for finding Christ.

The three kings had their star. We have Mary, Star of the Sea, Star of the East. We say to her today: Holy Mary, Star of the Sea, Morning Star, help your children. Our zeal for souls must know no frontiers, for no one is excluded from Christ's love. The three kings were the first among the gentiles to be called. But once the redemption had been accomplished, "there is neither male nor female"— there is no discrimination of any type—"for you are all one in Christ Jesus."[33]

We Christians cannot exclude anyone; we cannot segregate or classify souls. "Many will come from the East and West."[34] All find a place in Christ's heart. His arms, as we admire him

[33] Gal 3:28.
[34] Mt 8:11.

again in the manger, are those of a child; but they are the same arms that will be extended on the cross drawing all men to himself.[35]

And a last thought for that just man, our father and lord St Joseph, who apparently has a very minor role in the Epiphany—as usual. I can imagine him recollected in prayer, lovingly protecting the Son of God made man who has been entrusted to his paternal care. With the marvelous refinement of one who does not live for himself, the holy patriarch spends himself in silent prayer and effective service.

We have talked today about practising a life of prayer and concern for apostolate. Who could be a better teacher for us than St Joseph? If you want my advice, which I have never tired of repeating these many years, *Ite ad Ioseph*: "Go to Joseph."[36] He will show us definite ways, both human and divine, to approach Jesus. And soon you will dare, as he did, "to take up in his arms, kiss, clothe, and look after"[37] this child

---

[35] Cf. Jn 12:32.

[36] Gen 41:55.

[37] From the prayer to St Joseph as a preparation for holy Mass, found in the Roman Missal: *O felicem virum, beatum Ioseph, cui datum est, Deum, quem multi reges voluerunt videre et non viderunt, audire et non audierunt, non solum videre et audire, sed portare, deosculari, vestire et custodire!*

God who has been born unto us. As an homage of their veneration, the Magi offered gold, frankincense, and myrrh to Jesus. Joseph gave all his youthful and loving heart.

IN JOSEPH'S WORKSHOP*

The whole Church recognizes St Joseph as
a patron and guardian. For centuries many
different features of his life have caught the
attention of believers. He was a man ever
faithful to the mission God gave him. That is
why, for many years now, I have liked to
address him affectionately as "our father and
lord."

St Joseph really is a father and lord. He
protects those who revere him and accompanies
them on their journey through this life—just as
he protected and accompanied Jesus when he
was growing up. As you get to know him, you
discover that the holy patriarch is also a master
of the interior life—for he teaches us to know
Jesus and share our life with him, and to realize
that we are part of God's family. St Joseph can

---

* A homily given on March 19, 1963, the feast of St Joseph.

teach us these lessons, because he is an ordinary man, a family man, a worker who earned his living by manual labor—all of which has great significance and is a source of happiness for us.

As we celebrate his feast day, I should like to remind you of him and of what the Gospel says about him. This will help us find out what God is telling us through the simple life of Mary's husband.

ST JOSEPH IN THE GOSPEL

40 Both St Matthew and St Luke tell us that Joseph came from a noble line—the house of David and Solomon, kings of Israel. The details of his ancestry are not quite clear. We don't know which of the Gospel's two genealogies refers to Joseph, Jesus' father according to Jewish law, and which to Mary, his Mother according to the flesh. Nor do we know if Joseph came from Bethlehem, where he went for the census, or Nazareth, where he lived and worked.

On the other hand, we do know that he was not well-to-do: he was just a worker, like so many millions of people throughout the world.

He worked at the same demanding and humble job which God chose for himself when he took our flesh and came to live just like the rest of us for thirty years.

Scripture tells us St Joseph was a craftsman. Some Fathers of the Church add that he was a carpenter. When talking of the life of Jesus, St Justin says that he made ploughs and yokes.[1] Perhaps that's why St Isidore of Seville concludes that St Joseph was a blacksmith. In any event, he was a workman who supplied the needs of his fellow citizens with a manual skill acquired through years of toil and sweat.

The Gospels give us a picture of Joseph as a remarkably sound man who was in no way frightened or shy of life. On the contrary, he faced up to problems, dealt with difficult situations, and showed responsibility and initiative in whatever he was asked to do.

I don't agree with the traditional picture of St Joseph as an old man, even though it may have been prompted by a desire to emphasize the perpetual virginity of Mary. I see him as a strong young man, perhaps a few years older

---

[1] Cf. St Justin, *Dialogus cum Tryphone*, 88, 2, 8 (PG 6, 687).

than our Lady, but in the prime of his life and work.

You don't have to wait to be old or lifeless to practice the virtue of chastity. Purity comes from love; and the strength and gaiety of youth are no obstacle for noble love. Joseph had a young heart and a young body when he married Mary, when he learned of the mystery of her divine motherhood, when he lived in her company, respecting the integrity God wished to give the world as one more sign that he had come to share the life of his creatures. Anyone who cannot understand a love like that knows very little of true love and is a complete stranger to the Christian meaning of chastity.

Joseph was, we have said, a craftsman from Galilee, just one man among many. What had life to offer to someone from a forgotten village like Nazareth? Nothing but work: work every day, with the same constant effort. And at the end of the day, a poor little house in which to rest and regain energy for the next day.

But the name Joseph, in Hebrew, means "God will add." God adds unsuspected dimensions to the holy lives of those who do his will. He adds the one important dimension which gives meaning to everything, the divine dimension. To the humble and holy life of Joseph he added—if I may put it this way—the lives of the Virgin Mary and of Jesus, our Lord. God does not allow himself to be outdone in generosity. Joseph could make his own the words of Mary, his wife: "He has looked graciously upon the lowliness of his hand-maid... because he who is mighty, he whose name is holy, has wrought for me his won-ders."[2]

St Joseph was an ordinary sort of man on whom God relied to do great things. He did exactly what the Lord wanted him to do, in each and every event that went to make up his life. That is why Scripture praises Joseph as "a just man."[3] And in Hebrew a just man means a good and faithful servant of God, someone who fulfills the divine will,[4] or who is hon-orable and charitable toward his neighbor.[5] So a just man is someone who loves God and proves his love by keeping God's command-ments and directing his whole life toward the service of his brothers, his fellow men.

[2] Lk 1:48-49: *Quia respexit humilitatem ancillae suae.*
[3] Mt 1:19.
[4] Cf. Gen 7:1; 18:23-32; Ezek 18:5ff; Prov 12:10.
[5] Cf. Tob 7:5; 9:9.

JOSEPH'S FAITH, HOPE, AND LOVE

41   To be just is not simply a matter of obeying rules. Goodness should grow from the inside; it should be deep and vital—for "the just man lives by faith."[6] These words, which later became a frequent subject of St Paul's meditation, really did apply in the case of St Joseph. He didn't fulfill the will of God in a routine or perfunctory way; he did it spontaneously and wholeheartedly. For him the law which every practicing Jew lived by was not a code or a cold list of precepts, but an expression of the will of the living God. So he knew how to recognize the Lord's voice when it came to him so unexpectedly and so surprisingly.

St Joseph's life was simple, but it was not easy. After considerable soul-searching, he learned that the son of Mary had been conceived through the Holy Spirit. And this child, the Son of God, the descendant of David according to the flesh, was born in a cave. Angels celebrated his birth, and distinguished people from distant countries came to adore him. But the King of Judea wanted to kill him,

[6] Hab 2:4.

and they had to flee. The Son of God was, it appeared, a defenseless child who would live in Egypt.

When relating these events in his Gospel, St Matthew continually emphasizes Joseph's faithfulness. He kept the commandments of God without wavering, even though the meaning of those commandments was sometimes obscure or their relation to the rest of the divine plan hidden from him.

The Fathers of the Church and other spiritual writers frequently emphasize the firmness of Joseph's faith. Referring to the angel's command to fly from Herod and take refuge in Egypt,[7] St John Chrysostom comments: "On hearing this, Joseph was not shocked nor did he say: 'This is strange. You yourself made it known not long ago that he would save his people, and now you are incapable even of saving him—we have to flee, to set out on a long journey and spend a long while in a strange place; that contradicts your promise.' Joseph does not think in this way, for he is a man who trusts God. Nor does he ask when he will return, even though the angel left it so

---

[7] Cf. Mt 2:13.

42

vague: 'Stay there, until I tell you to return.'
Joseph does not object; he obeys and believes
and joyfully accepts all the trials."[8]

Joseph's faith does not falter, he obeys
quickly and to the letter. To understand this
lesson better, we should remember that Joseph's faith is active, that his docility is not a
passive submission to the course of events. For
the Christian's faith has nothing whatever to do
with conformity, inertia or lack of initiative.

Joseph entrusted himself unreservedly to the
care of God, but he always reflected on events
and so was able to reach that level of understanding of the works of God which is true
wisdom. In this way he learned little by little
that supernatural plans have a logic which at
times upsets human plans.

In the different circumstances of his life, St
Joseph never refuses to think, never neglects his
responsibilities. On the contrary, he puts his
human experience at the service of faith. When
he returns from Egypt, "learning that Archelaus
had succeeded his father Herod as ruler of
Judea, he was afraid to go there."[9] In other

[8] *In Matthaeum homiliae*, 8, 3 (PG 57, 85).
[9] Mt 2:22.

words, he had learned to work within the divine plan. And to confirm that he was doing the right thing, Joseph received an instruction to return to Galilee.

That's the way St Joseph's faith was: full, confident, complete. And it expressed itself in an effective dedication to the will of God and an intelligent obedience. With the faith went love. His faith nurtured his love of God, who was fulfilling the promises made to Abraham, Jacob and Moses, and his affection for Mary his wife and her Son. This faith, hope, and love would further the great mission which God was beginning in the world through, among others, a carpenter in Galilee: the redemption of man.

Faith, hope, love: these are the supports of 43 Joseph's life and of all Christian lives. Joseph's self-giving is an inter-weaving of faithful love, loving faith, and confident hope. His feast is thus a good opportunity for us to renew our commitment to the Christian calling God has given each of us.

When you sincerely desire to live by faith, hope, and love, the renewal of your commitment is not a matter of picking up again something neglected. When there really is faith, hope, and love, renewal means staying in God's hands, despite our personal faults, mistakes, and defects. It is a confirmation of our faithfulness. Renewing our commitment means renewing our fidelity to what God wants of us: it means expressing our love in deeds.

Love has certain standard features. Sometimes we speak of love as if it were an impulse to self-satisfaction or a mere means to selfish fulfillment of one's own personality. But that's not love. True love means going out of oneself, giving oneself. Love brings joy, but a joy whose roots are in the shape of a cross. As long as we are on earth and have not yet arrived at the fullness of the future life, we can never have true love without sacrifice and pain. This pain becomes sweet and lovable; it is a source of interior joy. But it is an authentic pain, for it involves overcoming one's own selfishness and taking Love as the rule of each and every thing we do.

44   Anything done out of love is important, however small it might appear. God has come to us, even though we are miserable creatures, and he has told us that he loves us: "My delight is to be among the sons of men."[10] Our Lord

---

[10] Prov 8:31: *Deliciae meae esse cum filiis hominum.*

tells us that everything is valuable—those actions which from a human point of view we regard as extraordinary and those which seem unimportant. Nothing is wasted. No man is worthless to God. All of us are called to share the kingdom of heaven—each with his own vocation: in his home, his work, his civic duties, and the exercise of his rights.

St Joseph's life is a good example of this: it was simple, ordinary, and normal, made up of years of the same work, of days—just one day after another—which were monotonous from a human point of view. I have often thought about this, meditating on St Joseph's life; it is one of the reasons why I have a special devotion to him.

When Pope John XXIII closed the first session of Vatican Council II and announced that the name of St Joseph was going to be included in the canon of the Mass, a very important churchman telephoned me to say, "Congratulations. Listening to the Pope's announcement, I thought immediately of you and of how happy you'd be." And indeed I was happy, for in that conciliar gathering, which represented the whole Church brought together in the Holy Spirit, there was proclaimed the

great supernatural value of St Joseph's life, the
value of an ordinary life of work done in God's
presence and in total fulfillment of his will.

SANCTIFY WORK AND IT WILL
SANCTIFY YOU AND OTHERS

45   In describing the spirit of the association* to
which I have devoted my life, Opus Dei, I have
said that it hinges upon ordinary work, *professional work* carried out in the midst of the world.
God's calling gives us a mission: it invites us
to share in the unique task of the Church, to
bear witness to Christ before our fellowmen
and so draw all things toward God.

Our calling discloses to us the meaning of
our existence. It means being convinced,
through faith, of the reason for our life on earth.
Our life, the present, past, and future, acquires
a new dimension, a depth we did not perceive

---

* When Blessed Josemaría Escrivá gave this homily, the
juridical status of Opus Dei was still provisional, not suited
to its nature. He had to resort to using generic terms like
"association", which was the most adequate at the time,
given the lack of appropriate terminology. The situation
changed in 1982 when Pope John Paul II established Opus
Dei as a personal prelature.

before. All happenings and events now fall into their true perspective: we understand where God is leading us, and we feel ourselves borne along by this task entrusted to us.

God draws us from the shadows of our ignorance, our groping through history, and, no matter what our occupation in the world, he calls us with a strong voice, as he once called Peter and Andrew: "Follow me and I will make you fishers of men."[11]

He who lives by faith may meet with difficulty and struggle, suffering and even bitterness, but never depression or anguish, because he knows that his life is worthwhile, he knows why he has been born. "I am the light of the world," Christ exclaimed. "He who follows me does not walk in the darkness, but will have the light of life."[12]

To deserve this light from God, we must love. We must be humble enough to realize we need to be saved, and we must say with Peter: "Lord, to whom shall we go? You have words of life everlasting, and we have come to believe

[11] Mt 4:19: *Venite post me, et faciam vos fieri piscatores hominum.*

[12] Jn 8:12: *Ego sum lux mundi: qui sequitur me non ambulat in tenebris, sed habebit lumen vitae.*

and to know that you are the Christ, the Son of God."[13] If we really do this, if we allow God's word to enter our hearts, we can truly say that we do not walk in darkness, for the light of God will shine out over our weakness and our personal defects, as the sun shines above the storm.

46   Christian faith and calling affect our whole existence, not just a part of it. Our relations with God necessarily demand giving ourselves, giving ourselves completely. The man of faith sees life, in all its dimensions, from a new perspective: that which is given us by God.

You, who celebrate with me today this feast of St Joseph, are men who work in different human professions; you have your own homes, you belong to so many different countries and have different languages. You have been educated in lecture halls or in factories and offices. You have worked in your profession for years, established professional and personal friendships with your colleagues, helped to solve the problems of your companies and your communities.

[13] Jn 6:69-70.

Well then: I remind you once again that all this is not foreign to God's plan. Your human vocation is a part—and an important part—of your divine vocation. That is the reason why you must strive for holiness, giving a particular character to your human personality, a style to your life; contributing at the same time to the sanctification of others, your fellow men; sanctifying your work and your environment: the profession or job that fills your day, your home and family and the country where you were born and which you love.

Work is part and parcel of man's life on 47 earth. It involves effort, weariness, exhaustion: signs of the suffering and struggle which accompany human existence and which point to the reality of sin and the need for redemption. But in itself work is not a penalty or a curse or a punishment: those who speak of it that way have not understood sacred Scripture properly.

It is time for us Christians to shout from the rooftops that work is a gift from God and that it makes no sense to classify men differently, according to their occupation, as if some jobs were nobler than others. Work, all work, bears witness to the dignity of man, to his dominion

over creation. It is an opportunity to develop
one's personality. It is a bond of union with
others, the way to support one's family, a
means of aiding in the improvement of the
society in which we live and in the progress of
all humanity.

For a Christian these horizons extend and
grow wider. For work is a participation in the
creative work of God. When he created man
and blessed him, he said: "Be fruitful, multiply,
fill the earth, and conquer it. Be masters of the
fish of the sea, the birds of heaven, and all
living animals on the earth."[14] And, moreover,
since Christ took it into his hands, work has
become for us a redeemed and redemptive
reality. Not only is it the background of man's
life, it is a means and path of holiness. It is
something to be sanctified and something
which sanctifies.

48   It is well to remember that the dignity of
work is based on Love. Man's great privilege
is to be able to love and to transcend what is
fleeting and ephemeral. He can love other
creatures, pronounce an "I" and a "you" which
are full of meaning. And he can love God, who

[14] Gen 1:28.

opens heaven's gates to us, makes us members of his family and allows us also to talk to him in friendship, face to face.

This is why man ought not to limit himself to material production. Work is born of love; it is a manifestation of love and is directed toward love. We see the hand of God, not only in the wonders of nature, but also in our experience of work and effort. Work thus becomes prayer and thanksgiving, because we know we are placed on earth by God, that we are loved by him and made heirs to his promises. We have been rightly told, "In eating, in drinking, in all that you do, do everything for God's glory."[15]

Professional work is also an apostolate, an   49 opportunity to give ourselves to others, to reveal Christ to them and lead them to God the Father—all of which is the overflow of the charity which the Holy Spirit pours into our hearts. When St Paul explained to the Ephesians how their conversion to Christianity should affect their lives, one of the things he said was: "Anyone who was a thief must stop stealing; he should try to find some useful manual work

[15] 1 Cor 10:31.

instead and be able to do some good by helping
others that are in need."[16] Men need earthly
bread to sustain them in their lives on earth;
they also need bread from heaven to enlighten
their minds and inflame their hearts. With your
work, taking advantage of the opportunities it
offers, in your conversations and your dealings
with others, you can and should carry out this
apostolic precept.

If we work with this attitude, our life,
despite its human limitations, will be a foretaste
of the glory of heaven, of that communion with
God and his saints where self-giving, faithfulness, friendship, and joy reign supreme. Your
ordinary professional work will provide the
true, solid, noble material out of which you will
build a truly Christian life. You will use your
work to make fruitful the grace which comes
to us from Christ.

Faith, hope, and charity will come into play
in your professional work done for God. The
incidents, the problems, the friendships which
your work brings with it, will give you food
for prayer. The effort to improve your own
daily occupation will give you the chance to

[16] Eph 4:28.

experience the cross which is essential for a Christian. When you feel your weakness, the failures which arise even in human undertakings, you will gain in objectivity, in humility, and in understanding for others. Successes and joys will prompt you to thanksgiving and to realize that you do not live for yourself, but for the service of others and of God.

IF YOU WANT TO BE USEFUL, SERVE

If we want to live this way, sanctifying our 50 profession or job, we really must work well, with human and supernatural intensity. I would like to remind you now, by way of contrast, of a story from the apocryphal gospels: "Jesus' father, who was a carpenter, made ploughs and yokes." Once, the story continues, "a certain important person asked him to make a bed. But it happened that one of the shafts was shorter than the other, so Joseph did not know what to do. Then, the child Jesus said to his Father: 'Put the two shafts on the ground and make them even at one end.' And Joseph did so. Jesus got at the other end, took the shorter beam of wood and stretched it until it was the same length as the other. Joseph, his

father, was full of astonishment at this miracle
and showered embraces and kisses on the
Child, saying: 'How fortunate am I that God
has given me this Child!'"[17]

Joseph would give God no such thanks, he
would never work in this way. He was not one
for easy solutions and little miracles, but a man
of perseverance, effort and, when needed,
ingenuity. The Christian knows that God works
miracles, that he did them centuries ago, that
he has continued doing them since, and that he
still works them now, because "the Lord's hand
is not shortened."[18] But miracles are a sign of
the saving power of God, not a cure for incom-
petence nor an easy way to dodge effort. The
"miracle" which God asks of you is to persevere
in your Christian and divine vocation, sanctifying each day's work: the miracle of turning
the prose of each day into heroic verse by the
love which you put into your ordinary work.
God waits for you there. He expects you to be
a responsible person, with the zeal of an apostle
and the competence of a good worker.

---

[17] *Gospel of the Childhood*, falsely attributed to St Thomas,
n. 13.
[18] Is 59:1: *Ecce non est abbreviata manus Domini.*

And so, as the motto of your work, I can give you this one: *If you want to be useful, serve.* For, in the first place, in order to do things properly, you must know *how* to do them. I cannot see the integrity of a person who does not strive to attain professional skills and to carry out properly the task entrusted to his care. It's not enough to want to do good; we must know how to do it. And, if our desire is real, it will show itself in the effort we make to use the right methods, finishing things well, achieving human perfection.

But human usefulness and technique, our 51 knowledge of our job, should have a feature which was basic to St Joseph's work and should be so for every Christian: the spirit of service, the desire to contribute to the well-being of other people. Joseph's work was not self-centered, even though his active life made him a strong and forceful personality. When he worked, he was aware that he was carrying out God's will; he was thinking of his people, of Jesus and Mary, and of everyone in Nazareth.

Joseph was one of the few craftsmen in Nazareth, if not the only one—a carpenter perhaps. But, as normally happens in villages, he must have felt called upon to turn his attention to other things: fixing a mill that was not working or, with the coming of winter, repairing the tiles of a roof. I am sure Joseph knew how to lend a hand in many difficulties, with work well done. His skilled work was in the service of others, to brighten the lives of other families in the town; and with a smile, a friendly word, or what might have seemed to be just a passing remark, he would restore faith and happiness to those in danger of losing them.

52   Sometimes, in the case of people poorer than himself, Joseph would charge only a little—just enough for his customer to feel that he had paid. But normally he would charge a reasonable amount—not too much or too little. He would demand what was justly owed him, for faithfulness to God cannot mean giving up rights which in fact are duties. St Joseph had to be properly paid, since this was his means of supporting the family which God had entrusted to him.

We should demand our rights, but not for selfish reasons. We do not love justice if we do not wish to see it fulfilled in the lives of others. In the same way, it is wrong to shut oneself up in comfortable religiosity, forgetting the needs of others. The man who wishes to be just in God's eyes also tries to establish the reign of justice among men. And not only for the good of God's name, but because to be a Christian means to work at fulfilling all the noble yearnings of men. Paraphrasing a well-known text of St John,[19] we can say that the man who says he acts justly toward God, but does not do so with other men, is a liar: and there is no truth in him.

Like all Christians at that time, I too was happy and grateful at the Church's decision to declare a liturgical feast in honor of St Joseph the Worker. This feast, which ratifies the divine value of work, shows how the Church publicly echoes central truths of the Gospel which God wishes men to meditate, especially in our own time.

I have often spoken of it before, but let me 53 insist once again on the naturalness and simplicity of St Joseph's life, which was in no way remote from that of his neighbors, and which raised no artificial obstacles to his dealings with them.

---

[19] Cf. 1 Jn 4:20.

So, though it may be proper to some periods or situations, I do not like to talk of Catholic workers, Catholic engineers, Catholic doctors and so on, as if describing a species within a genus, as if Catholics formed a little group separate from others. That creates the impression that there is a chasm between Christians and the rest of society. While respecting the contrary opinion, I think it more correct to speak of workers who are Catholics, or Catholics who are workers or engineers. For a man of faith who practices a profession, whether intellectual, technical or manual, feels himself and is in fact at one with others; he is the same as others, with the same rights and obligations, the same desire to improve, the same interest in facing and solving common problems.

The Catholic who is prepared to live in this way will, through his daily life, give a proof of his faith, hope, and charity: a simple and normal testimony without need of pomp and circumstance. The vitality of his life will show the constant presence of the Church in the world, since all Catholics are themselves the Church, because they are members in their own right of the one People of God.

HOW JOSEPH RELATES TO JESUS

For some time now I have enjoyed using a 54
moving invocation to St Joseph, which the
Church has offered us, in the preparatory
prayers of the Mass: "Joseph, blessed and
happy man, who was permitted to see and hear
the God whom many kings wished in vain to
see and hear, and not only to see and hear him,
but carry him in your arms, kiss him, clothe him
and look after him: pray for us." This prayer
will help us to begin the last topic on which
I would like to touch today: Joseph's affectionate dealings with Jesus.

The life of Jesus was, for St Joseph, a recur-
ring discovery of his own vocation. We recalled
earlier those first years full of contrasting circumstances: glorification and flight, the majesty
of the wise men and the poverty of the manger,
the song of the angels and the silence of
mankind. When the moment comes to present
the child in the temple, Joseph, who carries the
modest offering of a pair of doves, sees how
Simeon and Anna proclaim Jesus as the Messiah: "His father and mother listened with
wonder," says St Luke.[20] Later, when the child

[20] Lk 2:33.

stays behind in Jerusalem, unknown to Mary
and Joseph, and they find him again after three
days' search, the same evangelist tells us, "They
were astonished."[21]

Joseph is surprised and astonished. God
gradually reveals his plans to him, and he tries
to understand them. As with every soul who
wishes to follow Jesus closely, he soon discov-
ers that here is no laggard's pace, no room for
the halfhearted. For God is not content with our
achieving a certain level and staying there. He
doesn't want us to rest on our laurels. God
always asks more: his ways are not the ways
of men. St Joseph, more than anyone else before
or since, learned from Jesus to be alert to
recognize God's wonders, to have his mind and
heart awake.

55   But if Joseph learned from Jesus to live in a
divine way, I would be bold enough to say
that, humanly speaking, there was much he
taught God's Son. There is something I do not
quite like in that title of foster father which is
sometimes given to Joseph, because it might
make us think of the relationship between
Joseph and Jesus as something cold and exter-

---

[21] Lk 2:48.

nal. Certainly our faith tells us that he was not his father according to the flesh, but this is not the only kind of fatherhood.

"Joseph," we read in a sermon of St Augustine, "not only claims the name of father, but he has a greater claim to it than any other." And then he adds: "How was he father? All the more effectively, the more chaste the paternity. Some thought that he was the father of our Lord Jesus Christ in the same way as other fathers who beget sons carnally and do not receive them only as the fruit of a spiritual love. This is why St Luke says: 'People thought he was the father of Jesus.' Why does he say only they thought? Because this thought and human judgment refer to what is usual among men. And our Lord was not born of the seed of Joseph. Yet of the piety and charity of Joseph a son was born to him, of the Virgin Mary, and this was the Son of God."[22]

Joseph loved Jesus as a father loves his son and showed his love by giving him the best he had. Joseph, caring for the child as he had been commanded, made Jesus a craftsman, transmitting his own professional skill to him.

[22] *Sermo* 51, 20 (PL 38, 351).

So the neighbors of Nazareth will call Jesus both *faber* and *fabri filius:* the craftsman and the son of the craftsman.[23] Jesus worked in Joseph's workshop and by Joseph's side. What must Joseph have been, how grace must have worked through him, that he should be able to fulfill this task of the human upbringing of the Son of God!

For Jesus must have resembled Joseph: in his way of working, in the features of his character, in his way of speaking. Jesus' realism, his eye for detail, the way he sat at table and broke bread, his preference for using everyday situations to give doctrine—all this reflects his childhood and the influence of Joseph.

It's not possible to ignore this sublime mystery: Jesus who is man, who speaks with the accent of a particular district of Israel, who resembles a carpenter called Joseph, is the Son of God. And who can teach God anything? But he is also truly man and lives a normal life: first, as a child, then as a boy helping in Joseph's workshop, finally as a grown man in the prime of life. "Jesus advanced in wisdom and age and grace before God and men."[24]

---

[23] Mk 6:3; Mt 13:55.
[24] Lk 2:52.

In human life, Joseph was Jesus' master in 56 their daily contact, full of refined affection, glad to deny himself to take better care of Jesus. Isn't that reason enough for us to consider this just man, this holy patriarch, in whom the faith of the old covenant bears fruit, as a master of interior life? Interior life is nothing but continual and direct conversation with Christ, so as to become one with him. And Joseph can tell us many things about Jesus. Therefore, never neglect devotion to him—*Ite ad Ioseph:* "Go to Joseph"—as Christian tradition puts it in the words of the old testament .[25]

A master of interior life, a worker deeply involved in his job, God's servant in continual contact with Jesus: that is Joseph. *Ite ad Ioseph.* With St Joseph, the Christian learns what it means to belong to God and fully to assume one's place among men, sanctifying the world. Get to know Joseph and you will find Jesus. Talk to Joseph and you will find Mary, who always sheds peace about her in that attractive workshop in Nazareth.

[25] Gen 41:55.

in human life, Joseph, who is so masterly in
labor, only a man, full of reflective attention, glad
to deny himself to take better care of Jesus. Isn't
that reason enough for us to consider that this is
a new theology patriarch, now from the faith of
the old covenant, bears fruit has a measure of
interior life? Interior life is nothing but a continual and direct conversation with Christ Jesus
to become one with him. And Joseph can tell
us many times about Jesus. Therefore, never
reject devotion to him – to St. Joseph. "Go to
Joseph." As Christian teaching puts it, in the
words of the old testament.

A master of interior life, a worker deeply
involved in his job, God's servant in continual
contact with Jesus: that is Joseph. Ite ad Ioseph.

With St. Joseph, the Christian learns what it
means to belong to God and fully to assume,
one's place among men, sanctifying the world.
Get to know Joseph and you will find Jesus.
Talk to Joseph and you will find Mary, who
always shed peace about her in that attractive
workshop in Nazareth.

THE CONVERSION OF
THE CHILDREN OF GOD*

We are at the beginning of Lent: a time of penance, purification, and conversion. It is not an easy program, but then Christianity is not an easy way of life. It is not enough just to *be* in the Church, letting the years roll by. In our life, in the life of Christians, our first conversion—that unique moment which each of us remembers, when we clearly understood everything the Lord was asking of us—is certainly very significant. But the later conversions are even more important, and they are increasingly demanding. To facilitate the work of grace in these conversions, we need to keep our soul young; we have to call upon our Lord, know how to listen to him and, having found out what has gone wrong, know how to ask his pardon.

* A homily given on March 2, 1952, the first Sunday of Lent.

"If you call upon me, I will listen to you,"[1] we read in this Sunday's liturgy. Isn't it wonderful how God cares for us and is always ready to listen to us—waiting for man to speak? He hears us at all times, but particularly now. Our heart is ready and we have made up our minds to purify ourselves. He hears us and will not disregard the petition of a "humble and contrite heart."[2]

The Lord listens to us. He wants to intervene and enter our lives to free us from evil and fill us with good. "I will rescue him and honor him,"[3] he says of man. So we must hope for glory. Here again we have the beginning of the interior movement that makes up our spiritual life. Hope of glory increases our faith and fosters our charity; the three theological virtues, godly virtues which make us like our Father God, have been set in motion.

What better way to begin Lent? Let's renew our faith, hope, and love. The spirit of penance and the desire for purification come from these virtues. Lent is not only an opportunity for

---

[1] Ps 90:15 (introit of the Mass): *Invocabit me et ego exaudiam eum.*

[2] Ps 50:19.

[3] Ps 90:15 (introit).

increasing our external practices of self-denial.
If we thought it were only that, we would miss
the deep meaning it has in Christian living, for
these external practices are—as I have said—
the result of faith, hope, and charity.

THE RISKY SECURITY OF CHRISTIANS

"He that dwells in the aid of the Most High 58
shall abide under the protection of the God of
heaven."[4]   This is the risky security of the
Christian. We must be convinced that God
hears us, that he is concerned about us. If we
are, we will feel completely at peace. But living
with God is indeed a risky business, for he will
not share things: he wants everything. And if
we move toward him, it means we must be
ready for a new conversion, to take new
bearings, to listen more attentively to his inspirations—those holy desires that he provokes in
every soul—and to put them into practice.

Since our first conscious decision really to
follow the teaching of Christ, we have no doubt

[4] Ps 90:1: *Qui habitat in adiutorio Altissimi, in protectione Dei
coeli commorabitur.*

made good progress along the way of faithfulness to his word. And yet isn't it true that there is still much to be done? Isn't it true, particularly, that there is still so much pride in us? We need, most probably, to change again, to be more loyal and humble, so that we become less selfish and let Christ grow in us, for "He must become more and more, I must become less and less."[5]

We cannot stay still. We must keep going ahead toward the goal St Paul marks out: "It is not I who live, it is Christ that lives in me."[6] This is a high and very noble ambition, this identification with Christ, this holiness. But there is no other way if we are to be consistent with the divine life God has sown in our souls in baptism. To advance we must progress in holiness. Shying away from holiness implies refusing our Christian life its natural growth. The fire of God's love needs to be fed. It must grow each day, gathering strength in our soul; and a fire is maintained by burning more things. If we don't feed it, it may die.

[5] Jn 3:30: *Illum oportet crescere, me autem minui.*
[6] Gal 2:20.

Remember what St Augustine said: "If you say 'enough,' you are lost. Go further, keep going. Don't stay in the same place, don't go back, don't go off the road."[7] Lent should suggest to us these basic questions: Am I advancing in my faithfulness to Christ, in my desire for holiness, in a generous apostolate in my daily life, in my ordinary work among my colleagues?

Each one of us, silently, should answer these questions, and he will see that he needs to change again if Christ is to live in him, if Jesus' image is to be reflected clearly in his behavior. "If any man has a mind to come my way, let him renounce self, and take up his cross daily and follow me."[8] Christ is saying this again, to us, whispering it in our ears: the cross *each day*. As St Jerome puts it: "Not only in time of persecution or when we have the chance of martyrdom, but in all circumstances, in everything we do and think, in everything we say, let us deny what we used to be and let us confess what we now are, reborn as we have been in Christ."[9]

[7] *Sermo* 169, 15 (PL 38, 926).
[8] Lk 9:23.
[9] *Epistola* 121, 3 (PL 22, 1013).

It's an echo of St Paul's words: "Once you were all darkness. Now, in the Lord, you are all daylight. You must live as children of the light. Where light has its effect, men walk in all goodness, holiness, and truth, seeking those things which please God."[10]

Conversion is the task of a moment; sanctification is the work of a lifetime. The divine seed of charity, which God has sown in our souls, wants to grow, to express itself in action, to yield results which continually coincide with what God wants. Therefore, we must be ready to begin again, to find again—in new situations—the light and the stimulus of our first conversion. And that is why we must prepare with a deep examination of conscience, asking our Lord for his help, so that we'll know him and ourselves better. If we want to be converted again, there's no other way.

HERE IS THE TIME OF PARDON

59   "We entreat you not to offer God's grace an ineffectual welcome."[11] Yes, God's grace can fill

10 Eph 5:8-10.
11 2 Cor 6:1 (epistle of the Mass): *Exhortamur ne in vacuum gratiam Dei recipiatis.*

us this Lent, provided we do not close the doors of our heart. We must be well-disposed, we must really want to change; we cannot play with God's grace.

I don't like to speak of fear, for the Christian is moved by the charity of God, which has been shown to us in Christ and teaches us to love all men and the whole of creation. However, we should speak about being responsible, being serious. "Make no mistake about it; you cannot cheat God,"[12] the Apostle Paul warns us.

We must decide. It's wrong to have two candles lighted—one to St Michael and another to the devil. We must snuff out the devil's candle: we must spend our life completely in the service of the Lord. If our desire for holiness is sincere, if we are docile enough to place ourselves in God's hands, everything will go well. For he is always ready to give us his grace, especially at a time like this—grace for a new conversion, step forward in our lives as Christians.

We cannot regard this Lent as just another liturgical season which has simply happened to come around again. It is a unique time: a divine

[12] Gal 6:7.

aid which we should accept. Jesus is passing by and he hopes that we will take a great step forward—today, now.

"Here is the time of pardon; the day of salvation has come already."[13] Once again we hear the voice of the good shepherd calling us tenderly: "I have called you by your name."[14] He calls each of us by our name, the familiar name used only by those who love us. Words cannot describe Jesus' tenderness toward us.

Just think about the wonder of God's love. Our Lord comes out to meet us, he waits for us, he's by the roadside where we cannot but see him, and he calls each of us personally, speaking to us about our own things—which are also his. He stirs us to sorrow, opens our conscience to be generous; he encourages us to want to be faithful, so that we can be called his disciples. When we hear these intimate words of grace, which are by way of an affectionate reproach, we realize at once that our Lord has not forgotten us during all the time in which, through our fault, we did not see him. Christ loves us with all the inexhaustible charity of God's own heart.

---

[13] 2 Cor 6:2 (epistle of the Mass).
[14] Is 43:1: *Ego vocavi te nomine tuo.*

Look how he keeps insisting: "I have answered your prayer in a time of pardon, I have
brought you help in a day of salvation."[15] Since
he promises you glory, his love, and gives it
to you at the right time; since he calls you, what
are you in turn going to give to the Lord, how
are you going to respond, and how will I
respond, to this love of Jesus who has come out
to meet us?

The day of salvation is here before us. The
call of the good shepherd has reached us: "I
have called you by your name." Since love
repays love, we must reply: "Here I am, for you
called me."[16] I have decided not to let this Lent
go by like rain on stones, leaving no trace. I
will let it soak into me, changing me. I will be
converted, I will turn again to the Lord and love
him as he wants to be loved.

"You shall love the Lord your God with your
whole heart and your whole soul and your
whole mind."[17] And St Augustine comments:
"What is left of your heart for loving yourself?
What is left of your soul, of your mind? He says

[15] 2 Cor 6:2 (epistle of the Mass).
[16] 1 Kings 3:9: *Ecce ego quia vocasti me.*
[17] Mt 22:37.

'the whole.' He who made you requires you to give yourself completely."[18]

60   After this affirmation of love, we must behave as lovers of God. "In everything we do, let us behave as servants of the Lord."[19] If you give yourself as he wishes, the influence of grace will be apparent in your professional conduct, in your work, in your effort to divinize human things—be they great or small. For Love gives a new dimension to everything.

But during this Lent, let us not forget that to be servants of God is no easy matter. The text from this Sunday's epistle continues: "As God's ministers we have to show great patience, in times of affliction, of need, of difficulty; under the lash, in prison, in the midst of tumult; when we are tired out, sleepless, and fasting. We have to be pure-minded, enlightened, forgiving, and gracious to others; we have to rely on the Holy Spirit, on unaffected love, on the truth of our message, on the power of God."[20]

---

[18] *Sermo* 34, 4, 7 (PL 38, 212).
[19] 2 Cor 6:4 (epistle of the Mass): *In omnibus exhibeamus nosmetipsos sicut Dei ministros.*
[20] 2 Cor 6:4-7.

In the most varied activities of our day, in all situations, we must act as God's servants, realizing that he is with us, that we are his children. We must be aware of the divine roots burrowing into our life and act accordingly.

These words of the Apostle should make you happy, for they are, as it were, a ratification of your vocation as ordinary Christians in the middle of the world, sharing with other men— your equals—the enthusiasms, the sorrows, and the joys of human life. All this is a way to God. What God asks of you is that you should, always, act as his children and servants.

But these ordinary circumstances of life will be a divine way only if we really change ourselves, if we really give ourselves. For St Paul uses hard words. He promises that the Christian will have a hard life, a life of risk and of constant tension. How we disfigure Christianity if we try to turn it into something nice and comfortable! But neither is it true to think that this deep, serious way of life, which is totally bound up with all the difficulties of human existence, is something full of anguish, oppression or fear.

The Christian is a realist. His supernatural and human realism helps him appreciate all the aspects of his life: sorrow and joy, his own and other people's suffering, certainty and doubt, generosity and selfishness. The Christian experiences all this, and he confronts it all, with human integrity and with the strength he receives from God.

CHRIST IS TEMPTED

61   Lent commemorates the forty days Jesus spent in the desert in preparation for his years of preaching, which culminated in the cross and in the triumph of Easter. Forty days of prayer and penance. At the end: the temptations of Christ, which the liturgy recalls for us in today's Gospel.[21]

The whole episode is a mystery which man cannot hope to understand: God submitting to temptation, letting the evil one have his way. But we can meditate upon it, asking our Lord to help us understand the teaching it contains.

Jesus Christ being tempted... Tradition likes to see Christ's trials in this way: our Lord, who came to be an example to us in all things, wants

---

[21] Cf. Mt 4:1-11.

to suffer temptation as well. And so it is, for Christ was perfect man, like us in everything except sin.[22] After forty days of fasting, with perhaps no food other than herbs and roots and a little water, he feels hungry—he is really hungry, as anyone would be. And when the devil suggests he turn stones into bread, our Lord not only declines the food which his body requires, but he also rejects a greater temptation: that of using his divine power to solve, if we can express it so, a personal problem.

You have noticed how, throughout the Gospels, Jesus doesn't work miracles for his own benefit. He turns water into wine for the wedding guests at Cana;[23] he multiplies loaves and fish for the hungry crowd.[24] But he earns his bread, for years, with his own work. And later, during his journeys through the land of Israel, he lives with the help of those who follow him.[25]

St John tells how after a long journey when Jesus arrived at the well of Sichar, he sent his

---

[22] Cf. Heb 4:15.
[23] Cf. Jn 2:1-11.
[24] Cf. Mk 6:33-46.
[25] Cf. Mt 27:55.

disciples into town to buy food. And when he sees the Samaritan woman coming, he asks her for water, since he has no way of getting it.[26] His body, worn out from a long journey, feels weary. On other occasions he has to yield to sleep to regain his strength.[27] How generous our Lord is in humbling himself and fully accepting his human condition! He does not use his divine power to escape from difficulties or effort. Let's pray that he will teach us to be tough, to love work, to appreciate the human and divine nobility of savoring the consequences of self-giving.

In the second temptation, when the devil suggests Jesus throw himself off the temple tower, Christ again rejects the suggestion to make use of his divine power. Christ isn't looking for vainglory, for show. He teaches us not to stage God as the backdrop for our own excellence. Jesus Christ wants to fulfill the will of his Father without anticipating God's plans, without advancing the time for miracles; he simply plods the hard path of men, the lovable way of the cross.

[26] Cf. Jn 4:4ff.
[27] Cf. Lk 8:23.

Something very similar happens in the third temptation: he is offered kingdoms, power, and glory. The devil tries to extend to human ambitions that devotion which should be reserved wholly for God; he promises us an easy life if we fall down before him, before idols. Our Lord insists that the only true end of adoration is God; and he confirms his will to serve: "Away with you, Satan; it is written, you shall worship the Lord your God, and serve none but him."[28]

We should learn from Jesus' attitude in these 62 trials. During his life on earth he did not even want the glory that belonged to him. Though he had the right to be treated as God, he took the form of a servant, a slave.[29] And so the Christian knows that all glory is due to God and that he must not make use of the sublimity and greatness of the Gospel to further his own interests or human ambitions.

We should learn from Jesus. His attitude in rejecting all human glory is perfectly in keeping with the greatness of his unique mission as the beloved Son of God who takes flesh to save

---

[28] Mt 4:10.
[29] Cf. Phil 2:6-7.

men. He has a mission which the Father affectionately guides with tender care: "You are my
son; I have begotten you this day. Only ask, and
you shall have the nations for your patri-
mony."[30]

And the Christian who, following Christ, has
this attitude of complete adoration of the
Father, also experiences our Lord's loving care:
"He trusts in me, mine it is to rescue him; he
acknowledges my name, from me he shall have
protection."[31]

63   Jesus says "no" to the devil, the prince of
darkness. And immediately all is light. "Then
the devil left him alone; and thereupon angels
came and ministered to him."[32] Jesus has stood
up to the test. And it was a real test, because,
as St Ambrose comments: "He did not act as
God, using his power. If he had, what use
would his example have been? No. As a man
he uses those aids which he shared with us."[33]

The devil, with twisted intention, quoted the
old testament: God will send his angels to

---

[30] Ps 2:7-8: *Filius meus es tu, ego hodie genui te. Postula a me
et dabo tibi gentes haereditatem tuam.*

[31] Ps 90:14 (tract of the Mass).

[32] Mt 4:11.

[33] *Expositio Evangelii secundum Lucam*, 1, 4, 20 (PL 15, 1525).

protect the just man wherever he goes.[34] But Jesus refuses to tempt his Father; he restores true meaning to this passage from the Bible. And, as a reward for his fidelity, when the time comes, ministers of God the Father appear and wait upon him.

It's worth thinking about the method Satan uses with our Lord Jesus Christ: he argues with texts from the sacred books, twisting and distorting their meaning in a blasphemous way. Jesus doesn't let himself be deceived: the Word made flesh knows well the divine word, written for the salvation of men—not their confusion and downfall. So, we can conclude that anyone who is united to Jesus Christ through Love will never be deceived by manipulation of the holy Scripture, for he knows that it is typical of the devil to try to confuse the Christian conscience, juggling with the very words of eternal wisdom, trying to turn light into darkness.

Let us look for a moment at this appearance of angels in Jesus' life, for it will help us to better understand their role—their angelic mission—in all human life. Christian tradition describes the guardian angels as powerful

[34] Ps 90:11 (tract of the Mass).

friends, placed by God alongside each one of us, to accompany us on our way. And that is why he invites us to make friends with them and get them to help us.

In suggesting that we meditate on these passages of the life of Christ, the Church reminds us that during Lent, when we recognize our sins, our wretchedness, and our need for purification, there is also room for joy. Lent is a time for both bravery and joy; we have to fill ourselves with courage, for the grace of God will not fail us. God will be at our side and will send his angels to be our travelling companions, our prudent advisers along the way, our cooperators in all that we take on. The angels "will hold you up with their hands lest you should chance to trip on a stone,"[35] as the psalm says.

We must learn to speak to the angels. Turn to them now, tell your guardian angel that these spiritual waters of Lent will not flow off your soul but will go deep, because you are sorry. Ask them to take up to the Lord your good will, which, by the grace of God, has grown out of

---

[35] Ps 90:12 (tract of the Mass): *In manibus portabunt te, ne forte offendas ad lapidem pedem tuum.*

your wretchedness like a lily grown on a dunghill. Holy angels, our guardians: "defend us in battle so that we do not perish at the final judgment."[36]

CHILDREN OF GOD

How do you explain this confident prayer— 64 this knowledge that we shall not perish in the battle? It is a conviction rooted in something which is always a cause of wonder to me: our divine filiation. Our Lord, who during this Lent is asking us to change, is not a tyrannical master or a rigid and implacable judge: he is our Father. He speaks to us about our lack of generosity, our sins, our mistakes; but he does so in order to free us from them, to promise us his friendship and his love. Awareness that God is our Father brings joy to our conversion: it tells us that we are returning to our Father's house.

This divine filiation is the basis of the spirit of Opus Dei. All men are children of God. But

[36] *Missale Romanum*, prayer to St Michael: *Defende nos in proelio: ut non pereamus in tremendo iudicio.*

a child can look upon his father in many ways. We must try to be children who realize that the Lord, by loving us as his children, has taken us into his house, in the middle of the world, to be members of his family, so that what is his is ours, and what is ours is his, and to develop that familiarity and confidence which prompts us to ask him, like children, for the moon!

A child of God treats the Lord as his Father. He is not obsequious and servile, he is not merely formal and well-mannered: he is completely sincere and trusting. Men do not scandalize God. He can put up with all our infidelities. Our Father in heaven pardons any offense when his child returns to him, when he repents and asks for pardon. The Lord is such a good Father that he anticipates our desire to be pardoned and comes forward to us, opening his arms laden with grace.

Now I'm not inventing anything. Remember the parable which Jesus told to help us understand the love of our Father who is in heaven: the parable of the prodigal son?[37] "But while he was still a long way off, his father saw him

---

[37] Cf. Lk 15:11ff.

and took pity on him; running up, he threw his arms around his neck and kissed him."[38] That's what the sacred text says: he covered him with kisses. Can you put it more humanly than that? Can you describe more graphically the paternal love of God for men?

When God runs toward us, we cannot keep silent, but with St Paul we exclaim: *Abba, Pater*: "Father, my Father!"[39], for, though he is the creator of the universe, he doesn't mind our not using high-sounding titles, nor worry about our not acknowledging his greatness. He wants us to call him Father; he wants us to savor that word, our souls filling with joy.

Human life is in some way a constant returning to our Father's house. We return through contrition, through the conversion of heart which means a desire to change, a firm decision to improve our life and which, therefore, is expressed in sacrifice and self-giving. We return to our Father's house by means of that sacrament of pardon in which, by confessing our sins, we put on Jesus Christ again and become his brothers, members of God's family.

---

[38] Lk 15:20.
[39] Rom 8:15.

God is waiting for us, like the father in the parable, with open arms, even though we don't deserve it. It doesn't matter how great our debt is. Just like the prodigal son, all we have to do is open our heart, to be homesick for our Father's house, to wonder at and rejoice in the gift which God makes us of being able to call ourselves his children, of really being his children, even though our response to him has been so poor.

65   What a strange capacity man has to forget even the most wonderful things, to become *used* to mystery! Let's remind ourselves, this Lent, that the Christian cannot be superficial. While being fully involved in his everyday work, among other men, his equals; busy, under stress, the Christian has to be at the same time totally involved with God, for he is a child of God.

Divine filiation is a joyful truth, a consoling mystery. It fills all our spiritual life, it shows us how to speak to God, to know and to love our Father in heaven. And it makes our interior struggle overflow with hope and gives us the trusting simplicity of little children. More than that: precisely because we are children of God, we can contemplate in love and wonder everything as coming from the hands of our Father, God the Creator. And so we become contemplatives in the middle of the world, loving the world.

In Lent, the liturgy recalls the effect of Adam's sin in the life of man. Adam did not want to be a good son of God; he rebelled. But we also hear the echoing chant of that *felix culpa*: "O happy fault,"[40] which the whole Church will joyfully intone at the Easter vigil.

God the Father, in the fullness of time, sent to the world his only-begotten Son, to re-establish peace; so that by his redeeming men from sin, "we might become sons of God,"[41] freed from the yoke of sin, capable of sharing in the divine intimacy of the Trinity. And so it has become possible for this new man, this new grafting of the children of God,[42] to free all creation from disorder, restoring all things in Christ,[43] who has reconciled them to God.[44]

It is, then, a time of penance, but, as we have seen, this is not something negative. Lent

---

[40] *Missale Romanum, paschal Praeconium.*
[41] Gal 4:5: *adoptionem filiorum reciperemus.*
[42] Cf. Rom 6:4-5.
[43] Cf. Eph 1:5-10.
[44] Cf. Col 1:20.

should be lived in the spirit of filiation, which Christ has communicated to us and which is alive in our soul.[45] Our Lord calls us to come nearer to him, to be like him: "Be imitators of God, as his dearly beloved children,"[46] cooperating humbly but fervently in the divine purpose of mending what is broken, of saving what is lost, of bringing back order to what sinful man has put out of order, of leading to its goal what has gone astray, of re-establishing the divine balance of all creation.

66   At times the lenten liturgy, with its emphasis on the consequences of man's abandonment of God, has a suggestion of tragedy, but that is not all. It is God who has the last word—and it is the word of his saving and merciful love and, therefore, the word of our divine filiation. Therefore, I repeat to you today, with St John: "See how greatly the Father has loved us; that we should be counted as God's children, should be indeed his children."[47] Children of God, brothers of the Word made flesh, of him of whom it was said, "In him was life, and that

---

[45] Cf. Gal 4:6.
[46] Eph 5:1.
[47] 1 Jn 3:1.

life was the light of man."[48] Children of the light, brothers of the light: that is what we are. We bear the only flame capable of setting fire to hearts made of flesh.

I'm going to stop now and continue the Mass, and I want each of us to consider what God is asking of him, what resolution, what decisions grace wants to encourage in him. And as you note these supernatural and human demands of self-giving and continuing struggle, remember that Jesus Christ is our model. And that Jesus, being God, allowed himself to be tempted, so that we might be in better spirits and feel certain of victory. For God does not lose battles, and if we are united to him, we will never be overcome. On the contrary, we can call ourselves victors and indeed be victors: good children of God.

Let us be happy. I am happy. I shouldn't be, looking at my life, making that personal examination of conscience which Lent requires. But I do feel happy, for I see that the Lord is seeking me again, that the Lord is still my Father. I know that you and I will surely see, with the light and help of grace, what things

---

[48] Jn 1:4.

must be burned and we will burn them; what things must be uprooted and we will uproot them; what things have to be given up and we will give them up.

It's not easy. But we have a clear guide, which we should not and cannot do without. We are loved by God, and we will let the Holy Spirit act in us and purify us, so that we can embrace the Son of God on the cross, and rise with him, because the joy of the resurrection is rooted in the cross.

Mary, our Mother, "help of Christians, refuge of sinners": intercede with your Son to send us the Holy Spirit, to awaken in our hearts the decision to go ahead confidently, making us hear deep in our soul the call which filled with peace the martyrdom of one of the first Christians: "Come, return to your Father,"[49] he is waiting for you.

---

[49] St Ignatius of Antioch, *Epistola ad Romanos*, 7, 2 (PG 5, 694): *Veni ad Patrem*.

CHRISTIAN RESPECT
FOR PERSONS
AND THEIR FREEDOM*

We have just read in this holy Mass a text
from St John's Gospel: the scene of the miraculous cure of the man born blind. I imagine that
all of us have once again been moved by the
power and mercy of God, who cannot look indifferently upon human misfortune. But I
should like to fix our attention on other considerations. Specifically, let us try to see that,
when there is love of God, a Christian cannot
be indifferent to the lot of other men. He must
show respect in his dealings with all men. For
he knows that when love shrinks, there arises
the danger of thoughtlessly, mercilessly invad-
ing the conscience of others.

* A homily given on March 15, 1961.

"And Jesus saw," says the holy Gospel, "as he passed on his way, a man who had been blind from his birth."[1] Jesus is passing by. How often have I marveled at this simple way of describing divine mercy! Jesus is headed somewhere, yet he is not too busy to spot human suffering. Consider, on the other hand, how different was the reaction of his disciples. They ask him: "Master, was this man guilty of sin, or was it his parents, that he should have been born blind?"[2]

JUDGING ON IMPULSE

We cannot be surprised that many persons, even those who think themselves Christians, act in the same way. Their first impulse is to think badly of someone or something. They don't need any proof; they take it for granted. And they don't keep it to themselves, they air their snap judgments to the winds.

Trying to be benevolent about it, we could call the disciples' behavior short-sighted. Then as now, for little has changed, there were

[1] Jn 9:1.
[2] Jn 9:2.

others, the Pharisees, who consistently adopted this attitude. Remember how Jesus Christ denounced them? "When John came, he would neither eat nor drink, and they say of him that he is possessed. When the Son of Man came, he ate and drank with them, and of him they said, Here is a glutton; he loves wine; he is a friend of publicans and sinners."[3]

Jesus suffered a campaign of slurs on his name, defamation of his irreproachable conduct, biting and wounding criticism. It is not unusual for some people to accord the same treatment to those who wish to follow the Master while fully conscious of their natural shortcomings and personal mistakes which, given human weakness, are so common and even inevitable. But our experience of human limitations cannot lead us to condone sins and injustices against the good name of anyone, even though their authors try to cover their tracks by just "wondering" aloud. Jesus says that if the father of the family has been labeled Beelzebub, members of the household cannot expect to fare any better.[4] But he also adds that

[3] Mt 11:18-19.
[4] Cf. Mt 10:25.

"whoever calls his brother a fool shall be in danger of hell fire."[5]

Where does this unjust, carping attitude come from? It almost seems as though some people are now wearing glasses that disfigure their vision. In principle, they reject the possibility of a virtuous life or, at least, the constant effort to do the right thing. Everything they take in is colored by their own previous deformation. For them, even the most noble and unselfish actions are only hypocritical contortions designed to appear good. "When they clearly discover goodness," writes St Gregory the Great, "they scrutinize it in the hope of finding hidden defects."[6]

68   When such a deformation has become almost second nature it is difficult to help people to see that it is both more human and more truthful to think well of others. St Augustine recommends the following rule-of-thumb: "Try to acquire the virtues you believe lacking in your brothers. Then you will no longer see their defects, for you will no longer have them yourselves."[7] Some would find this

[5] Mt 5:22.
[6] Moralia, 6, 22 (PL 75, 750).
[7] Enarrationes in psalmos, 30, 2, 7 (PL 36, 243).

way of acting naïve. They are wiser, more "realistic."

Setting their prejudices up as criteria, they are quick to criticize anybody and slow to listen. Afterwards perhaps, out of "openmind-edness" or "fair play," they extend to the accused the possibility of defending himself. Flying in the face of the most elementary justice and morality—for he who accuses must bear the burden of proof—they "grant" the innocent party the "privilege" of proving himself blame-less.

I must confess that these thoughts are not borrowed from textbooks on law or moral theology. They are based on the experience of many people who have borne these blows. Time and again, over a number of years, they, like many others, have served as a bull's-eye for the target-practice of those who specialize in gossip, defamation, and calumny. The grace of God and a nature little given to recrimination have spared them from the slightest trace of bitterness. "To me it is a very small thing to be judged by you,"[8] they could say with St Paul. Using a more common expression, they could

[8] 1 Cor 4:3: *Mihi pro minimo est, ut a vobis iudicer.*

have added that the whole thing was just a storm in a tea-cup. And that's the truth.

Nonetheless, I can't deny that I am saddened by those who unjustly attack the integrity of others, for the slanderer destroys himself. And I suffer, too, for all those who, in the face of arbitrary and outrageous accusations, do not know where to turn. They are frightened. They do not believe it is possible, they wonder if the whole thing is not a nightmare.

Several days ago we read in the epistle of the holy Mass the story of Susanna, that chaste woman so falsely accused of wrongdoing by two lustful old men. "Susanna groaned deeply; there is no escape for me, she said, either way. It is death if I consent, and if I refuse I shall be at your mercy."[9] How often does the trickery of those moved by envy and intrigue force many noble Christians into the same corner? They are offered only one choice: offend God or ruin their reputation. The only acceptable and upright solution is, at the same time, highly painful. Yet they must decide: "Let me rather fall into your power through no act of mine, than commit sin in the Lord's sight."[10]

[9] Dan 13:22.
[10] Dan 13:23.

RIGHT TO PRIVACY

Let us return to the scene of the curing of 69
the blind man. Jesus Christ answered his
disciples by pointing out that the blind man's
misfortune is not the result of sin, but an
occasion to manifest God's power. And with
marvelous simplicity, he decides to give the
blind man his sight.

Thereupon begins that poor man's happiness, but also his anguish. People simply will
not leave him alone. First it is his "neighbors
and those who had been accustomed to see him
begging."[11] The Gospel doesn't say that they
even bothered to rejoice; they couldn't bring
themselves to believe it, in spite of the fact that
the once blind man claimed that he was the
man who before couldn't see and now does.
Rather than let him enjoy in peace his new-
found fortune, they drag him to the Pharisees,
who again inquire how this could have come
about. And once again he replies: "He put clay
on my eyes; and then I washed, and now I can
see."[12]

[11] Jn 9:8.
[12] Jn 9:15.

And the Pharisees seek to show that what
has happened—a great favor and miracle—
didn't happen. Some of them turn to petty,
hypocritical, illogical arguments—this man has
cured on the Sabbath and, since working on the
Sabbath is unlawful, they deny the wonder.
Others start taking what today we would call
a poll. They first approach the parents of the
blind man: "Is this your son, who, you say, was
born blind? How then does he now see?"[13]
Fearing the authorities, his parents give an
answer that is technically correct: "We can tell
you that this is our son, and that he was blind
when he was born. We cannot tell how he is
able to see now. We have no means of knowing
who opened his eyes for him. Ask the man
himself; he is of age. Let him tell you his own
story."[14]

Those taking the poll cannot believe, because
they have chosen not to believe. "So once more
they summoned the man who had been blind
and said to him... 'This man'—Jesus Christ—'to
our knowledge, is a sinner'."[15]

[13] Jn 9:19.
[14] Jn 9:20-21.
[15] Jn 9:24.

In a few words St John's account illustrates in a typical way an unscrupulous assault upon a basic natural right of all men, that of being treated with respect.

This way of acting is not a thing of the past. It would be no trouble at all to point out present-day cases of aggressive curiosity which pries morbidly into the private lives of others. A minimum of justice demands that, even when actual wrongdoing is suspected, an investigation of this sort be carried out with caution and moderation, lest mere possibility be converted into certainty. It is clear that an unhealthy curiosity to perform autopsies on actions that are not illicit but positively good should be ranked under the heading of perversion.

Faced with traders in suspicion who prey on the intimacy of others, we must defend the dignity of every person, his right to peace. All honest men, Christians or not, agree on the need for this defense, for a common value is at stake: the legitimate right to be oneself, to avoid ostentation, to keep within the family its joys, sorrows, and difficulties. We are defending, no less, the right to do good without publicity, to help the disadvantaged out of pure love, without feeling obliged to publicize one's efforts to serve others, much less to bare the intimacy of one's soul to the indiscreet and twisted gaze of persons who know nothing and want to know nothing of disinterested generosity, except to mock it mercilessly.

But how difficult it is to be free of this meddlesome sleuthing! The means invented to prevent man from being left alone have multiplied. I am referring not only to the technical means, but also to accepted forms of argument, which are so cunning that one endangers his reputation if he but answers them. Thus, for example, a familiar way of arguing assumes that everyone acts from motives that leave something to be desired. Following this gratuitous train of thought, one is obliged to pronounce a *mea culpa* over his own actions, to indulge in self-criticism. And if someone does not sling a ton of mud upon himself, his critics immediately assume that, in addition to being a devious villain, he is also hypocritical and arrogant.

On other occasions, a different procedure is followed. The writer or speaker, with libelous intent, "admits" that you are an upright individual, but, he says, other people won't be willing to admit this and they might argue that you are a thief. Now how do you prove that you are not a thief? Another example: "You are always claiming that your conduct is clean, noble, and upright. Would you mind examining the matter again to see if, on the contrary, it might not be dirty, twisted, and ignoble?"

I haven't pulled these examples out of the hat. I am absolutely convinced that any person or moderately well-known institution could greatly add to the list. A mistaken idea has arisen in certain environments that grants to the public or the media or whatever they wish to call it, the right to know and to judge the most intimate details of the lives of others.

May I mention something close to my heart? For more than thirty years I have said and written in thousands of different ways that Opus Dei does not seek any worldly or political aims, that it only and exclusively seeks to foster—among all races, all social conditions, all countries—the knowledge and practice of the saving teachings of Christ. It only wants to contribute to there being more love of God on earth and, therefore, more peace and justice among all men, children of a common Father.

Many thousands and millions of people throughout the world have understood this.

Some apparently have not, for a variety of reasons. If my heart goes out more to those who understand, still I honor and love the others too, for their dignity is worthy of respect and esteem, just as all of them are likewise called to the glory of being children of God.

But there will always be a partisan minority who are ignorant of what I and so many of us love. They would like us to explain Opus Dei in their terms, which are exclusively political, foreign to supernatural realities, attuned only to power plays and pressure groups. If they do not receive an explanation that suits their erroneous and twisted taste they continue to allege that here you have deception and sinister designs.

Let me assure you that, when I am faced with such situations, I become neither sad nor concerned. I should add that I would almost be amused, if I could legitimately overlook the fact that they have committed an injustice and a sin, which cries out to heaven for redress. I am from a region of Spain known for its frankness, and even humanly speaking I place great store on sincerity. I instinctively react against anything that resembles deceit. When accused, I have always tried to tell the truth, without pride or disdain, even if those who vilified me were uncouth, arrogant, hostile, bereft of a minimum of humanity.

A SALVE FOR OUR EYES

To my mind frequently comes the reply of 71 the man born blind who was asked by the Pharisees for the umpteenth time how the miracle had taken place: "I have told you already, and you would not listen to me. Why must you hear it over again? Would you too become his disciples?"[16]

The sin of the Pharisees did not consist in not seeing God in Christ, but in voluntarily shutting themselves up within themselves, in not letting Jesus, who is the light, open their eyes.[17] This closed-mindedness immediately affects our relations with others. The Pharisee, who believes himself to be light and does not let God open his eyes, will treat his neighbor unjustly, pridefully: "I thank you, God, that I am not like the rest of men, who steal and cheat

[16] Jn 9:27.
[17] Cf. Jn 9:39-41.

and commit adultery, or like this publican here."[18] Thus does he pray. And they hurl insults upon the once blind man, who persists in his truthful account of the miraculous cure: "What, they answered, are we to have lessons from you, all steeped in sin from your birth? And they cast him out from their presence."[19]

Among those who do not know Christ, there are many honest persons who have respect for others and know how to conduct themselves properly and are sincere, cordial, and refined. If neither they nor we prevent Christ from curing our blindness, if we let our Lord apply the clay which, in his hands, becomes a cleansing salve, we shall come to know earthly realities and we shall look upon the divine realities with new vision, with the light of faith. Our outlook will have become Christian.

This is the vocation of a Christian. We are called to the fullness of charity which "is patient, is kind. Charity feels no envy; charity is never perverse or proud, never insolent; does not claim its rights, cannot be provoked, does not brood over an injury; takes no pleasure

[18] Lk 18:11.
[19] Jn 9:34.

in wrongdoing, but rejoices at the victory of truth; sustains, believes, hopes, endures, to the last."[20]

The charity of Christ is not merely a benevolent sentiment for our neighbor; it is not limited to a penchant for philanthropy. Poured out in our soul by God, charity transforms from within our mind and will. It provides the supernatural foundation for friendship and the joy of doing what is right.

Contemplate the scene of the cure of the paralytic, as told to us in the Acts of the Apostles. Peter and John were going up to the temple, and on their way they came across a man seated at the gate. It turns out he had been lame from birth. Everything resembles the cure of the blind man. But now the disciples no longer think that the misfortune is due to the paralytic's sins or to the faults of his parents. And they say to him: "In the name of Jesus Christ of Nazareth, rise up and walk."[21] Before they poured out scorn, now mercy. Before they had judged contemptuously, now they cure miraculously in the name of the Lord.

[20] 1 Cor 13:4-7.
[21] Acts 3:6.

Christ is always passing by! Christ continues to pass through the streets and squares of the world, in the person of his apostles and disciples. And I fervently beg him to "pass through" the souls of you who are listening to me now.

RESPECT AND CHARITY

72   At the beginning we were surprised at the attitude of Jesus' disciples toward the man born blind. They were consistent with that unfortunate saying: "Think badly and you'll be right." Afterwards, as they come to know the Master better, and realize what it means to be a Christian, their thoughts are gradually tempered by understanding.

"In any man," writes St Thomas Aquinas, "there is an aspect under which others can consider him superior to themselves, according to the Apostle's words, 'Each of you must have the humility to think others better men than himself' (Phil 2:3). It is in this spirit that all men should honor one another."[22] Humility is the

---

[22] *S. Th.*, II-II, q. 103, a. 2-3.

virtue that teaches us that the signs of respect for others—for their good name, their good faith, their privacy—are not external conventions, but the first signs of charity and justice.

Christian charity cannot be limited to giving things or money to the needy. It seeks, above all, to respect and understand each person for what he is, in his intrinsic dignity as a man and child of God. Consequently, those who impugn the reputation and honor of others show that they are ignorant of some truths of our Christian faith and, in any case, lacking in an authentic love of God. "The charity by which we love God and our neighbor is the same virtue, for God is the reason for our loving our neighbor, and we love God when we love our neighbor with charity."[23]

I hope we will be able to derive some very practical consequences from this conversation with God. Let us especially resolve not to judge others, not to doubt their good will, to drown evil in an abundance of good, sowing loyal friendship, justice, and peace all around us.

And let us resolve never to become sad if our upright conduct is misunderstood by

---

[23] St Thomas Aquinas, *ibid*.

others; if the good which, with the continuous help of our Lord, we try to accomplish is misinterpreted by others, who delight in unjustly guessing at our motives and accuse us of wicked designs and deceitful behavior.

Let us forgive always, with a smile on our lips. Let us speak clearly, without hard feelings, when in conscience we think we ought to speak. And let us leave everything in the hands of our Father God, with a divine silence—"Jesus was silent"[24]—if we are confronted with personal attacks, no matter how brutal and shameful they might be. Let us concern ourselves only with doing good deeds. God will see to it that they "shine before men."[25]

---

[24] Mt 26:63.
[25] Mt 5:16.

INTERIOR STRUGGLE*

Like every Christian celebration, today's is one of peace. The palm branches, with their ancient symbolism, recall a scene of the book of Genesis: "After waiting seven more days, Noah again sent out the dove from the ark. In the evening, the dove came back to him and there was a new olive branch in its beak. So Noah realized that the waters were receding from the earth."[1] Today we remember that the alliance between God and his people is confirmed and established in Christ, for "he is our peace."[2] In the liturgy of our holy Catholic Church—which so wonderfully unites and sums up the old in the new—we read today the joyful words which remind us of how Jesus was greeted at his birth in Bethlehem: "The sons

73

* A homily given on April 4, 1971, Palm Sunday.
[1] Gen 8:10-11.
[2] Eph 2:14.

of the Hebrews, raising olive branches, went out to meet the Lord, crying out, 'Glory in high heaven'."[3] As he moved off, St Luke tells us, "people spread their cloaks in the road, and now, as he was approaching the downward slope of the Mount of Olives, the whole group of disciples joyfully began to praise God at the top of their voices for all the miracles they had seen. They cried out: 'Blessed is the king who comes in the name of the Lord, peace in heaven and glory in the highest'."[4]

PEACE ON EARTH

Peace in heaven. But let's take a look at the earth. Why is there no peace in the world? That's right, there is no peace, only a certain appearance of peace—a balance created by fear and precarious compromises. There is no peace even in the Church. It is rent by tensions which tear the white robe of the Spouse of Christ. And there is no peace in many hearts which vainly strive to make up for their intranquility of soul by continuous activity, by seeking a thin satis-

---

[3] Antiphon during distribution of palms.
[4] Lk 19:36-38.

faction in things which do not fill them but only leave a bitter aftertaste of sorrow.

"The palm leaves," writes St Augustine, "symbolize homage, for they stand for victory. Our Lord is on the point of conquering by dying on the cross. Under the sign of the cross, he is about to triumph over the devil, the prince of death."[5] Christ is our peace because he is the victor. He has won the victory because he has fought, in a hard struggle, against the accumulated evil of human hearts.

Christ, who is our peace, is also the way.[6] If we seek peace we have to follow his footsteps. Peace is a consequence of war, of struggle, of the intimate ascetical struggle which each Christian must keep up against everything in his life which does not belong to God. He is called to overcome pride, sensuality, selfishness, superficiality, and meanness of heart. It is useless to call for exterior calm if there is no calm in men's consciences, in the center of their souls, for "from the heart come evil intentions: murder, adultery, fornication, theft, perjury, slander."[7]

[5] *In Ioannis Evangelium tractatus*, 51, 2 (PL 35, 1764).
[6] Jn 14:6.
[7] Mt 15:19.

STRUGGLE: A DEMAND OF LOVE AND JUSTICE

74   But is not this rather an old-fashioned way
of talking? Has it not been replaced by a more
contemporary language, a language which
cloaks personal defects in pseudo-scientific
terms? Surely people tacitly agree that the really
valuable things are money which buys everything; influence; shrewdness which leaves you
always on top; human maturity which defines
itself as "adult," thinking it has outgrown the
sacred?

I am not and never have been a pessimist,
for the faith teaches me that Christ has conquered once and for all. He has given us, as
a pledge of his victory, a commandment which
is also a commitment: "Fight." We Christians
have a commitment of love to the calling of
divine grace, which we have freely accepted, an
obligation which urges us to fight tenaciously.
We know that we are as weak as other men,
but we cannot forget that if we use the means
available to us, we will become salt and light
and leaven of the world; we will be the consolation of God. Our determination to persevere
in this resolution of Love is, moreover, an
obligation of justice. This obligation—common

to all Christians—implies a constant battle. The entire tradition of the Church has described Christians as *milites Christi*: soldiers of Christ. Soldiers who bring serenity to others while continually fighting against their own bad inclinations. Sometimes because we are short on supernatural outlook, in effect short on faith, we do not want to hear any talk of life on earth as a kind of war. We maliciously insinuate that if we think of ourselves as *milites Christi*, there is a danger that we might use the faith for earthly purposes, bringing pressure to bear, creating little isolated groups. This very naïve line of thought is completely illogical and usually goes hand in hand with cowardice and love of comfort.

There is nothing further from the Christian faith than fanaticism—that unholy alliance of the sacred and the profane, whatever guise it takes. That danger just does not exist if we understand our struggle as Christ has taught us to: as a war each of us makes on himself. It is a constantly renewed effort to love God better, to root out selfishness, to serve all men. Turning your back on this conflict, no matter what the excuse, means surrendering before you have begun to fight. Anyone who does so is brought low, without faith, depressed in his heart, blown this way and that by miserable pleasures.

Our spiritual combat in the presence of God and of all our brothers in the faith is a necessary result of being a Christian. So if you do not fight, you are betraying Jesus Christ and the whole Church, his mystical body.

AN UNCEASING STRUGGLE

75   A Christian's struggle must be unceasing, for interior life consists in beginning and beginning again. This prevents us from proudly thinking that we are perfect already. It is inevitable that we should meet difficulties on our way. If we did not come up against obstacles, we would not be creatures of flesh and blood. We will always have passions which pull us downwards; we will always have to defend ourselves against more or less self-defeating urges.

We should not be surprised to find, in our body and soul, the needle of pride, sensuality, envy, laziness, and the desire to dominate others. This is a fact of life, proven by our personal experience. It is the point of departure and the normal context for winning in this intimate sport, this race toward our Father's house. St Paul says: "That is how I run, intent on winning; that is how I fight, not beating the air. I treat my body hard and make it obey me for, having preached to others, I do not want to be disqualified."[8]

To begin or sustain this conflict a Christian should not wait for external signs or nice inner feelings. Interior life does not consist in feelings but in divine grace, willingness, and love. All the disciples were quite capable of following Christ on the day of his triumph in Jerusalem, but almost all of them left him at the shameful hour of the cross.

If you are really going to love, you have to be strong and loyal; your heart has to be firmly anchored in faith, hope, and charity. Only people who are inconstant and superficial change the object of their love from one day to the next: that's not love at all, it's the pursuit of selfishness. When love exists there is a kind of wholeness—a capacity for self-giving, sacrifice, and renunciation. In the midst of that self-denial, along with painful difficulties, we find

[8] 1 Cor 9:26-27.

joy and happiness, a joy which nothing and no
one can take away from us.

In this adventure of love we should not be
depressed by our falls, not even by serious falls,
if we go to God in the sacrament of penance
contrite and resolved to improve. A Christian
is not a neurotic collector of good behavior
reports. Jesus Christ our Lord was moved as
much by Peter's repentance after his fall as by
John's innocence and faithfulness. Jesus understands our weakness and draws us to himself
on an inclined plane. He wants us to make an
effort to climb a little each day. He seeks us
out, just as he did the disciples of Emmaus,
whom he went out to meet. He sought Thomas,
showed himself to him and made him touch
with his fingers the open wounds in his hands
and side. Jesus Christ is always waiting for us
to return to him; he knows our weakness.

THE INTERIOR STRUGGLE

76   "Put up with your share of difficulties, like
a good soldier of Jesus Christ,"[9] St Paul tells

---

[9] 2 Tim 2:3.

us. A Christian's life is a fight, a war, a beautiful war of peace and completely different from human warfare which results from division and often hatred. The war of the sons of God is a war against their own selfishness. It is based on unity and love. "Though we live in the world, we are not carrying on a worldly war, for the weapons of our warfare are not worldly but have divine power to destroy strongholds. We destroy arguments and every proud obstacle to the knowledge of God."[10] The Apostle is referring to our relentless fight against pride, against our tendency to do evil and our exaltation of self.

On this Palm Sunday, when our Lord begins the week which is so decisive for our salvation, let us put aside the more superficial aspects of the question and go right to the core, to what is really important. Look: what we have to try to do is to get to heaven. If we don't, nothing is worth while. Faithfulness to Christ's doctrine is absolutely essential to our getting to heaven. To be faithful it is absolutely essential to strive doggedly against anything that blocks our way to eternal happiness.

[10] 2 Cor 10:3-5.

I know that the moment we talk about fighting we recall our weakness and we foresee falls and mistakes. God takes this into account. As we walk along it is inevitable that we will raise dust; we are creatures and full of defects. I would almost say that we will always *need* defects. They are the shadow which shows up the light of God's grace and our resolve to respond to God's kindness. And this *chiaroscuro* will make us human, humble, understanding, and generous.

Let's not deceive ourselves: in our life we will find vigor and victory *and* depression and defeat. This has always been true of the earthly pilgrimage of Christians, even of those we venerate on the altars. Don't you remember Peter, Augustine, Francis? I have never liked biographies of saints which naïvely—but also with a lack of sound doctrine—present their deeds as if they had been confirmed in grace from birth. No. The true life stories of Christian heroes resemble our own experience: they fought and won; they fought and lost. And then, repentant, they returned to the fray.

We should not be surprised to find ourselves defeated relatively often, usually or even always in things of little importance which we tend to take seriously. If we love God and are humble, if we persevere relentlessly in our struggle, the defeats will never be very important. There will also be abundant victories which bring joy to God's eyes. There is no such thing as failure if you act with a right intention, wanting to fulfill God's will and counting always on his grace and your own nothingness.

However, a powerful enemy is lying in wait 77 for us, an enemy which counters our desire to incarnate Christ's doctrine in our lives. This enemy is pride, which grows if we do not reach out for the helping and merciful hand of God after each failure and defeat. In that case the soul remains in the shadows, in an unhappy darkness, and thinks it is lost. Its imagination creates all sorts of obstacles which have no basis in fact, which would disappear if it just looked at them with a little humility. Prompted by pride and wild imagination, the soul sometimes creates painful calvaries for itself. But Christ is not on these calvaries, for joy and peace always accompany our Lord even when the soul is nervous and surrounded by darkness.

There is another hypocritical enemy of our sanctification: the idea that this interior struggle has to be against extraordinary obstacles, against fire-belching dragons. This is another sign of pride. We are ready to fight, but we want to do it noisily, with the clamor of trumpets and the waving of standards. We must convince ourselves that the worst enemy of a rock is not a pickaxe or any other such implement, no matter how sharp it is. No, its worst enemy is the constant flow of water which drop by drop enters the crevices until it ruins the rock's structure. The greatest danger for a Christian is to underestimate the importance of fighting skirmishes. The refusal to fight the little battles can, little by little, leave him soft, weak, and indifferent, insensitive to the accents of God's voice.

Let's listen to our Lord: "He who is faithful in a very little is faithful also in much; and he who is dishonest in very little is dishonest also in much."[11] It is as if he were saying to us: "Fight continuously in the apparently unimportant things which are to my mind important; fulfill your duty punctually; smile at whoever needs cheering up, even though there is sorrow in your soul; devote the necessary time to

[11] Lk 16:10.

prayer, without haggling; go to the help of anyone who looks for you; practice justice and go beyond it with the grace of charity."

These and many others are the inspirations we feel inside us every day, little silent reminders encouraging us to outdo ourselves in the supernatural sport of overcoming our self. May the light of God show us the way to understand his directions. May he help us to fight and be with us in victory. May he not leave us when we fall but always help us to get up and return to the struggle.

We cannot take it easy. Our Lord wants us to fight more, on a broader front, more intensely each day. We have an obligation to outdo ourselves, for in this competition the only goal is to arrive at the glory of heaven. And if we did not reach heaven, the whole thing would have been useless.

THE SACRAMENTS OF DIVINE GRACE

Anyone who wants to fight has to use the 78 available means, which have not changed in twenty centuries of Christianity. They are prayer, mortification and frequent use of the sacraments. Since mortification is also prayer—prayer of the senses—we can sum up these means in two words: prayer and sacraments.

I would like us to reflect now on the sacraments, which are fountains of divine grace. They are a wonderful proof of God's loving kindness. Just meditate calmly on the Catechism of Trent's definition: "certain sensible signs which cause grace and at the same time declare it by putting it before our eyes."[12] God our Lord is infinite; his love is inexhaustible; his clemency and tenderness toward us are limitless. He grants us his grace in many other ways, but he has expressly and freely established, as only he can do, seven effective signs to enable men to share in the merits of the redemption in a stable, simple, and accessible way.

If the sacraments are abandoned, genuine Christian life disappears. Yet we should realize that particularly today there are many people who seem to forget about the sacraments and who even scorn this redeeming flow of Christ's grace. It is painful to have to speak of this sore

[12] *Catechism of the Council of Trent*, 2:1, 3.

in a so-called Christian society, but we must do so for it will encourage us to approach these sources of sanctification more gratefully and more lovingly.

Without the slightest scruple people decide to postpone the baptism of newly born children. Yet by doing so they seriously go against justice and charity by depriving children of the grace of faith, of the incalculable treasure of the indwelling of the Blessed Trinity in a soul which comes into the world stained by original sin. They also try to change the true nature of the sacrament of confirmation, which tradition has unanimously seen as a strengthening of the spiritual life. By giving more supernatural strength to the soul, through a quiet and fruitful outpouring of the Holy Spirit, confirmation enables the Christian to fight as *milites Christi*, as a soldier of Christ, in his intimate battle against selfishness and lust of all sorts.

If you lose sensitivity for the things of God, it is very difficult to appreciate the sacrament of penance. Sacramental confession is not a human but a divine dialogue. It is a tribunal of divine justice and especially of mercy, with a loving judge who "has no pleasure in the

death of the wicked; I desire that the wicked
turn back from his way and live."[13]

The tenderness of our Lord is truly infinite.
See how gently he treats his sons. He has made
marriage a holy bond, the image of the union
of Christ and his Church,[14] a great sacrament
on which is based the Christian family that has
to be, with God's grace, a place of peace and
harmony, a school of sanctity. Parents are the
cooperators of God. That is the reason why
children have the obligation of loving them. It
is quite right to describe, as I wrote many years
ago, the fourth commandment as the sweetest
precept of the decalogue. If you live marriage
as God wishes you to, in a holy way, your
house will be a bright and cheerful home, full
of peace and joy.

79   In the sacrament of holy orders our Father
God has made it possible for some members of
the faithful, by virtue of a further and ineffable
communication of the Holy Spirit, to receive an
indelible character on their soul which config-
ures them to Christ the priest so that they can
act in the name of Jesus Christ, head of his

---

[13] Ezek 33:11.
[14] Cf. Eph 5:32.

mystical body.[15] By virtue of this ministerial priesthood—which differs essentially and not only in degree[16] from the common priesthood of the faithful—the sacred ministers can consecrate the body and blood of Christ, offering God the holy sacrifice. They can pardon sins in sacramental confession and carry out the ministry of teaching the peoples "about everything that refers to God"[17]—and nothing more.

A priest should be exclusively a man of God. He should reject any desire to shine in areas where other Christians do not need him. A priest is not a psychologist or a sociologist or an anthropologist. He is another Christ, Christ himself, who has to look after the souls of his brothers. It would be a sad thing if a priest thought himself equipped to pontificate on dogmatic or moral theology on the basis of some human science—which if he were really dedicated to his priestly work he could only know as an amateur or an observer. This would only show his double ignorance—in human science and theological science—even though a

---

[15] Cf. Council of Trent, Session 23, c. 4; Vatican II, Decree *Presbyterorum ordinis*, n. 2.

[16] Cf. Vatican II, Const. *Lumen gentium*, n. 10.

[17] Heb 5:1: *in iis quae sunt ad Deum*.

superficial air of wisdom might deceive a few
naïve readers or listeners.

It is public knowledge that some ecclesiastics
today seem to want to create a new Church.
By doing so they betray Christ, for they change
spiritual aims—the salvation of souls, one by
one—into temporal aims. If they do not resist
this temptation, they will leave their sacred
ministry unfulfilled, lose the confidence and
respect of the people, and create havoc in the
Church. Moreover, by interfering intolerably
with the political freedom of Christians and
other men, they will sow confusion in civil
society and make themselves dangerous. Holy
orders is the sacrament of supernatural service
of one's brothers in the faith; some seem to be
trying to turn it into the earthly instrument of
a new despotism.

80   But let's continue contemplating the marvel
of the sacraments. In the anointing of the sick,
as extreme unction is now called, we find a
loving preparation for the journey which ends
in the Father's house. And in the Eucharist,
which we might call the sacrament of divine
extravagance, God gives his grace and himself
to us: Jesus Christ, who is always really present—not just during Mass—with his body,

with his soul, with his blood, and with his divinity.

I think very often about the responsibility that lies with priests to preserve the divine channel of the sacraments for all Christians. God's grace comes to the aid of every soul, for every person needs specific, personal help. You cannot treat souls *en masse!* It is not right to offend human dignity and the dignity of the sons of God by not going personally to the aid of each one. The priest must do just that, with the humility of a man who knows he is only an instrument, the vehicle of Christ's love. For every soul is a wonderful treasure; every man is unique and irreplaceable. Every single person is worth all the blood of Christ.

We were talking previously about the need to fight. But fighting calls for training, a proper diet, urgent medical attention in the case of illness, bruises, and wounds. The sacraments are the main medicine the Church has to offer. They are not luxuries. If you voluntarily abandon them, it is impossible to advance on the road, to follow Jesus Christ. We need them as we need air to breathe, the circulation of the blood, and light to appreciate at every moment what our Lord wants of us.

A Christian's asceticism requires strength, which is found in the Creator. We are darkness and he is radiant light. We are infirmity and he is robust good health. We are poverty and he is infinite wealth. We are weakness and he sustains us, "for you are, O God, my strength."[18] Nothing on earth is capable of stemming the impatient gushing forth of the redeeming blood of Christ. Yet human limitations can veil our eyes so that we do not notice the grandeur of God. Hence the responsibility of all the faithful, especially those who have the role of governing—serving—the People of God spiritually, of not blocking the sources of grace, of not being ashamed of Christ's cross.

PASTORS' RESPONSIBILITY

81   In the Church of Christ, everyone is obliged to make a tenacious effort to remain loyal to the teaching of Christ. No one is exempt. If the shepherds do not themselves strive to acquire a sensitive conscience and to remain faithful to dogma and moral teaching—which make up

[18] Ps 42:2: *quia tu es, Deus, fortitudo mea.*

the deposit of faith and the inheritance of all—then the prophetic words of Ezechiel will be borne out: "Son of man, prophesy against the shepherds of Israel, prophesy, and say to them, even to the shepherds, thus says the Lord God: Ho, shepherds of Israel who have been feeding yourselves! Should not shepherds feed the sheep? You eat the fat of the sheep, you clothe yourselves with the wool... the weak you have not strengthened, the sick you have not healed, the crippled you have not bound up, the strayed you have not brought back, the lost you have not sought, and with force and harshness you have ruled them."[19]

This is a strong reproof, but the offense against God is even worse when those who have received the task of promoting the spiritual welfare of everyone abuse souls instead, depriving them of the crystal water of baptism, which regenerates the soul; of the soothing oil of confirmation, which strengthens it; of the tribunal which pardons; of the food which gives eternal life.

Such is the result when one abandons the war of peace. Anyone who does not put up a

[19] Ezek 34:2-4.

fight exposes himself to one or other of the slaveries which can chain hearts of flesh—the slavery of a purely human outlook, the slavery of a zealous desire for temporal influence and prestige, the slavery of vanity, the slavery of money, the slavery of sensuality....

Should God permit you to undergo this test, should you come across shepherds unworthy of the name, do not be scandalized. Christ has promised his Church infallible and unfailing help, but he has not guaranteed the fidelity of the men who compose it. They will never be short of grace, abundant and generous grace, if they do the little God asks of them: if they strive with the help of God's grace to remove the obstacles which get in the way of holiness. If that effort is missing, even he who seems to be very high up, may be very low in God's eyes. "I know your works; you have the name of being alive, and you are dead. Awake, and strengthen what remains of your flock, which is on the point of death, for I have not found your works perfect in the sight of my God. Remember then what you have received and heard; keep that and repent."[20]

[20] Rev 3:1-3.

This exhortation, which comes from St John in the first century, is addressed to the person in charge of the church in the city of Sardis. So, a weakening of some shepherds' sense of responsibility is not a modern phenomenon. You find it also at the time of the Apostles, in the very century in which our Lord Jesus Christ lived on earth. It is simply that no one is safe if he ceases to strive against himself. Nobody can save himself by his own efforts. Everyone in the Church needs specific means to strengthen himself: humility which disposes us to accept help and advice; mortifications which temper the heart and allow Christ to reign in it; the study of abiding, sound doctrine which leads us to conserve and spread our faith.

NOW AS BEFORE

The liturgy of Palm Sunday puts these 82 words on our lips: "Swing back, doors, higher yet; reach higher, immemorial gates, to let the king enter in triumph!"[21] Anyone who barricades himself in the citadel of his own selfish-

---

[21] Antiphon during distribution of palms.

ness will never come down onto the battlefield.
But if he raises the gates of his fortress and lets
in the king of peace, then he will go out with
the king to fight against all that misery which
blurs the eyes and numbs the conscience.
"Reach higher, immemorial gates." The fact that
Christianity requires us to fight is nothing new.
It has always been that way. If we do not fight,
we will not win and if we do not win, we will
not obtain peace. Without peace human joy is
illusory, fake, barren, and it is not translated
into service of men, or works of charity and
justice, of pardon and mercy, or the service of
God.

Today, inside and outside the Church, high
and low, one gets the impression that many
people have given up the struggle—that personal war against one's own weaknesses—and
have surrendered bag and baggage to slaveries
which debase the soul. It is a danger which
always confronts Christians.

That is why we must insistently go to the
Holy Trinity asking God to have compassion
on everyone. When talking about this subject,
I hesitate to refer to God's justice. I appeal to
his mercy, his compassion, so that he will not
look at our sins but will rather see the merits

of Christ and of his holy Mother, who is also our mother, the merits of the patriarch St Joseph whom he made his father, and the merits of the saints.

A Christian can rest completely assured that if he wants to fight, God will take him by the right hand, as we read in today's Mass. It is Jesus the king of peace who says on entering Jerusalem astride a miserable donkey: "The kingdom of heaven has been subjected to violence and the violent are taking it by storm."[22] This violence is not directed against others. It is violence used to fight your own weaknesses and miseries, a fortitude which prevents you from camouflaging your own infidelities, a boldness to own up to the faith even when the environment is hostile.

Today, as yesterday, heroism is expected of the Christian. A heroism in great struggles, if the need arises. Normally, however, heroism in the little skirmishes of each day. When you put up a continuous fight, with love, in apparently insignificant things, the Lord is always present at your side, as a loving shepherd: "I myself pasture my sheep, I myself will show them

[22] Mt 11:12.

where to rest—it is the Lord Yahweh who speaks. I shall look for the lost one, bring back the stray, bandage the wounded, and make the weak strong.... They will feel safe in their own pastures. And men will learn that I am Yahweh when I break their yoke straps and release them from their captivity."[23]

---

[23] Ezek 34:15-16, 27.

THE EUCHARIST, MYSTERY OF FAITH AND LOVE*

"Now before the feast of the Passover, when 83 Jesus knew that his hour had come to depart out of this world to the Father, having loved his own who were in the world, he loved them to the end."[1] The reader of this verse from St John's Gospel is brought to understand that a great event is about to take place. The introduction, full of tender affection, is similar to that which we find in St Luke: "I have earnestly desired," says our Lord, "to eat this Passover with you before I suffer."[2]

Let us begin by asking the Holy Spirit, from this moment on, to give us the grace to understand every word and gesture of Christ—

---

* A homily given on April 14, 1960, Holy Thursday.
[1] Jn 13:1.
[2] Lk 22:15.

because we want to live a supernatural life, because our Lord has shown his desire to give himself to us as nourishment for our soul, and because we acknowledge that only he has "words of eternal life."[3]

Faith makes us profess in the words of Peter that "we have come to believe and to know that you are the Christ, the Son of God."[4] It is this faith, together with our devotion, that leads us to emulate the daring of John, to come close to Jesus and to rest on the breast of the Master,[5] who loved those who were with him ardently, and who was to love them, as we have just read, to the end.

Any words we might use to explain the mystery of Holy Thursday are inadequate. But it is not hard to imagine the feelings of Jesus' heart on that evening, his last evening with his friends before the sacrifice of Calvary.

Think of the human experience of two people who love each other, and yet are forced to part. They would like to stay together forever, but duty—in one form or another—forces them to separate. They are unable to fulfil their

[3] Jn 6:69.
[4] Jn 6:70.
[5] Cf. Jn 13:25.

desire of remaining close to each other, so man's love—which, great as it may be, is limited—seeks a symbolic gesture. People who make their farewells exchange gifts or perhaps a photograph with a dedication so ardent that it seems almost enough to burn that piece of paper. They can do no more, because a creature's power is not as great as its desire.

What we cannot do, our Lord is able to do. Jesus Christ, perfect God and perfect man, leaves us, not a symbol, but a reality. He himself stays with us. He will go to the Father, but he will also remain among men. He will leave us, not simply a gift that will make us remember him, not an image that becomes blurred with time, like a photograph that soon fades and yellows, and has no meaning except for those who were contemporaries. Under the appearances of bread and wine, he is really present, with his body and blood, with his soul and divinity.

THE JOY OF HOLY THURSDAY

How well we understand the song that 84 Christians of all times have unceasingly sung to the sacred host: "Sing, my tongue, the mystery of the glorious body and of the precious blood, that the king of all nations, born of the generous womb of the Virgin, has offered for the redemption of the world."[6] We must adore devoutly this God of ours, hidden in the Eucharist[7]—it is Jesus himself, born of the Virgin Mary, who suffered and gave his life in the sacrifice of the cross; Jesus, from whose side, pierced by a lance, flowed water and blood.[8]

This is the sacred banquet, in which we receive Christ himself. We renew the memory of his passion, and through him the soul is brought to an intimate relationship with God and receives a promise of future glory.[9] The liturgy of the Church has summarized, in a few words, the culminating points of the history of our Lord's love for us.

The God of our faith is not a distant being who contemplates indifferently the fate of men—their desires, their struggles, their sufferings. He is a Father who loves his children so much that he sends the Word, the Second

---

[6] Hymn *Pange, lingua*.
[7] Cf. hymn *Adoro te devote*.
[8] Cf. hymn *Ave, verum*.
[9] Cf. hymn *O sacrum convivium*.

Person of the most Blessed Trinity, so that by taking on the nature of man he may die to redeem us. He is the loving Father who now leads us gently to himself, through the action of the Holy Spirit who dwells in our hearts.

This is the source of the joy we feel on Holy Thursday—the realization that the Creator has loved his creatures to such an extent. Our Lord Jesus Christ, as though all the other proofs of his mercy were insufficient, institutes the Eucharist so that he can always be close to us. We can only understand up to a point that he does so because Love moves him, who needs nothing, not to want to be separated from us. The Blessed Trinity has fallen in love with man, raised to the level of grace and made "to God's image and likeness."[10] God has redeemed him from sin—from the sin of Adam, inherited by all his descendants, as well as from his personal sins— and desires ardently to dwell in his soul: "If anyone love me, he will keep my word; and my Father will love him, and we will come to him and make our abode with him."[11]

[10] Gen 1:26.
[11] Jn 14:23.

THE EUCHARIST AND

THE MYSTERY OF THE TRINITY

85   The Blessed Trinity's love for man is made
permanent in a sublime way through the
Eucharist. Many years ago, we all learned from
our catechism that the Eucharist can be considered as a sacrifice and as a sacrament; and that
the sacrament is present to us both in communion and as a treasure on the altar, in the
tabernacle. The Church dedicates another feast
to the eucharistic mystery—the feast of the
body of Christ, *Corpus Christi*, present in all the
tabernacles of the world. Today, on Holy
Thursday, we can turn our attention to the holy
Eucharist as our sacrifice and as our nourishment, in the holy Mass and in communion.

I was talking to you about the love of the
Blessed Trinity for man. And where can we see
this more clearly than in the Mass? The three
divine Persons act together in the holy sacrifice
of the altar. This is why I like to repeat the final
words of the collect, secret and postcom-
munion: "Through Jesus Christ, your Son, our
Lord," we pray to God the Father, "who lives
and reigns with you in the unity of the Holy
Spirit, one God, forever and ever. Amen."

In the Mass, our prayer to God the Father is constant. The priest represents the eternal high priest, Jesus Christ, who is, at the same time, the victim offered in this sacrifice. And the action of the Holy Spirit in the Mass is truly present, although in a mysterious manner. "By the power of the Holy Spirit," writes St John Damascene, "the transformation of the bread into the body of Christ takes place."[12]

The action of the Holy Spirit is clearly expressed when the priest invokes the divine blessing on the offerings: "Come, Sanctifier, almighty and eternal God, and bless this sacrifice prepared in honor of your holy name"[13]— the holocaust that will give to the holy name of God the glory that is due. The sanctification we pray for is attributed to the Paraclete, who is sent to us by the Father and the Son. And we also recognize the active presence of the Holy Spirit in this sacrifice, as we say, shortly before communion: "Lord Jesus Christ, who, by the will of the Father, with the cooperation of the Holy Spirit, by your death have brought life to the world..."[14]

---

[12] *De fide orthodoxa*, 13 (PG 94, 1139).

[13] *Roman Missal*, offertory, invocation to the Holy Spirit.

[14] *Ibid.*, prayer preparing for communion.

86   The three divine Persons are present in the
sacrifice of the altar. By the will of the Father,
with the cooperation of the Holy Spirit, the Son
offers himself in a redemptive sacrifice. We
learn how to personalize our relationship with
the most Blessed Trinity, one God in three
Persons: three divine Persons in the unity of
God's substance, in the unity of his love and
of his sanctifying action.

Immediately after the Lavabo, the priest
prays: "Receive, Holy Trinity, this offering that
we make in memory of the passion, resurrection, and ascension of our Lord Jesus Christ."[15]
And, at the end of the Mass, there is another
prayer of homage to the Trinity of God: "May
the tribute of my service be pleasing to you, O
Holy Trinity; and grant that the sacrifice that
I, who am unworthy, have offered to your
majesty, may be acceptable to you; and that
through your mercy it may bring forgiveness
to me and to all those for whom I have offered
it."[16]

The Mass is, I insist, an action of God, of
the Trinity. It is not a merely human event. The

---

[15] Ibid., offertory, offering to the Blessed Trinity.
[16] Ibid., prayer before the final blessing.

priest who celebrates fulfils the desire of our Lord, lending his body and his voice to the divine action. He acts, not in his own name, but *in persona et in nomine Christi*: in the person of Christ and in his name.

Because of the Blessed Trinity's love for man, the presence of Christ in the Eucharist brings all graces to the Church and to mankind. This is the sacrifice announced by the prophet Malachy: "From the rising of the sun to its setting my name is great among the nations, and a fragrant sacrifice and a pure offering is made to me in all places."[17] It is the sacrifice of Christ, offered to the Father with the cooperation of the Holy Spirit—an offering of infinite value, which perpetuates the work of the redemption in us and surpasses the sacrifices of the old law.

HOLY MASS IN THE CHRISTIAN'S LIFE

The holy Mass brings us face to face with 87 one of the central mysteries of our faith, because it is the gift of the Blessed Trinity to the Church. It is because of this that we can consider the

[17] Mal 1:11.

Mass as the center and the source of a Christian's spiritual life.

It is the aim of all the sacraments.[18] The life of grace, into which we are brought by baptism, and which is increased and strengthened by confirmation, grows to its fullness in the Mass. "When we participate in the Eucharist," writes St Cyril of Jerusalem, "we are made spiritual by the divinizing action of the Holy Spirit, who not only makes us share in Christ's life, as in baptism, but makes us entirely Christ-like, incorporating us into the fullness of Christ Jesus."[19]

This pouring out of the Holy Spirit unites us to Christ and makes us acknowledge that we are children of God. The Paraclete, who is Love, teaches us to saturate our life with the virtue of charity. Thus *consummati in unum*: "made one with Christ,"[20] we can be among men what the Eucharist is for us, in the words of St Augustine: "a sign of unity, a bond of love."[21]

I will not surprise anyone if I say that some Christians have a very poor concept of the holy

[18] Cf. St Thomas, *S. Th.*, III, q. 65, a. 3.

[19] *Catechesis*, 22, 3.

[20] Jn 17:23.

[21] *In Ioannis Evangelium tractatus*, 26, 13 (PL 35, 1613).

Mass. For them it is a purely external rite, if not a mere social convention. This is because our poor hearts are capable of treating the greatest gift of God to man as routine. In the Mass, in this Mass that we are now celebrating, the most Holy Trinity intervenes, I repeat, in a very special way. To correspond to such great love, we must give ourselves completely, in body and in soul. We hear God, we talk to him, we see him, we taste him. And when words are not enough, we sing, urging our tongue—*Pange, lingua!*—to proclaim to all mankind the greatness of the Lord.

To *live* the holy Mass means to pray continu- 88 ally, and to be convinced that, for each one of us, this is a personal meeting with God. We adore him, we praise him, we give thanks to him, we atone for our sins, we are purified, we feel ourselves united in Christ with all Christians.

We may have asked ourselves, at one time or another, how we can respond to the greatness of God's love. We may have wanted to see a program for Christian living clearly explained. The answer is easy, and it is within reach of all the faithful: to participate lovingly in the holy Mass, to learn to deepen our

personal relationship with God in the sacrifice
that summarizes all that Christ asks of us.

Let me remind you of what you have seen
on so many occasions: the succession of prayers
and actions as they unfold before our eyes at
Mass. As we follow them, step by step, our
Lord may show us aspects of our lives in which
each one of us must improve, vices we must
conquer, and the kind of brotherly attitude that
we should develop with regard to all men.

The priest draws near to the altar of God,
"of God who gives joy to our youth." The holy
Mass begins with a song of joy, because God
is here. It is the joy that is shown, together with
love and gratitude, as the priest kisses the altar,
symbol of Christ and reminder of the saints—
a small surface, sanctified because this is where
the sacrament of infinite worth is made present
to us.

The Confiteor makes us aware of our
unworthiness; not an abstract reminder of guilt,
but the actual presence of our sins and weaknesses. This is why we repeat: *Kyrie, eleison,
Christe, eleison*: Lord, have mercy, Christ, have
mercy. If the forgiveness we need had to be
won by our own merits, we would only be
capable of a bitter sadness. But, because of

God's goodness, forgiveness comes from his mercy, and we praise him—*Gloria!*: "for you alone are the holy one, you alone are Lord, you alone, O Jesus Christ, are the most high, with the Holy Spirit in the glory of God the Father."

We now listen to the word of Scripture, the epistle and the gospel—light from the Holy Spirit, who speaks through human voices so as to make our intellect come to know and contemplate, to strengthen our will and make our desire for action effective. And because we are one people, "gathered together in the unity of the Father, and of the Son, and of the Holy Spirit,"[22] we recite the Creed, affirming the unity of our faith.

Then, the offering: the bread and wine of men. It is very little, but it is accompanied by prayer: "Lord God, we ask you to receive us and be pleased with the sacrifice we offer you with humble and contrite hearts: and that the sacrifice which today we offer you, O God, our Lord, may be brought to your presence and be made acceptable." Again, a reminder of our smallness and of the desire to cleanse and purify all that is offered to God: "I will wash

---

[22] St Cyprian, *De dominica oratione*, 23 (PL 4, 553).

my hands... I have loved the beauty of your house...."

A moment ago, just before the Lavabo, we invoked the Holy Spirit, asking him to bless the sacrifice offered to his holy name. After washing his hands, the priest, in the name of all those present, prays to the Holy Trinity—*Suscipe, Sancta Trinitas*—to accept our offering in memory of the life of Christ and of his passion, resurrection and ascension; and in honor of Mary, ever-Virgin, and of all the saints.

May this offering be effective for the salvation of all men—*Orate, fratres*, the priest invites the people to pray—because this sacrifice is yours and mine, it is the sacrifice of the whole Church. Pray, brethren, although there may not be many present, although materially there may be only one person there, although the celebrant may find himself alone; because every Mass is a universal sacrifice, the redemption of every tribe and tongue and people and nation.[23]

Through the communion of the saints, all Christians receive grace from every Mass that is celebrated, regardless of whether there is an attendance of thousands of persons, or whether

[23] Cf. Rev 5:9.

it is only a boy with his mind on other things who is there to serve. In either case, heaven and earth join with the angels of the Lord to sing: *Sanctus, Sanctus, Sanctus...*

I adore and praise with the angels—it is not difficult, because I know that, as I celebrate the holy Mass, they surround me, adoring the Blessed Trinity. And I know that in some way the Blessed Virgin is there, because of her intimate relationship with the most Blessed Trinity and because she is the Mother of Christ, of his flesh and blood—the Mother of Jesus Christ, perfect God and perfect man. Jesus was conceived in the womb of Mary most holy, not through the intervention of man, but by the power of the Holy Spirit alone. In his veins runs the blood of his Mother, the blood that is offered in the sacrifice of the redemption, on Calvary and in the Mass.

Thus we begin the canon, with the confidence of children of God, calling him our most loving Father: *clementissime*. We pray for the Church and for all those who are a part of the Church—the pope, our families, our friends and companions. And a Catholic, with his heart open to all men, will pray for all men, because no one can be excluded from his love. We ask

God to hear our prayers. We call on the memory of the glorious ever-Virgin Mary and of a handful of men who were among the first to follow Christ and to die for him, and we recall our union with them.

Quam oblationem... the moment of the consecration draws near. Now, in the Mass, it is Christ who acts again, through the priest: "This is my body"... "This is the cup of my blood." Jesus is with us! The transubstantiation is a renewal of the miracle of God's infinite love. When that moment takes place again today, let us tell our Lord, without any need for words, that nothing will be able to separate us from him; that, as he puts himself into our hands, defenseless, under the fragile appearances of bread and wine, he has made us his willing slaves. "Make me live always through you, and taste the sweetness of your love."[24]

More prayers, because we human beings almost always feel the need to ask for things— prayers for our deceased brothers, for ourselves. We have brought all our weaknesses, our lack of faithfulness. The weight is heavy,

---

[24] Hymn *Adoro te devote: praesta meae menti de te vivere, et te illi semper dulce sapere.*

but he wants to bear it for us and with us. The canon ends with another invocation to the Blessed Trinity: *Per Ipsum, et cum Ipso, et in Ipso...*: Through Christ, and with Christ, and in Christ, who is all our love, in the unity of the Holy Spirit, all honor and glory is yours, almighty Father, for ever and ever.

Jesus is the way, the mediator. In him are 91 all things; outside of him is nothing. In Christ, taught by him, we dare to call God our Father— he is the Almighty who created heaven and earth, and he is a loving Father who waits for us to come back to him again and again, as the story of the prodigal son repeats itself in our lives.

Ecce Agnus Dei... Domine, non sum dignus... We are going to receive our Lord. On this earth, when we receive an important person, we bring out the best—lights, music, formal dress. How should we prepare to receive Christ into our soul? Have we ever thought about how we would behave if we could only receive him once in a lifetime?

When I was a child, frequent communion was still not a widespread practice. I remember how people used to prepare to go to communion. Everything had to be just right, body and soul: the best clothes, hair well-combed—even physical cleanliness was important—maybe even a few drops of cologne... These were manifestations of love, full of finesse and refinement, on the part of manly souls who knew how to repay Love with love.

With Christ in our soul, we end the holy Mass. The blessing of the Father, of the Son, and of the Holy Spirit accompanies us all day long, as we go about our simple, normal task of making holy all honest human activity.

As you attend Mass, you will learn to deepen your friendship with each one of the three divine Persons: the Father who begets the Son; the Son, begotten by the Father; the Holy Spirit, who proceeds from the Father and the Son. When we approach any one of the divine Persons, we approach the one God. And when we come close to all three Persons—Father, Son, and Holy Spirit—again we come into the presence of the one true God. Love the Mass, my children, love the Mass. And be hungry to receive our Lord in communion, although you may be cold inside, although your emotions may not correspond to your desires. Receive communion with faith, with hope, with burning charity.

CONTACT WITH JESUS

A man who fails to love the Mass fails to 92 love Christ. We must make an effort to *live* the Mass with calm and serenity, with devotion and affection. Those who love acquire a finesse, a sensitivity of soul that makes them notice details that are sometimes very small, but that are important because they express the love of a passionate heart. This is how we should attend the holy Mass. And this is why I have always suspected that those who want the Mass to be over quickly show, with this insensitive attitude, that they have not yet realized what the sacrifice of the altar means.

If we love Christ, who offers himself for us, we will feel compelled to find a few minutes after Mass for an intimate personal thanksgiving, which will prolong in the silence of our hearts that other thanksgiving which is the Eucharist. How are we to approach him, what are we to say, how should we behave?

Christian life is not made up of rigid norms, because the Holy Spirit does not guide souls collectively, but inspires each one with resolutions, inspirations, and affections that will help it to recognize and fulfill the will of the Father.

Still, I feel that, on many occasions, the central theme of our conversation with Christ, in our thanksgiving after holy Mass, can be the consideration that our Lord is our king, physician, teacher, and friend.

93   He is our king. He desires ardently to rule our hearts, because we are children of God. But we should not try to imagine a human sort of rule—Christ does not dominate or seek to impose himself, because he "has not come to be served but to serve."[25]

His kingdom is one of peace, of joy, of justice. Christ our king does not expect us to spend our time in abstract reasoning; he expects deeds, because "not everyone who says to me, 'Lord, Lord!' shall enter the kingdom of heaven; but he who does the will of my Father in heaven shall enter the kingdom of heaven."[26]

He is our physician, and he heals our selfishness, if we let his grace penetrate to the depths of our soul. Jesus has taught us that the worst sickness is hypocrisy, the pride that leads us to hide our own sins. We have to be totally

[25] Mt 20:28.
[26] Mt 7:21.

sincere with him. We have to tell the whole truth, and then we have to say: "Lord, if you will"—and you are always willing—"you can make me clean."[27] You know my weaknesses; I feel these symptoms; I suffer from these failings. We show him the wound, with simplicity, and if the wound is festering, we show the pus too. Lord, you have cured so many souls; help me to recognize you as the divine physician, when I have you in my heart or when I contemplate your presence in the tabernacle.

He is a teacher, with a knowledge that only he possesses—the knowledge of unlimited love for God, and, in God, for all men. In Christ's teaching we learn that our existence does not belong to us. He gave up his life for all men and, if we follow him, we must understand that we cannot take possession of our own lives in a selfish way, without sharing the sorrows of others. Our life belongs to God. We are here to spend it in his service, concerning ourselves generously with souls, showing, through our words and our example, the extent of the Christian dedication that is expected of us.

[27] Mt 8:2: *Domine, si vis, potes me mundare.*

Jesus expects us to nourish the desire to acquire this knowledge, so that he can repeat to us: "If anyone thirst, let him come to me and drink."[28] And we answer: teach us to forget ourselves, so that we may concern ourselves with you and with all souls. In this way, our Lord will lead us forward with his grace, just as when we were learning to write. Do you remember that childish scrawl, guided by the teacher's hand? And we will begin to taste the joy of showing our faith, which is yet another gift from God, and showing it with clear strokes of Christian conduct, in which all will be able to read the wonders of God.

He is our friend, *the* Friend: *vos autem dixi amicos*,[29] he says. He calls us his friends; and he is the one who took the first step, because he loved us first. Still, he does not impose his love—he offers it. He shows it with the clearest possible sign: "Greater love than this no one has, that one lay down his life for his friends."[30] He was Lazarus' friend. He wept for him when he saw him dead, and he raised him from the

---

[28] Jn 7:37.
[29] Jn 15:15.
[30] Jn 15:13.

dead. If he sees us cold, unwilling, rigid perhaps with the stiffness of a dying interior life, his tears will be our life—"I say to you, my friend, arise and walk,"[31] leave that narrow life which is no life at all.

Our Holy Thursday meditation draws to a 94 close. If our Lord has helped us—and he is always ready to do so, as long as we open our hearts to him—we will feel the need to correspond in what is most important, and that is love. And we will know how to spread that love among other men, with a life of service. "I have given you an example,"[32] he tells his disciples after washing their feet, on the night of the last supper. Let us reject from our hearts any pride, any ambition, any desire to dominate; and peace and joy will reign around us and within us, as a consequence of our personal sacrifice.

Finally, a loving thought directed to Mary, Mother of God and our Mother. Forgive me if I go back to another childhood memory—a picture that became very common in my own country when St Pius X was encouraging the

---

[31] Cf. Jn 11:43; Lk 5:24.
[32] Jn 13:15.

practice of frequent communion. It represented Mary adoring the sacred host. Today, as in those days and as always, our Lady teaches us to come to Jesus, to recognize him and to find him in all the different situations of our day. And nowhere is she more a teacher than in the supreme moment of the holy sacrifice of the Mass, where time blends with eternity. Jesus, with the gesture of a high priest, attracts all things to himself and places them, with the breath of the Holy Spirit, in the presence of God the Father.

CHRIST'S DEATH IS THE CHRISTIAN'S LIFE*

During this week which Christians tradition-
ally call Holy Week, we are given another
chance to reflect on and to re-live the last hours
of Jesus' life. All the things brought to our mind
by the different expressions of piety which
characterize these days are of course directed
to the resurrection, which is, as St Paul says,
the foundation of our faith.[1] But we should not
tread this path too hastily, lest we lose sight of
a very simple fact which we might easily
overlook. We will not be able to share in our
Lord's resurrection unless we unite ourselves
with him in his passion and death.[2] If we are
to accompany Christ in his glory at the end of

---

* A homily given on April 15, 1960, Good Friday.
[1] Cf. 1 Cor 15:14.
[2] Cf. Rom 8:17.

Holy Week, we must first enter into his holocaust and be truly united to him, as he lies dead
on Calvary.

Christ's generous self-sacrifice is a challenge
to sin. We find it hard to accept the reality of
sin, although its existence is undeniable. Sin is
the *mysterium iniquitatis*: the mystery of evil, the
inexplicable evil of the creature whose pride
leads him to rise up against God. The story is
as old as mankind. It began with the fall of our
first parents; then came the unending depravi-
ties which punctuate the behavior of mankind
down the ages; and, finally, our own personal
rebellions. It is very difficult to realize just how
perverse sin is and to understand what our faith
tells us. We should remember that even in the
human context the scale of an offense is frequently determined by the importance of the
injured party—his social standing, his qualities.
But with sin man offends God, the creature
repudiates his Creator.

But "God is love."[3] The abyss of malice
which sin opens wide has been bridged by his
infinite charity. God did not abandon men. His
plans foresaw that the sacrifices of the old law

---

[3] 1 Jn 4:8.

would be insufficient to repair our faults and re-establish the unity which had been lost. A man who was God would have to offer himself up. To help us grasp in some measure this unfathomable mystery, we might imagine the Blessed Trinity taking counsel together in its uninterrupted intimate relationship of infinite love. As a result of its eternal decision, the only-begotten Son of God the Father takes on our human condition and bears the burden of our wretchedness and sorrows, to end up sewn with nails to a piece of wood.

Christ's whole life, from his birth in Bethlehem, was filled with a burning desire to carry out the saving decree of God the Father. Throughout the three years his disciples lived with him, they constantly heard him say that his food was to do the will of him who sent him.[4] And so it was, right up to the afternoon of the first Good Friday when his sacrifice was completed. "Bowing his head, he gave up his spirit."[5] That is how St John the Apostle describes Christ's death. Jesus dies on the cross beneath the weight of all the faults of men,

---

[4] Cf. Jn 4:34.
[5] Jn 19:30.

crushed by the sheer force and wickedness of
our sins.

Let us meditate on our Lord, wounded from
head to foot out of love for us. Using a phrase
which approaches the truth, although it does
not express its full reality, we can repeat the
words of an ancient writer: "The body of Christ
is a portrait in pain." At the sight of Christ
bruised and broken—just a lifeless body taken
down from the cross and given to his Mother—
at the sight of Jesus destroyed in this way, we
might have thought he had failed utterly.
Where are the crowds that once followed him,
where is the kingdom he foretold? But this is
victory, not defeat. We are nearer the resurrection than ever before; we are going to see the
triumph which he has won with his obedience.

CHRIST'S DEATH CALLS US
TO A FULLER CHRISTIAN LIFE

96   We have just been re-living the drama of
Calvary, which I would dare to describe as the
first, the original Mass, celebrated by Jesus
Christ. God the Father delivers his Son up to
death. Jesus, the only Son of God, embraces the

cross on which they have condemned him to die, and his sacrifice is accepted by his Father. As a result of that sacrifice, the Holy Spirit is poured out upon mankind.[6]

The tragedy of the passion brings to fulfillment our own life and the whole of human history. We can't let Holy Week be just a kind of commemoration. It means contemplating the mystery of Jesus Christ as something which continues to work in our souls. The Christian is obliged to be *alter Christus, ipse Christus*: another Christ, Christ himself. Through baptism all of us have been made priests of our lives, "to offer spiritual sacrifices acceptable to God through Jesus Christ."[7] Everything we do can be an expression of our obedience to God's will and so perpetuate the mission of the Godman.

Once we realize this, we are immediately reminded of our wretchedness and our personal failings. But they should not dishearten us; we should not become pessimistic and put our ideals aside. Our Lord is calling us, in our present state, to share his life and make an

[6] Cf. Rom 3:24ff; Heb 10:5ff; Jn 7:39.
[7] 1 Pet 2:5.

effort to be holy. I know holiness can sound like an empty word. Too many people think it is unattainable, something to do with ascetical theology—but not a real goal for them, a living reality. The first Christians didn't think that way. They often used the word "saints" to describe each other in a very natural manner: "greetings to all the saints",[8] "my greetings to every one of the saints in Jesus Christ."[9]

Take a look now at Calvary. Jesus has died and there is as yet no sign of his glorious triumph. It is a good time to examine how much we really want to live as Christians, to be holy. Here is our chance to react against our weaknesses with an act of faith. We can trust in God and resolve to put love into the things we do each day. The experience of sin should lead us to sorrow. We should make a more mature and deeper decision to be faithful and truly identify ourselves with Christ, persevering, no matter what it costs, in the priestly mission that he has given every single one of his disciples. That mission should spur us on to be the salt and light of the world.[10]

[8] Rom 16:15.
[9] Phil 4:21.
[10] Cf. Mt 5:13-14.

So, in thinking about Christ's death, we find 97
ourselves invited to take a good hard look at
our everyday activities and to be serious about
the faith we profess. Holy Week cannot be a
kind of "religious interlude", time taken out
from a life which is completely caught up in
human affairs. It must be an opportunity to
understand more profoundly the love of God,
so that we'll be able to show that love to other
people through what we do and say.

But for this our Lord lays down certain
conditions. We cannot ignore his words that St
Luke recorded for us: "If anyone comes to me
and does not hate his own father and mother
and wife and children and brothers and sisters,
yes and even his own life, he cannot be my disciple."[11] They are hard words. True, "hate" in
English does not exactly express what Jesus
meant. Yet he did put it very strongly, because
he doesn't just mean "love less," as some people
interpret it in an attempt to tone down the
sentence. The force behind these vigorous
words does not lie in their implying a negative
or pitiless attitude, for the Jesus who is speaking here is none other than that Jesus who

[11] Lk 14:26.

commands us to love others as we love ourselves and who gives up his life for mankind.
These words indicate simply that we cannot be
half-hearted when it comes to loving God.
Christ's words could be translated as "love
more, love better," in the sense that a selfish
or partial love is not enough—we have to love
others with the love of God.

That's the key. Jesus says we must also hate
our life, our very soul—that is what our Lord
is asking of us. If we are superficial, if the only
thing we care about is our own personal well-
being, if we try to make other people, and even
the world, revolve around our own little self,
we have no right to call ourselves Christians
or think we are disciples of Christ. We have to
give ourselves really, not just in word but in
deed and truth.[12] Love for God invites us to
take up the cross and feel on our own shoulders
the weight of humanity. It leads us to fulfill the
clear and loving plans of the Father's will in
all the circumstances of our work and life. In
the passage we've just read Jesus goes on to
say: "Whoever does not bear his own cross and
come after me, cannot be my disciple."[13]

[12]Cf. 1 Jn 3:18.
[13] Lk 14:27.

Let us accept God's will and be firmly resolved to build all our life in accordance with what our faith teaches and demands. We can be sure this involves struggle and suffering and pain, but if we really keep faith we will never feel we have lost God's favor. In the midst of sorrow and even calumny, we will experience a happiness which moves us to love others, to help them share in our supernatural joy.

THE CHRISTIAN AND HUMAN HISTORY

Being a Christian is not simply a way to 98 personal contentment; it implies a mission. We have already recalled that God invites all Christians to be the salt and light of the world. Echoing that commandment and using texts from the old testament, St Peter spells out its implications in forthright language: "You are a chosen race, a royal priesthood, a holy nation, God's own people, that you may declare the wonderful deeds of him who called you out of darkness into his marvelous light."[14]

Being a Christian is not something incidental; it is a divine reality that takes root deep

[14] 1 Pet 2:9.

in our life. It gives us a clear vision and strengthens our will to act as God wants. So we learn that the Christian's pilgrimage in the world must express itself in a continuous service in all kinds of ways, varying with each person's circumstances, but always motivated by love of God and of our neighbor. Being a Christian means forgetting petty objectives of personal prestige and ambition and even possibly nobler aims, like philanthropy and compassion for the misfortunes of others. It means setting our mind and heart on reaching the fullness of love which Jesus Christ showed by dying for us.

Let me give you an example of the kind of attitude which develops if one is unable to penetrate this mystery of Jesus. Some people tend to see Christianity as a collection of devout practices, failing to realize the relation between them and the circumstances of ordinary life, including the urgency to meet the needs of other people and remedy injustice. I would say that anyone who has that attitude has not yet understood the meaning of the incarnation. The Son of God has taken the body and soul and voice of a man; he has shared our fate, even to the extent of experiencing the excruciating anguish of death. Yet perhaps without wanting to, some people regard Christ as a stranger in the world of man.

Others tend to imagine that in order to remain human we need to play down some central aspects of Christian dogma. They act as if the life of prayer, continual relationship with God, implied fleeing from responsibilities and forsaking the world. But they forget that it was none other than Jesus who showed us the extreme to which we should go in love and service. Only if we try to understand the mystery of God's love—a love which went as far as death—will we be able to give ourselves totally to others and not let ourselves be overcome by difficulties or indifference.

What illuminates our conscience is faith in 99 Christ, who has died and risen and is present in every moment of life. Faith moves us to play our full part in the changing situations and in the problems of human history. In this history, which began with the creation of the world and will reach its fulfillment at the end of time, the Christian is no expatriate. He is a citizen of the city of men, and his soul longs for God. While still on earth he has glimpses of God's love and comes to recognize it as the goal to which all men on earth are called.

If my own personal experience is of any help, I can say that I have always seen my work as a priest and shepherd of souls as being aimed at helping each person to face up to all the demands of his life and to discover what God wants from him in particular—without in any way limiting that holy independence and blessed personal responsibility which are the features of a Christian conscience. This way of acting and this spirit are based on respect for the transcendence of revealed truth and on love for the freedom of the human person. I might add that they are also based on a realization that history is undetermined and open to a variety of human options—all of which God respects.

Following Christ does not mean taking refuge in the temple, shrugging one's shoulders at social development, ignoring the achievements and aberrations alike of men or nations. On the contrary, Christian faith makes us see the world as God's creation and appreciate all its nobility and beauty, recognizing the dignity of each person made in the image of God. It makes us admire the splendid gift of freedom which gives us power over our own actions and enables us—with heaven's grace—to build our eternal destiny. You would belittle the faith if you reduced it to a human ideology, if you raised a political-religious standard to condemn—on who knows what divine authority—those who think differently from you in matters which by their very nature can be solved in a wide variety of ways.

UNDERSTANDING CHRIST'S DEATH

The only purpose of the digression I have 100 just made was to emphasize a central truth: I wanted to remind you that Christian life finds its meaning in God. Men have not been created just to build the best possible world. We have been put here on earth for a further purpose: to enter into communion with God himself. Jesus has promised us not a life of ease or worldly achievement, but the house of his Father God, which awaits us at the end of the way.[15]

The liturgy of Good Friday contains a wonderful hymn, *Crux Fidelis*. It invites us to sing and celebrate the glorious struggle of our

[15] Cf. Jn 14:2.

Lord, the victory of the cross, the splendid triumph of Christ. The redeemer of the universe is sacrificed and triumphs. God, the Lord of all creation, does not make his presence felt by force of arms or by the temporal power of his followers, but by the nobility of his infinite love.

The Lord does not destroy man's freedom; it is precisely he who has made us free. That is why he does not want to wring obedience from us. He wants our decisions to come from the depths of our heart. And he wants Christians to live in such a way that the people we deal with will find in our conduct—despite our weaknesses, faults, and failings—an echo of the drama of love that was Calvary. Everything we have comes from God; he wants us to be salt which flavors and light which brings the happy news that he is a Father who loves without measure. The Christian is the salt and light of the world, not because he conquers or triumphs, but because he bears witness to God's love. And he won't be salt if he can't give flavor. Nor will he be light if he doesn't bear witness to Jesus through his example and word, if he loses sight of the purpose of his life.

101   It is good for us to try to understand better the meaning of Christ's death. We must get

beyond external appearances and clichés. We need to put ourselves really and truly into the scenes which we are re-living during these days: Jesus' sorrow, his Mother's tears, the disciples' flight, the courage of the holy women, the daring of Joseph and Nicodemus who ask Pilate for the body of our Lord.

Let us, above all, come close to Jesus in his death and to his cross which stands out in silhouette above the summit of Golgotha. But we must approach him sincerely and with the interior recollection that is a sign of Christian maturity. The divine and human events of the passion will then pierce our soul as words spoken to us by God to uncover the secrets of our heart and show us what he expects of our lives.

Many years ago I saw a painting which made a deep impression on me. It showed the cross of Christ with three angels beside it. One was weeping disconsolately; one held a nail in his hand, as if trying to convince himself it was true; and the third was rapt in prayer. Here we have a program for each of us: to cry, believe, and pray.

Here before the cross, we should have sorrow for our sins and for those of all men, for they are responsible for Jesus' death. We should have faith to penetrate deep into this sublime truth which surpasses our understanding and to fill ourselves with amazement at God's love. And we should pray so that Christ's life and death may become the model and motivation for our own life and self-giving. Only thus will we earn the name of conquerors: for the risen Christ will conquer in us, and death will be changed into life.

CHRIST'S PRESENCE
IN CHRISTIANS*

"Christ is alive." This is the great truth 102
which fills our faith with meaning. Jesus, who
died on the cross, has risen. He has triumphed
over death; he has overcome sorrow, anguish
and the power of darkness. "Do not be terrified" was how the angels greeted the women
who came to the tomb. "Do not be terrified. You
are looking for Jesus of Nazareth, who was crucified. He has risen; he is not here."[1] "This is
the day which the Lord has made; let us rejoice
and be glad in it."[2]

Easter is a time of joy—a joy not confined
to this period of the liturgical year, for it should
always be present in the Christian's heart. For

---

* A homily given on March 26, 1967, Easter Sunday.

[1] Mk 16:6 (gospel of Easter Sunday Mass).

[2] Ps 117:24 (gradual of the Mass): *Haec est dies quam fecit
Dominus, exultemus et laetemur in ea.*

Christ is alive. He is not someone who has gone, someone who existed for a time and then passed on, leaving us a wonderful example and a great memory.

No, Christ is alive. Jesus is the Emmanuel: God with us. His resurrection shows us that God does not abandon his own. He promised he would not: "Can a woman forget her baby that is still unweaned, pity no longer the son she bore in her womb? Even these may forget, yet I will not forget you."[3] And he has kept his promise. His delight is still to be with the sons of men.[4]

Christ is alive in his Church. "I tell you the truth: it is to your advantage that I go away, for if I do not go away, the Counsellor will not come to you; but if I go, I will send him to you."[5] That was what God planned: Jesus, dying on the cross, gave us the Spirit of truth and life. Christ stays in his Church, its sacraments, its liturgy, its preaching—in all that it does.

In a special way Christ stays with us in the daily offering of the holy Eucharist. That is why

---

[3] Is 49:14-15.
[4] Cf. Prov 8:31.
[5] Jn 16:7.

the Mass is the center and source of Christian life. In each and every Mass the complete Christ, head and body, is present. *Per Ipsum et cum Ipso et in Ipso.* For Christ is the way; he is the mediator; in him we find everything. Outside of him our life is empty. In Jesus Christ, and taught by him, "we dare to say: Our Father." We dare to call the Lord of heaven and earth our Father. The presence of the living Christ in the host is the guarantee, the source and the culmination of his presence in the world.

Christ is alive in Christians. Our faith teaches us that man, in the state of grace, is divinized— filled with God. We are men and women, not angels. We are flesh and blood, people with sentiments and passions, with sorrows and joys. And this divinization affects everything human; it is a sort of foretaste of the final resurrection. "Christ has risen from the dead, the first-fruits of those who have fallen asleep. For since by a man came death, by a man also comes resurrection of the dead. For as in Adam all die, so in Christ all will be made to live."[6]

103

[6] 1 Cor 15:20-22.

Christ's life is our life, just as he promised his Apostles at the last supper: "If anyone love me, he will keep my word, and my Father will love him, and we will come to him and make our home with him."[7] That is why a Christian should live as Christ lived, making the affections of Christ his own, so that he can exclaim with St Paul: "It is now no longer I that live, but Christ lives in me."[8]

JESUS, THE SOURCE OF CHRISTIAN LIVING

104   I wanted to review with you, briefly, some of the ways in which Christ is alive today— "Jesus Christ, yesterday and today, yes and forever"[9]—because this is the basis of all Christian living. If we take a look at the course of human history, we will see progress and advances. Science has made man more aware of his power. Technology today controls the world much more than in the past, helping men to reach their dream of a greater level of culture, unity, and material well-being.

---

[7] Jn 14:23.
[8] Gal 2:20: *Non vivo ego, vivit vero in me Christus.*
[9] Heb 13:8: *Iesus Christus heri et hodie, ipse et in saecula.*

Some people are perhaps inclined to tone down this optimism, reminding us that men still suffer from injustice and wars, at times worse than those of the past. They may well be right. But, above and beyond these considerations, I prefer to remember that in the religious sphere man is still man and God is still God. In this sphere the peak of progress has already been reached. And that peak is Christ, alpha and omega, the beginning of all things and their end.[10]

In the spiritual life, there is no new era to come. Everything is already there, in Christ who died and rose again, who lives and stays with us always. But we have to join him through faith, letting his life show forth in ours to such an extent that each Christian is not simply *alter Christus*: another Christ, but *ipse Christus*: Christ himself!

St Paul gave a motto to the Christians at   105 Ephesus: *Instaurare omnia in Christo*:[11] to fill everything with the spirit of Jesus, placing Christ at the center of everything. "And I, when I am lifted up from the earth, will draw all

---

[10] Rev 21:6.
[11] Eph 1:10.

things to myself."[12] Through his incarnation, through his work at Nazareth and his preaching and miracles in the land of Judea and Galilee, through his death on the cross, and through his resurrection, Christ is the center of the universe, the firstborn and Lord of all creation.

Our task as Christians is to proclaim this kingship of Christ, announcing it through what we say and do. Our Lord wants men and women of his own in all walks of life. Some he calls away from society, asking them to give up involvement in the world, so that they remind the rest of us by their example that God exists. To others he entrusts the priestly ministry. But he wants the vast majority to stay right where they are, in all earthly occupations in which they work: the factory, the laboratory, the farm, the trades, the streets of the big cities and the trails of the mountains.

In this connection I like to think of Christ's conversation with the disciples going to Emmaus. As he is walking along, he meets two men who have nearly lost all hope. They are beginning to feel that life has no meaning for

---

[12] Jn 12:32: *Si exaltatus fuero a terra, omnia traham ad meipsum.*

them. Christ understands their sorrow; he sees into their heart and communicates to them some of the life he carries within himself.

When they draw near the village, he makes as if he is going on, but the two disciples stop him and practically force him to stay with them. They recognize him later when he breaks the bread. The Lord, they exclaimed, has been with us! "And they said to each other: 'Was not our heart burning within us while he was speaking on the road and explaining to us the Scriptures?'"[13] Every Christian should make Christ present among men. He ought to act in such a way that those who know him sense "the fragrance of Christ."[14] Men should be able to recognize the Master in his disciples.

A Christian knows that he is grafted onto 106 Christ through baptism. He is empowered to fight for Christ through confirmation, called to act in the world sharing the royal, prophetic and priestly role of Christ. He has become one and the same thing with Christ through the Eucharist, the sacrament of unity and love. And so, like Christ, he has to live for other men,

[13] Lk 24:32.
[14] Cf. 2 Cor 2:15: *bonus odor Christi.*

loving each and every one around him and indeed all humanity.

Faith helps us recognize that Christ is God; it shows that he is our savior; it brings us to identify ourselves with him and to act as he acted. When the risen Christ frees the apostle Thomas from his doubts, showing him his wounds, Jesus exclaims: "Blessed are they who have not seen, and yet have believed."[15] And St Gregory the Great comments that "he is referring in particular to us, for we possess spiritually him whom we have not seen in the body. He is referring to us, provided our behavior agrees with our faith. A person does not truly believe unless he puts into practice what he believes. That is why St Paul says of those whose faith is limited to words: 'They profess recognition of God, but in their behavior they deny him' (Tit 1:16)."[16]

You cannot separate the fact that Christ is God from his role as redeemer. The Word became flesh and came into the world "to save all men."[17] With all our personal defects and

---

[15] Jn 20:29.
[16] *In Evangelia homiliae*, 26, 9 (PL 76, 1202).
[17] Cf. 1 Tim 2:4: *ut omnes homines salvi fiant.*

limitations, we are other Christs, Christ himself, and we too are called to serve all men. We must hear and hear again his command which remains new throughout the centuries. "Beloved," writes St John, "I am writing you no new commandment, but an old commandment which you had from the beginning; the old commandment is the word which you have heard. Yet I am writing you a new commandment, which is true in him and in you, because the darkness is passing away and the true light is already shining. He who says he is in the light and hates his brother is in the darkness still. He who loves his brother abides in the light, and in it there is no cause for stumbling."[18]

Our Lord has come to bring peace, good news, and life to all men. Not only to the rich, nor only to the poor. Not only to the wise nor only to the simple. To everyone, to the brothers, for brothers we are, children of the same Father, God. So there is only one race, the race of the children of God. There is only one color, the color of the children of God. And there is only one language, the language which speaks to the

[18] 1 Jn 2:7-10.

heart and to the mind, without the noise of words, making us know God and love one another.

CONTEMPLATING CHRIST'S LIFE

107   This is the love of Christ which each of us should try to practice in his own life. But to be Christ himself, we must *see ourselves in him*. It's not enough to have a general idea of the spirit of Jesus' life; we have to learn the details of his life and, through them, his attitudes. And, especially, we must contemplate his life, to derive from it strength, light, serenity, peace.

When you love someone, you want to know all about his life and character, so as to become like him. That is why we have to meditate on the life of Jesus, from his birth in a stable right up to his death and resurrection. In the early years of my life as a priest, I used to give people presents of copies of the Gospel and books about the life of Jesus. For we do need to know it well, to have it in our heart and mind, so that at any time, without any book, we can close our eyes and contemplate his life, watching it like a movie. In this way the words and actions of our Lord will come to mind in all the different circumstances of our life.

In this way we become involved in his life. It is not a matter of just thinking about Jesus, of recalling some scenes of his life. We must be completely involved and play a part in his life. We should follow him as closely as Mary his Mother did, as closely as the first twelve, the holy women, the crowds that pressed about him. If we do this without holding back, Christ's words will enter deep into our soul and will really change us. For "the word of God is living and active, sharper than any two-edged sword, piercing to the division of the soul and spirit, of joints and marrow, and discerning the thoughts and intentions of the heart."[19]

If we want to bring other men and women to our Lord, we must first go to the Gospel and contemplate Christ's love. We could take the central events of his passion, for, as he himself said: "Greater love has no man than this, that a man lay down his life for his friends."[20] But we can also look at the rest of his life, his everyday dealings with the people he met.

---

[19] Heb 4:12.
[20] Jn 15:13.

In order to bring men his message of salvation and show them God's love, Christ, who was perfect God and perfect man, acted in a human and a divine way. God comes down to man's level. He takes on our nature completely, except for sin.

108   It makes me very happy to realize that Christ wanted to be fully a man, with flesh like our own. I am moved when I contemplate how wonderful it is for God to love with a man's heart. Let us choose some events from the Gospel, beginning with Jesus' relationships with the twelve. St John the Apostle, who pours into his narrative so much that is first-hand, tells of his first unforgettable conversation with Christ. "'Master, where are you staying?' He said to them, 'Come and see.' They went and saw where he was staying; and they stayed with him that day, for it was about the tenth hour."[21]

This divine and human dialogue completely changed the life of John and Andrew, and Peter and James and so many others. It prepared their hearts to listen to the authoritative call which Jesus gave them beside the Sea of Galilee. "As

---

[21] Jn 1:38-39.

he walked by the Sea of Galilee, he saw two brothers, Simon, who is called Peter, and Andrew his brother, casting a net into the sea; for they were fishermen. And he said to them, 'Follow me, and I will make you fishers of men.' Immediately they left their nets and followed him."[22]

During the next three years, Jesus shared his life with his disciples; he came to know them; he answered their questions and resolved their doubts. He is indeed the rabbi, the Master who speaks with authority, the Messiah sent by God. But he is also accessible; he is close to them. One day Jesus went off to pray and the disciples were near him, perhaps staring at him and trying to make out what he was saying. When Jesus came back, one of them said: "'Lord, teach us to pray, as John taught his disciples.' And he told them, 'When you pray, say, Father, hollowed be thy name...'."[23]

In the same way, with the authority of God and the affection of a human heart, our Lord meets the Apostles who were amazed at the

---

[22] Mt 4:18-20.

[23] Lk 11:1-2: *Domine, doce nos orare, sicut docuit et Ioannis discipulos suos.*

fruits of their first mission and eager to tell him about the immediate results of their apostolate: "Come away by yourselves to a lonely place, and rest a while."[24]

There is a similar scene toward the end of Jesus' life on earth, just before his ascension: "Just as day was breaking, Jesus stood on the beach; yet the disciples did not know that it was Jesus. 'Young men, have you any fish?' Jesus asked them." He asks the question as any man would, and then he speaks as God: "'Cast the net on the right side of the boat, and you will find some.' So they cast it, and now they were not able to haul it in, for the quantity of fish. The disciple whom Jesus loved said to Peter: 'It is the Lord'."

And God is waiting for them on the shore. "When they got out on land, they saw a charcoal fire there, with fish lying on it, and bread. 'Bring some of the fish that you have just caught,' Jesus said to them. So Simon Peter went aboard and hauled the net ashore, full of large fish, a hundred and fifty-three of them; and although there were so many, the net was not torn. Jesus said to them: 'Come and have

[24] Mk 6:31.

breakfast.' Now none of the disciples dared ask him, 'Who are you?' They knew it was the Lord. Jesus came and took the bread and gave it to them, and so with the fish."[25]

Jesus shows this refinement and affection not only to a small group of disciples, but to everyone: to the holy women, to representatives of the Sanhedrin, like Nicodemus, to tax collectors like Zachaeus; he shows it to sick and healthy people, to teachers of the law and pagans, to individuals and crowds.

The Gospels tell us that Jesus had no place to rest his head, but they also tell us that he had many good, close friends, eager to have him stay in their homes when he was in the vicinity. They tell us of his compassion for the sick, of his sorrow for those who were ignorant or in error, his anger at the money changers who profaned the temple; his heart was touched by the sorrow of the widow at Naim.

All this human behavior is the behavior of 109 God. "For in him dwells all the fullness of the godhead bodily."[26] Christ is God become man: a complete, perfect man. And through his

25 Jn 21:4-13.
26 Col 2:9.

human nature, he shows us what his divine nature is.

Recalling this human refinement of Christ, who spent his life in the service of others, we are doing much more than describing a pattern of human behavior; we are discovering God. Everything Christ did has a transcendental value. It shows us the nature of God and beckons us to believe in the love of God who created us and wants us to share his intimate life. "I have manifested your name to the men whom you gave me out of the world; yours they were, and you gave them to me, and they have kept your word. Now they know that everything you have given me is from you."[27]

Jesus' dealings with men go much further than words or superficial attitudes. Jesus takes them seriously and wants to make known to them the divine meaning of their life. Jesus knows how to be demanding, how to direct men to face up to their duties. If we listen to him, he weans us from comfort and conformity, and brings us to know the thrice-holy God. For Jesus is moved by hunger and sorrow, but what moves him most is ignorance. "As he landed

[27] Jn 17:6-7.

he saw a great throng, and he had compassion
on them, because they were like sheep without
a shepherd; and he began to teach them many
things."[28]

TURNING TO OUR EVERYDAY LIFE

We have gone to the Gospel to contemplate
Jesus' dealings with men and to learn to bring
him to our fellow men, being ourselves other
Christs. Let's apply this lesson to everyday life,
to our own life. For the ordinary life of a man
among his fellows is not something dull and
uninteresting. It is there that the Lord wants the
vast majority of his children to achieve sanctity.

It is important to keep reminding ourselves
that Jesus did not address himself to a privileged set of people; he came to reveal the *universal* love of God to us. God loves all men, and
he wants all to love him—everyone, whatever
his personal situation, his social position, his
work. Ordinary life is something of great value.
All the ways of the earth can be an opportunity
to meet Christ, who calls us to identify our-

---

[28] Mk 6:34.

selves with him and carry out his divine mission—right where he finds us.

God calls us through what happens during our day: through the suffering and happiness of the people we live with, through the human interests of our colleagues and the things that make up our family life. He also calls us through the great problems, conflicts, and challenges of each period of history, which attract the effort and idealism of a large part of mankind.

111 It is easy to understand the impatience, anxiety, and uneasiness of people whose naturally Christian soul[29] stimulates them to fight the personal and social injustice which the human heart can create. So many centuries of men living side by side and still so much hate, so much destruction, so much fanaticism stored up in eyes that do not want to see and in hearts that do not want to love!

The good things of the earth, monopolized by a handful of people; the culture of the world, confined to cliques. And, on the outside, hunger for bread and education. Human lives—holy, because they come from God—treated as mere

[29] Cf. Tertullian, *Apologeticus*, 17 (PL 1, 375).

things, as statistics. I understand and share this impatience. It moves me to look at Christ, who is continually inviting us to put his new commandment of love into practice.

All the circumstances in which life places us bring a divine message, asking us to respond with love and service to others. "When the Son of Man comes in his glory, and all the angels with him, then he will sit on his glorious throne. Before him will be gathered all the nations, and he will separate them one from another as a shepherd separates the sheep from the goats, and he will place the sheep at his right hand, but the goats at the left.

"Then the King will say to those at his right hand, 'Come, O blessed of my Father, inherit the kingdom prepared for you from the foundation of the world; for I was hungry and you gave me food, I was thirsty and you gave me drink, I was a stranger and you welcomed me, I was naked and you clothed me, I was sick and you visited me, I was in prison and you came to me.' Then the righteous will answer him, 'Lord, when did we see you hungry and feed you, or thirsty and give you drink? And when did we see you a stranger and welcome you, or naked and clothe you? And when did

we see you sick or in prison and visit you?' And
the King will answer them, 'Truly, I say to you,
as you did it to one of the least of these my
brothers, you did it to me'."[30]

We must learn to recognize Christ when he
comes out to meet us in our brothers, the people
around us. No human life is ever isolated. It
is bound up with other lives. No man or
woman is a single verse; we all make up one
divine poem which God writes with the cooperation of our freedom.

112   Nothing can be foreign to Christ's care. If we
enter into the theology of it instead of limiting
ourselves to functional categories, we cannot
say that there are things—good, noble or
indifferent—which are exclusively worldly.
This cannot be after the Word of God has lived
among the children of men, felt hunger and
thirst, worked with his hands, experienced
friendship and obedience and suffering and
death. "For in him all the fullness of God was
pleased to dwell, and through him to reconcile
to himself all things, whether on earth or in
heaven, making peace by the blood of his
cross."[31]

[30] Mt 25: 31-40.
[31] Col 1:19-20.

We must love the world and work and all human things. For the world is good. Adam's sin destroyed the divine balance of creation; but God the Father sent his only Son to re-establish peace, so that we, his children by adoption, might free creation from disorder and reconcile all things to God.

Each human situation is unique; it is the result of a unique vocation which should be lived intensely, giving expression to the spirit of Christ. And so, living among our equals in a Christian way, we will be Christ present among men. And we will do this in a natural way consistent with our faith.

When we consider the dignity of the voca- 113 tion God calls us to, we might become proud and presumptuous. If that happens, we have a wrong idea of the Christian mission. Our error prevents us from realizing that we are made of clay, that we are dust and wretchedness. We forget that there is evil not only around us, but right inside ourselves, nestled deep in our hearts, which makes us capable of vileness and selfishness. Only the grace of God is sure ground, we are sand, quicksand.

If we look at the history of mankind or at the present situation of the world, it makes us

sad to see that after twenty centuries there are
so few who claim to be Christians and fewer
still who are faithful to their calling. Many years
ago, a man with a good heart but who had no
faith, said to me, pointing to a map of the
world: "Look how Christ has failed! So many
centuries trying to give his teaching to men, and
there you have the result: there are no Christians."

There are many people nowadays who still
think that way. But Christ has not failed. His
word and his life continue to enrich the world.
Christ's work, which his Father entrusted to
him, is being carried out. His power runs right
through history, bringing true life with it, and
"when all things are subjected to him, then the
Son himself will also be subjected to him who
put all things under him, that God may be
everything to every one."[32]

God wants us to cooperate with him in
this task which he is carrying out in the
world. He *takes a risk with our freedom*. I am
deeply moved by the Jesus born in Bethlehem:
a defenseless, powerless child, incapable of
offering any resistance. God gives himself up

---

[32] 1 Cor 15:28.

to men; he comes close to us, down to our level.

"Though he was in the form of God, he did not count equality with God a thing to be grasped, but emptied himself, taking the form of a servant."[33] God respects and bows down to our freedom, our imperfection and wretchedness. He agrees to have his divine treasures carried in vessels of clay; he lets us make them known; God is not afraid of mixing his strength with our weaknesses.

Experience of sin, then, should not make us 114 doubt our mission. True, our sins can make it difficult to recognize Christ. That is why we must face up to our personal miseries and seek to purify ourselves. But in doing this, we must realize that God has not promised us a complete victory over evil in this life. Instead he asks us to fight. "My grace is sufficient for you,"[34] our Lord replied to St Paul, when he wanted to be freed of the "thorn in his flesh" which humiliated him.

The power of God is made manifest in our weakness and it spurs us on to fight, to battle

[33] Phil 2:6-7.
[34] 2 Cor 12:9: *sufficit tibi gratia mea.*

against our defects, although we know that we will never achieve total victory during our pilgrimage on earth. The Christian life is a continuous beginning again each day. It renews itself over and over.

Christ gives us his risen life, he rises in us, if we become sharers in his cross and his death. We should love the cross, self-sacrifice and mortification. Christian optimism is not something sugary, nor is it a human optimism that things will "work out well." No, its deep roots are awareness of freedom and faith in grace. It is an optimism which makes us be demanding with ourselves. It gets us to make a real effort to respond to God's call.

Not so much despite our wretchedness but in some way *through* it, through our life as men of flesh and blood and dust, Christ is shown forth: in our effort to be better, to have a love which wants to be pure, to overcome our selfishness, to give ourselves fully to others—to turn our existence into a continuous service.

115   I don't want to finish without another consideration. When a Christian makes Christ present among men by being Christ himself, it is not only a matter of being a considerate, loving person, but of making the Love of God

known through his human love. Jesus saw all his life as a revelation of this love. As he said to one of his disciples, "He who has seen me has seen the Father."[35]

St John applies this teaching when he tells Christians that, since they have come to know the love of God, they should show it in their deeds: "Beloved, let us love one another since love comes from God, and everyone who loves is begotten by God and knows God.

"He who does not love does not know God; for God is love. In this the love of God was made manifest among us, that God sent his only Son into the world, so that we might live through him. In this is love, not that we love God but that he loved us and sent his Son to be the expiation for our sins. Beloved, if God so loved us, we also ought to love one another."[36]

So, our faith must be living—a faith which 116 makes us really believe in God and keep up a continuous conversation with him. A Christian life should be one of constant prayer, trying to live in the presence of God from morning to

[35] Jn 14:9.
[36] 1 Jn 4:7-11.

night and from night to morning. A Christian can never be a lonely man, since he lives in continual contact with God, who is both near us and in heaven.

"Pray constantly," the Apostle tells us.[37] And Clement of Alexandria reminds us of this commandment: "He tells us to praise and honor the Word whom we know to be savior and king; and, through him, the Father, not on special days as some people do, but continually, right through all our life and in every kind of way."[38]

In the middle of his daily work, when he has to overcome his selfishness, when he enjoys the cheerful friendship of other people, a Christian should rediscover God. Through Christ and in the Holy Spirit, a Christian has access to the intimacy of God the Father, and he spends his life looking for the Kingdom which is not of this world, but which is initiated and prepared in this world.

We must seek Christ in the word and in the bread, in the Eucharist and in prayer. And we must treat him as a friend, as the real, living

[37] 1 Thess 5:17: *Sine intermissione orate.*
[38] *Stromata*, 7, 7, 35 (PG 9, 450).

person he is—for he is risen. Christ, we read in the Epistle to the Hebrews, "holds his priesthood permanently, because he continues forever. Consequently he is able for all time to save those who draw near to God, since he always lives to make intercession for them."[39]

Christ, the risen Christ, is our companion and friend. He is a companion whom we can see only in the shadows—but the fact that he is really there fills our whole life and makes us yearn to be with him forever. "The Spirit and the Bride say, 'Come.' And let him who hears say, 'Come.' And let him who is thirsty come, let him who desires take the water of life without price.... He who testifies to these things says, 'Surely I am coming soon. Amen. Come, Lord Jesus'."[40]

[39] Heb 7:24-25.
[40] Rev 22:17, 20.

THE ASCENSION
OF OUR LORD*

117

Once more the liturgy reminds us of the final
moment in Jesus' life among men, his ascension
into heaven. Many things have happened since
our Lord was born in Bethlehem. We have seen
him in the manger, worshipped by the shepherds and the Magi; we have contemplated
those long years of unpretentious work in
Nazareth; we have gone with him all through
the land of Palestine, as he preached the
kingdom of God to men and went about doing
good to all. And later on, during the days of
his passion, we have suffered on seeing him
accused and ill-treated and crucified.

Then, sorrow gave way to the joy and light
of the resurrection. What a clear and firm
foundation for our faith! But perhaps, like the

* A homily given on May 19, 1966, the feast of the Ascension.

Apostles in those days, we are still weak, and on the day of the ascension we ask Christ: "Lord, will you at this time restore the kingdom of Israel?"[1] Is it now that we can expect all our perplexity and all our weakness to vanish forever?

Our Lord answers by going up to heaven. Like the Apostles, we remain partly perplexed and partly saddened at his departure. It is not easy, in fact, to get accustomed to the physical absence of Jesus. I am moved when I think that, in an excess of love, he has remained with us, even when he has gone away. He has gone to heaven and, at the same time, he gives himself to us as our nourishment in the sacred host. Still, we miss his human speech, his way of acting, of looking, of smiling, of doing good. We would like to go back and regard him closely again, as he sits down at the edge of the well, tired from his journey;[2] as he weeps for Lazarus;[3] as he prays for a long time;[4] as he feels pity for the crowd.[5]

---

[1] Acts 1:6.
[2] Cf. Jn 4:6.
[3] Cf. Jn 11:35.
[4] Cf. Lk 6:12.
[5] Cf. Mt 15:32; Mk 8:2.

It has always seemed logical to me that the most holy humanity of Christ should ascend to the glory of the Father. The ascension has always made me very happy. But I think that the sadness that is particular to the day of the ascension is also a proof of the love that we feel for Jesus Christ, our Lord. He is God made man, perfect man, with flesh like ours, with blood like ours in his veins. Yet he leaves us and goes up to heaven. How can we help but miss his presence?

CHRIST IN THE BREAD AND IN THE WORD

If we have learned to contemplate the mystery of Christ, if we make an effort to see him clearly, we will realize that now we can come very near Jesus too, in body and soul. Christ has pointed out the way to us clearly. We can be with him in the bread and in the word, receiving the nourishment of the Eucharist and knowing and fulfilling all that he came to teach us, as we meet and deal with him in our prayer. "He who eats my flesh, and drinks my blood, abides in me and I in him."[6] "He

118

[6] Jn 6:57.

who has my commandments and keeps them,
he it is who loves me. But he who loves me
will be loved by my Father, and I will love him
and manifest myself to him."[7]

These are not mere promises. They are
something real, the essence of a true life, the
life of grace that leads us to deal with God
personally and directly. "If you keep my
commandments, you will abide in my love, as
I also have kept my Father's commandments,
and abide in his love."[8] These words that Jesus
said at the last supper are the best introduction
to the day of the ascension. Christ knew that
he had to go away, because, in a mysterious
way that we cannot fully understand, after the
ascension, a new outpouring of God's love
would bring the presence of the Third Person
of the Blessed Trinity. "I speak the truth to you:
it is expedient for you that I depart. For if I
do not go, the Advocate will not come to you;
but if I go, I will send him to you."[9]

Jesus has gone away. He sends us the Holy
Spirit, who directs and sanctifies our souls. The
action of the Paraclete within us confirms what

[7] Jn 14:21.
[8] Jn 15:10.
[9] Jn 16:7.

Christ had announced—that we are children of God, that we "have not received a spirit of bondage so as to be again in fear, but... a spirit of adoption as sons, by virtue of which we cry 'Abba! Father!'."[10]

You see? This is the action of the Blessed Trinity in our souls. A Christian always has access to God, who dwells in the innermost part of his being, if he corresponds to the grace that leads us to become one with Christ, in the bread and in the word, in the sacred host and in prayer. On two other occasions in the liturgical year—Holy Thursday and Corpus Christi—the Church sets aside important feast days to commemorate the reality of this living bread, which we are reminded of every day. On this feast of the ascension, let us turn our mind to conversation with our Lord. Let us attentively listen to his word.

A LIFE OF PRAYER

"A prayer to my living God."[11] If God is life 119 for us, we should not be surprised to realize

---

[10] Rom 8:15.
[11] Ps 41:9.

that our very existence as Christians must be interwoven with prayer. But don't imagine that prayer is an action to be carried out and then forgotten. The just man "delights in the law of the Lord, and meditates on his law day and night."[12] "Through the night I meditate on you"[13] and "my prayer comes to you like incense in the evening."[14] Our whole day can be a time for prayer—from night to morning and from morning to night. In fact, as holy Scripture reminds us, even our sleep should be a prayer.[15]

Remember what the Gospels tell us about Jesus. At times he spent the whole night in an intimate conversation with his Father. The Apostles were filled with love when they saw Christ pray; and, after seeing this constant attitude in their master, they asked him: "Lord, teach us to pray"[16] in this way. St Paul spreads the living example of Christ everywhere when he urges the faithful to be "constant in prayer."[17] And St Luke portrays the behavior

[12] Ps 1:2.
[13] Cf. Ps 62:7.
[14] Cf. Ps 140:2.
[15] Cf. Deut 6:6, 7.
[16] Lk 11:1: *Domine, doce nos orare.*
[17] Rom 12:12: *orationi instantes.*

of the first Christians with a phrase that is like the touch of an artist's brush: "they all, with one mind, continued steadfastly in prayer."[18]

A good Christian acquires his mettle, with the help of grace, in the training-ground of prayer. But prayer, our life-giving nourishment, is not limited to one form alone. Our heart will find a habitual expression in words, in the vocal prayers taught us by God himself— the Our Father—or by his angels—the Hail Mary. On other occasions, we will use the time-proven words that have expressed the piety of millions of our brothers in the faith: prayers from the liturgy—*lex orandi*; or others whose source is the love of an ardent heart, like the antiphons to our Lady: *Sub tuum praesidium; Memorare; Salve, Regina....*

There will be other occasions on which all we'll need will be two or three words, said with the quickness of a dart, *iaculata*—ejaculatory prayers, aspirations that we learn from a careful reading of Christ's life: "Lord, if you will, you can make me clean."[19] "Lord, you know all things, you know that I love you."[20] "Lord, I

---

[18] Acts 1:14.

[19] Mt 8:2: *Domine, si vis, potes me mundare.*

[20] Jn 21:17: *Domine, tu omnia nosti, tu scis quia amo te.*

do believe, but help my unbelief,"[21] strengthen
my faith. "Lord, I am not worthy."[22] "My Lord
and my God!"[23] ...or other short phrases, full
of affection, that spring from the soul's intimate
fervor and correspond to the different circumstances of each day.

Besides these occasions, our life of prayer
should also be based on some moments that are
dedicated exclusively to our conversation with
God, moments of silent dialogue, before the
tabernacle if possible, in order to thank our
Lord for having waited for us—so often alone—
for twenty centuries. This heart-to-heart dialogue with God is mental prayer, in which the
whole soul takes part; intelligence, imagination,
memory, and will are all involved. It is a
meditation that helps to give supernatural
value to our poor human life, with all its
normal, everyday occurrences.

Thanks to these moments of meditation and
to our vocal prayer, we will be able to turn our
whole day into a continuous praise of God, in
a natural way and without any outward dis-

---

[21] Mk 9:23: *Credo, Domine, sed adiuva incredulitatem meam.*
[22] Mt 8:8: *Domine, non sum dignus.*
[23] Jn 20:28: *Dominus meus et Deus meus.*

play. Just as people in love are always thinking about each other, we will be aware of God's presence. And all our actions, down to the most insignificant, will be filled with spiritual effectiveness.

This is why, as a Christian sets out on his way of uninterrupted dealing with our Lord, his interior life grows and becomes strong and secure. And he is led to engage in the demanding yet attractive struggle to fulfill completely the will of God. I might add that this is not a path for a privileged few; it is a way open to everyone.

It is through our life of prayer that we can understand the other aspect of today's feast: the apostolate, the carrying out of the commission Jesus gave to the disciples shortly before the ascension: "You shall be witnesses for me in Jerusalem and in all Judea and Samaria and even to the very ends of the earth."[24]

APOSTOLATE: REDEEMING WITH OUR LORD

With the amazing naturalness of the things 120 of God, the contemplative soul is filled with

[24] Acts 1:8.

apostolic zeal. "My heart was warmed within me, a fire blazed forth from my thoughts."[25] What could this fire be if not the fire that Christ talks about: "I have come to cast fire upon the earth, and what will I but that it be kindled?"[26] An apostolic fire that acquires its strength in prayer. There is no better way than this to carry on, throughout the whole world, the battle of peace to which every Christian is called, to fill up what is lacking in the sufferings of Christ.[27]

Jesus has gone up to heaven, as we have seen. But a Christian can deal with him, in prayer and in the Eucharist, as the twelve Apostles dealt with him. The Christian can come to burn with an apostolic fervor that will lead him to serve, to redeem with Christ, to sow peace and joy wherever he goes. To serve, that is what apostolate is all about. If we count on our own strength alone, we will achieve nothing in the supernatural order. But if we are God's instruments, we will achieve everything. "I can do all things in him who gives me strength."[28] God, in his infinite goodness, has

---

[25] Ps 38:4.
[26] Lk 12:49.
[27] Cf. Col 1:24.
[28] Phil 4:13.

chosen to use inadequate instruments; and so, the apostle has no other aim than to let the Lord work in him and through him, to put himself totally at God's disposition, allowing him to carry out his work of salvation through creatures, through that soul whom he has chosen.

An apostle—that is what a Christian is, when he knows that he has been grafted onto Christ, made one with Christ, in baptism. He has been given the capacity to carry on the battle in Christ's name, through confirmation. He has been called to serve God by his activity in the world, because of the common priesthood of the faithful, which makes him share to a certain degree in the priesthood of Christ. This priesthood—though essentially distinct from the ministerial priesthood—gives him the capacity to take part in the worship of the Church and to help other men in their journey to God, with the witness of his word and his example, through his prayer and work of atonement.

Each of us is to be *ipse Christus*: Christ himself. He is the one mediator between God and man.[29] And we make ourselves one with

---

[29] Cf. 1 Tim 2:5.

him in order to offer all things, with him, to
the Father. Our calling to be children of God,
in the midst of the world, requires us not only
to seek our own personal holiness, but also to
go out onto all the ways of the earth, to convert
them into roads that will carry souls over all
obstacles and lead them to the Lord. As we take
part in all temporal activities, as ordinary
citizens, we are to become leaven[30] acting on
the mass.[31]

Christ has gone up to heaven, but he has
given to all honest human things a specific
capacity to be redeemed. St Gregory the Great
expresses this reality in a striking way: "Thus
Jesus went away to where he had come from,
and came back from the place he continued to
dwell; for, in the very moment in which he
went up to heaven, he brought together, by his
activity, heaven and earth. On today's feast we
should proclaim solemnly that the decree of our
condemnation has been suppressed, and the
judgment which made us subject to corruption
has been lifted. That nature which heard the
words, 'You are dust, and to dust you shall

---

[30] Cf. Mt 13:33.
[31] Cf. 1 Cor 5:6.

return,' that same nature has gone up to heaven today with Christ."[32]

And so I keep on repeating to you that the world can be made holy. We Christians have a special role to play in sanctifying it. We are to cleanse it from the occasions of sin with which we human beings have soiled it. We are to offer it to our Lord as a spiritual offering, presented to him and made acceptable through his grace and with our efforts. Strictly speaking, we cannot say that there is any noble human reality that does not have a supernatural dimension, for the divine Word has taken on a complete human nature and consecrated the world with his presence and with the work of his hands. The great mission that we have received in baptism is to redeem the world with Christ. We are urged on by the charity of Christ[33] to take upon our shoulders a part of this task of saving souls.

Look. The redemption was consummated 121 when Jesus died on the cross, in shame and glory, "to the Jews a stumbling-block, and to the Gentiles foolishness."[34] But the redemption

---

[32] *In Evangelia homiliae*, 29, 10 (PL 76, 1218).
[33] Cf. 2 Cor 5:14.
[34] 1 Cor 1:23.

will, by the will of God, be carried out continually until our Lord's time comes. It is impossible to live according to the heart of Jesus Christ and not to know that we are sent, as he was, "to save all sinners,"[35] with the clear realization that we ourselves need to trust in the mercy of God more and more every day. As a result, we will foster in ourselves a vehement desire to live as co-redeemers with Christ, to save all souls with him, because we are, we want to be *ipse Christus*: Christ himself, and "He gave himself as a ransom for all."[36]

A great task awaits us. We cannot remain inactive, because our Lord has told us clearly, "Trade till I come."[37] As long as we are awaiting the Lord's return, when he will come to take full possession of his kingdom, we cannot afford to relax. Spreading the kingdom of God isn't only an official task of those members of the Church who represent Christ because they have received sacred powers from him. "You are also the body of Christ,"[38] says the Apostle, with a specific command to fulfill.

---

[35] 1 Tim 1:15: *peccatores salvos facere.*
[36] 1 Tim 2:6.
[37] Lk 19:13.
[38] 1 Cor 12:27: *Vos autem estis corpus Christi.*

There is so much to be done. Is it because in twenty centuries nothing has been done? In these two thousand years much work has been done. I don't think it would be fair or objective to discount, as some people want to do, the accomplishments of those who have gone before us. In two thousand years a great task has been accomplished, and it has often been accomplished very well. On other occasions there have been mistakes, making the Church lose ground, just as today there is loss of ground, fear and a timid attitude on the part of some, and at the same time no lack of courage and generosity in others. But, whatever the situation, the human race is being continually renewed. In each generation it is necessary to go on with the effort to help men realize the greatness of their vocation as children of God, to teach them to carry out the commandment of love for God and neighbor.

Christ has taught us in a definitive way how 122 to make this love for God real. Apostolate is love for God that overflows and communicates itself to others. The interior life implies a growth in union with Christ, in the bread and in the word. And apostolate is the precise and necessary outward manifestation of interior life.

When one tastes the love of God, one *feels* burdened with the weight of souls. There is no way to separate interior life from apostolate, just as there is no way to separate Christ, the God-man, from his role as redeemer. The Word chose to become flesh in order to save men, to make them one with him. This is why he came to the world; he came down from heaven "for us men and for our salvation," as we say in the creed.

For a Christian apostolate is something instinctive. It is not something added onto his daily activities and his professional work from the outside. I have repeated it constantly, since the day that our Lord chose for the foundation of Opus Dei! We have to sanctify our ordinary work, we have to sanctify others through the exercise of the particular profession that is proper to each of us, in our own particular state in life.

For a Christian apostolate is like breathing. A child of God cannot live without this supernatural life-force. Today's feast reminds us that our concern for souls is a response to a command of love given to us by our Lord. As he goes up to heaven, Jesus sends us out as his witnesses throughout the whole world. Our responsibility is great, because to be Christ's witness implies first of all that we should try to behave according to his doctrine, that we should struggle to make our actions remind others of Jesus and his most lovable personality. We have to act in such a way that others will be able to say, when they meet us: this man is a Christian, because he does not hate, because he is willing to understand, because he is not a fanatic, because he is willing to make sacrifices, because he shows that he is a man of peace, because he knows how to love.

THE WHEAT AND THE WEEDS

I have been describing to you, not my own 123 idea, but Christ's doctrine on the Christian ideal. You can see that it is demanding, sublime, attractive. Still some might ask: "Is it possible to live this way in today's society?"

Our Lord has called us, it is true, in a time when everyone talks about peace, and there is no peace—whether in souls or in institutions or in social life or among nations. Everyone talks about equality and democracy, and what we see all around are closed and impenetrable castes.

He has called us in a time when everyone demands understanding, and understanding is conspicuous only by its absence, even among persons who act in good faith and want to be charitable. Don't forget that charity, more than in giving, consists in *understanding*.

We are living in a period of time when the fanatics and the intransigent—those incapable of listening to the reasons of other people—use the device of accusing their victims of being violent and aggressive. Our Lord has called us, finally, in a time when we can hear all kinds of talk about unity, and it would be hard to imagine a greater disunion among Catholics themselves, not to speak of people in general.

I never make political remarks; that's not my job. If I were to describe the present situation of the world as a priest, all I need is to think again about one of our Lord's parables, that of the wheat and the weeds. "The kingdom of heaven is like a man who sowed good seed in his field; but while men were asleep, his enemy came and sowed weeds among the wheat, and went away."[39] The situation is clear—the field is fertile and the seed is good; the Lord of the

---

[39] Mt 13:24-25.

field has scattered the seed at the right moment and with great skill. He even has watchmen to make sure that the field is protected. If, afterwards, there are weeds among the wheat, it is because men have failed to respond, because they—and Christians in particular—have fallen asleep and allowed the enemy to approach.

When the careless servants ask the Lord why weeds have grown in his field, the explanation is obvious: "An enemy has done this."[40] We Christians should have been on guard to make sure that the good things placed in this world by the Creator were developed in the service of truth and good. But we have fallen asleep— a sad thing, that sluggishness of our heart!— while the enemy and all those who serve him acted without stopping. You can see how the weeds have grown abundantly everywhere.

My vocation is not that of a prophet of misfortune. With these words I do not wish to make you see a desolate and hopeless picture of reality. I do not want to complain about this time in which the Lord's providence has placed us. We love this time of ours because it is in this time when we are called to achieve our

[40] Mt 13:28: *inimicus homo hoc fecit*.

personal sanctification. We will not admit naïve longings that lead nowhere—the world has never been any better. From the very beginning, from the cradle of the Church, in the times when the twelve Apostles were still preaching, violent persecutions had already begun, the first heresies were springing up, lies were being spread and hatred was unleashed.

Still, it cannot be denied that evil seems to have prospered. Weeds have grown in this whole field of God, which is the earth, the inheritance of Christ. Not only have they grown, they are abundant. We cannot allow ourselves to be deceived by the myth of constant and irreversible progress. Progress, in an orderly manner, is good, and God wants it to take place. But people seem to consider more another kind of progress, which is false and blinds many persons, who often fail to realize that, in some of its movements, the human race moves backward and loses some of the ground it had conquered.

Our Lord, I insist, has given us the world for our inheritance. It is up to us to keep our souls and our minds wide awake. We have to be realistic, without being defeatist. Only a person with a callous conscience, made insen-

sitive by routine or dulled by a frivolous attitude, can allow himself to think that evil—
offense to God and harm, at times irreparable
harm, to souls—does not exist in the world he
sees. We have to be optimistic, but our optimism should come from our faith in the power
of God who does not lose battles, and not from
any human sense of satisfaction, from a stupid
and presumptuous complacency.

SOWERS OF PEACE AND JOY

What are we to do? I have told you that I 124
was not trying to describe social or political
crises or cultural declines or disruptions.
Looking at the world from the point of view
of Christian faith, I am referring to evil in its
precise meaning, as an offense against God.
Christian apostolate is not a political program
or a cultural alternative. It implies the spreading of good, "infecting" others with a desire
to love, sowing peace and joy. There is no
doubt that this apostolate will produce spiritual benefits for all: more justice, more understanding and a greater mutual respect among
men.

There are many souls all around us, and we have no right to be an obstacle to their eternal happiness. We have the obligation of leading a fully Christian life, of becoming saints, of not betraying God and all those who expect a Christian to be an example and a source of truth.

Our apostolate has to be based on understanding. I insist, as I have done before, on the fact that charity, more than in giving, consists in understanding. I cannot deny the fact that I have learned by my own experience what it means not to be understood. I have always tried to make myself understood, but there have been people who were bent on not understanding. This gives me one more reason, and a very practical one, for trying to be understanding toward everyone. But it is not this type of incidental reason that should prompt us to have a heart that is great, universal, catholic. The understanding we must show is a proof of Christian charity on the part of a good child of God. Our Lord wants us to be present in all the honest pursuits of the earth, so that there we may sow, not weeds, but the good seed of brotherhood, of forgiveness, of charity, and of peace. Never consider yourself anybody's enemy.

A Christian has to be ready to share his life with everyone at all times, giving to everyone the chance to come nearer to Christ Jesus. He has to sacrifice his own desires willingly for the sake of others, without separating people into watertight compartments, without pigeon-holing them or putting tags on them as though they were merchandise or dried-up insects. A Christian cannot afford to separate himself from others, because, if he did that, his life would be miserably selfish. He must become "all things to all men, in order to save all men."[41]

If only we lived like this, if only we knew how to saturate our behavior with the good seed of generosity, with a desire for understanding and peace! We would encourage the rightful independence of all men. Each person would take on his own responsibility for the tasks that correspond to him in temporal matters. Each Christian would defend other people's freedom in the first place, so that he could defend his own as well. His charity would lead him to accept others as they are—because everyone, without any exception, has his weaknesses and makes his mistakes. He

---

[41] 1 Cor 9:22.

would help them, with God's grace and his own human refinement, to overcome evil, to remove the weeds, so that we can all help each other in living according to our dignity as human beings and as Christians.

WHAT AWAITS US

125   The apostolic task that Christ entrusted to all his disciples leads to specific results in social matters. It is inconceivable that a Christian, in order to fulfill his task, should have to turn his back on the world and become a defeatist with regard to human nature. Everything, even the smallest occurrence, has a human and a divine meaning. Christ, who is perfect man, did not come to destroy what is human, but to raise it up. He took on himself our human nature, except for sin. He came to share all man's concerns, except for the sad experience of willful evil.

A Christian has to be ready, at all times, to sanctify society from within. He is fully present in the world, but without belonging to the world, when it denies God and opposes his lovable will of salvation, not because of its nature, but because of sin.

The feast of our Lord's ascension also 126 reminds us of another fact. The same Christ, who encourages us to carry out our task in the world, awaits us in heaven as well. In other words, our life on earth, which we love, is not definitive. "We do not have a permanent dwelling-place here, but we seek that which is to come,"[42] a changeless home, where we may live forever.

Still, we must be careful not to interpret the Word of God within limits that are too narrow. Our Lord does not expect us to be unhappy in our life on earth and await a reward only in the next life. God wants us to be happy on earth too, but with a desire for the other, total happiness that only he can give.

In this life, the contemplation of supernatural reality, the action of grace in our souls, our love for our neighbor as a result of our love for God—all these are already a foretaste of heaven, a beginning that is destined to grow from day to day. We Christians cannot resign ourselves to leading a double life—our life must be a strong and simple unity into which all our actions converge.

[42] Heb 13:14.

Christ awaits us. We are "citizens of heaven,"[43] and at the same time fully-fledged citizens of this earth, in the midst of difficulties, injustices and lack of understanding, but also in the midst of the joy and serenity that comes from knowing that we are children of God. Let us persevere in the service of our God, and we will see the growth in numbers and in sanctity of this Christian army of peace, of this co-redeeming people. Let us be contemplative souls, carrying on an unceasing dialogue with our Lord at all hours—from the first thought of the day to the last, turning our heart constantly toward our Lord Jesus Christ, going to him through our Mother, Holy Mary, and through him to the Father and the Holy Spirit.

If, in spite of everything, Jesus' ascension into heaven leaves a certain taste of sadness in our souls, let us go to his Mother, as the Apostles did. "They returned to Jerusalem... and they prayed with one mind... together with Mary, the Mother of Jesus."[44]

[43] Phil 3:20.
[44] Acts 1:12-14.

THE GREAT UNKNOWN*

Having just read in the Acts of the Apostles about Pentecost, the day when the Holy Spirit came down on the Lord's disciples, we are conscious of being present at the great display of God's power with which the Church's life began to spread among all nations. The victory Christ achieved through his obedience, his offering of himself on the cross, and his resurrection—his triumph over death and sin—is revealed here in all its divine splendor.

The disciples, witnesses of the glory of the risen Christ, were filled with the strength of the Holy Spirit. Their minds and hearts were opened to a new light. They had followed Christ and accepted his teachings with faith, but they were not always able to fathom the full meaning of his words. The Spirit of truth, who

* A homily given on May 25, 1969, Whit Sunday.

was to teach them all things,[1] had not yet come. They knew that Jesus alone could give them words of eternal life, and they were ready to follow him and to give their lives for him. But they were weak, and in the time of trial, they fled and left him alone.

On Pentecost all that is a thing of the past. The Holy Spirit, who is the Spirit of strength, has made them firm, strong, daring. The word of the Apostles resounds forcefully through the streets of Jerusalem.

The men and women who have come to the city from all parts of the world listen with amazement. "Parthians and Medes and Elamites, and inhabitants of Mesopotamia, Judea and Cappadocia, Pontus and Asia, Phrygia and Pamphylia, Egypt and the parts of Libya about Cyrene, and visitors from Rome, Jews as well as proselytes, Cretans and Arabs, we have heard them speaking in our own languages of the wonderful works of God."[2] These wonders, which take place before their own eyes, lead them to listen to the preaching of the Apostles. The Holy Spirit himself, who

[1] Cf. Jn 16:12-13.
[2] Acts 2:9-11.

is acting through our Lord's disciples, moves the hearts of their listeners and leads them to the faith.

St Luke tells us that after St Peter had spoken and proclaimed Christ's resurrection, many of those present came up to him and asked: "Brethren, what shall we do?" The apostle answered: "Repent and be baptized every one of you in the name of Jesus Christ for the forgiveness of your sins; and you will receive the gift of the Holy Spirit." And on that day, the sacred text tells us, about three thousand were added to the Church.[3]

The solemn coming of the Holy Spirit on Pentecost was not an isolated event. There is hardly a page in the Acts of the Apostles where we fail to read about him and the action by which he guides, directs, and enlivens the life and work of the early Christian community. It is he who inspires the preaching of St Peter,[4] who strengthens the faith of the disciples,[5] who confirms with his presence the calling of the gentiles,[6] who sends Saul and Barnabas to the

---

[3] Cf. Acts 2:37-41.
[4] Cf. Acts 4:8.
[5] Cf. Acts 4:31.
[6] Cf. Acts 10:44-47.

distant lands where they will open new paths
for the teaching of Jesus.[7] In a word, his
presence and doctrine are everywhere.

PENTECOST TODAY

128   The profound reality which we see in the
texts of holy Scripture is not a remembrance
from the past, from some golden age of the
Church which has since been buried in history.
Despite the weaknesses and the sins of every
one of us, it is the reality of today's Church and
the Church of all time. "I will ask the Father,"
our Lord told his disciples, "and he will give
you another Counsellor to dwell with you forever."[8] Jesus has kept his promise. He has risen
from the dead, and in union with the eternal
Father he sends us the Holy Spirit to sanctify
us and to give us life.

The strength and the power of God light up
the face of the earth. The Holy Spirit is present
in the Church of Christ for all time, so that it
may be, always and in everything, a sign raised

---

[7] Cf. Acts 13:2-4.
[8] Jn 14:16.

up before all nations, announcing to all men the goodness and the love of God.[9] In spite of our great limitations, we can look up to heaven with confidence and joy: God loves us and frees us from our sins. The presence and the action of the Holy Spirit in the Church are a foretaste of eternal happiness, of the joy and peace for which we are destined by God.

Like the men and women who came up to Peter on Pentecost, we too have been baptized. In baptism, our Father God has taken possession of our lives, has made us share in the life of Christ, and has given us the Holy Spirit. Holy Scripture tells us that God has saved us "through the baptism of regeneration and renewal by the Holy Spirit; whom he has abundantly poured out upon us through Jesus Christ our Savior, in order that, justified by this grace, we may be heirs in hope to life everlasting."[10]

The experience of our weakness and of our failings, the painful realization of the smallness and meanness of some who call themselves Christians, the apparent failure or aimlessness

[9] Cf. Is 11:12.
[10] Tit 3:5-7.

of some works of apostolate, all these things which bring home to us the reality of sin and human limitation, can still be a trial of our faith. Temptation and doubt can lead us to ask: where are the strength and the power of God? When that happens we have to react by practicing the virtue of hope with greater purity and forcefulness, and striving to be more faithful.

129   Let me tell you about an event of my own personal life which happened many years ago. One day I was with a friend of mine, a man with a good heart but who did not have faith. Pointing toward a globe he said, "Look, from North to South, from East to West." "What do you want me to look at?" I asked. His answer was: "The failure of Christ. For twenty centuries people have been trying to bring his doctrine to men's lives, and look at the result." I was filled with sadness. It is painful to think that many people still don't know our Lord, and that among those who do know him, many live as though they did not. But that feeling lasted only a moment. It was shortly overcome by love and thankfulness, because Jesus has wanted every man to cooperate freely in the work of redemption. He has not failed. His doctrine and life are effective in the world at all times. The

redemption carried out by him is sufficient, and more than sufficient.

God does not want slaves, but children. He respects our freedom. The work of salvation is still going on, and each one of us has a part in it. It is Christ's will, St Paul tells us in impressive words, that we should fulfill in our flesh, in our life, what is lacking in his passion, "for the good of his body, which is the Church."[11]

It is worthwhile putting our lives on the line, giving ourselves completely, so as to answer to the love and the confidence that God has placed in us. It is worth while, above all, to decide to take our Christian life seriously. When we recite the creed, we state that we believe in God the Father Almighty, in his Son Jesus Christ, who died and rose again, and in the Holy Spirit, the Lord and giver of life. We affirm that the Church, one, holy, catholic and apostolic, is the body of Christ, enlivened by the Holy Spirit. We rejoice in the forgiveness of sins and in the hope of the resurrection. But do those words penetrate to the depths of our own heart? Or do they remain only on our lips? The divine

---

[11] Cf. Col 1:24: *pro corpore eius, quod est Ecclesia.*

message of victory, the joy and the peace of
Pentecost, should be the unshakable foundation
for every Christian's way of thinking and acting
and living.

GOD'S STRENGTH AND OUR WEAKNESS

130   "The arm of the Lord has not been shortened."[12] God is no less powerful today than he
was in other times; his love for man is no less
true. Our faith teaches us that all creation, the
movement of the earth and the other heavenly
bodies, the good actions of creatures and all the
good that has been achieved in history, in short
everything, comes from God and is directed
toward him.

The action of the Holy Spirit can pass
unnoticed, because God does not reveal to us
his plans, and because man's sin clouds over
the divine gifts. But faith reminds us that God
is always acting. He has created us and main-
tains us in existence, and he leads all creation
by his grace toward the glorious freedom of the
children of God.[13]

[12] Is 59:1: *Non est abbreviata manus Domini.*
[13] Cf. Rom 8:21.

For this reason, Christian tradition has summarized the attitude we should adopt toward the Holy Spirit in just one idea: docility. That means we should be aware of the work of the Holy Spirit all around us, and in our own selves we should recognize the gifts he distributes, the movements and institutions he inspires, the affections and decisions he provokes in our hearts. The Holy Spirit carries out in the world the works of God. He is, as we read in a liturgical hymn, the giver of grace, the light of our hearts, the soul's guest, our rest in work, our consolation in sorrow. Without his help there is nothing innocent or valuable in man, since he is the one who cleanses the soiled, heals what is sick, sets on fire what is cold, straightens what is bent and guides men toward the safe harbor of salvation and eternal joy.[14]

But our faith in the Holy Spirit must be complete. It is not a vague belief in his presence in the world, but a grateful acceptance of the signs and realities into which he has poured forth his power in a special way. When the Spirit of truth comes, our Lord tells us, "he will

---

[14] Sequence *Veni Sancte Spiritus*, Mass of Whit Sunday.

glorify me, for he will take of what is mine and declare it to you."[15] The Holy Spirit is the Spirit sent by Christ to carry out in us the work of holiness that our Lord merited for us on earth.

And so, there cannot be faith in the Holy Spirit if there is not faith in Christ, in his sacraments, in his Church. A man cannot act in accordance with his Christian faith, cannot truly believe in the Holy Spirit, unless he loves the Church and trusts it. He cannot be a coherent Christian if he limits himself to pointing out the deficiencies and limitations of some who represent the Church, judging her from the outside, as though he were not her son. Moreover, consider the extraordinary importance and abundance of the Paraclete when the priest renews the sacrifice of Calvary by celebrating Mass on our altars.

131   We Christians carry the great treasures of grace in vessels of clay.[16] God has entrusted his gifts to the weakness and fragility of human freedom. We can be certain of the help of God's power, but our lust, our love of comfort, and our pride sometimes cause us to reject his grace

[15] Jn 16:14.
[16] Cf. 2 Cor 4:7.

and to fall into sin. For more than twenty-five years when I have recited the creed and asserted my faith in the divine origin of the Church: "One, holy, catholic, and apostolic," I have frequently added, "in spite of everything." When I mention this custom of mine and someone asks me what I mean, I answer, "I mean your sins and mine."

All this is true, but it does not authorize us in any way to judge the Church in a human manner, without theological faith. We cannot consider only the greater or lesser merits of certain churchmen or of some Christians. To do this would be to limit ourselves to the surface of things. What is most important in the Church is not how we humans react but how God acts. This is what the Church is: Christ present in our midst, God coming toward men in order to save them, calling us with his revelation, sanctifying us with his grace, maintaining us with his constant help, in the great and small battles of our daily life.

We might come to mistrust other men, and each one of us should mistrust himself and end each of his days with a *mea culpa*, an act of contrition that is profound and sincere. But we have no right to doubt God. And to doubt the

298 CHRIST IS PASSING BY

Church, its divine origin and its effectiveness
for our salvation through its doctrine and its
sacraments, would be the same as doubting
God himself, the same as not fully believing in
the reality of the coming of the Holy Spirit.

"Before Christ was crucified," writes St John
Chrysostom, "there was no reconciliation. And
while there was no reconciliation, the Holy
Spirit was not sent.... The absence of the Holy
Spirit was a sign of the anger of God. Now that
you see him sent in fullness, do not doubt the
reconciliation. But what if people should ask,
'Where is the Holy Spirit now? We can talk of
his presence when the miracles took place,
when the dead were raised and the lepers were
healed. But how are we to know that he is truly
present now?' Do not be concerned. I will show
you that the Holy Spirit is present among us
now as well.

"If the Holy Spirit were not present, we
would not be able to say, 'Jesus is the Lord,'
for no one can invoke Jesus as the Lord unless
it is in the Holy Spirit (1 Cor 12:3). If the Holy
Spirit were not present, we would not be able
to pray with confidence. For when we pray, we
say, 'Our Father, who art in heaven' (Mt 6:9).
If the Holy Spirit were not present, we could

not call God our Father. How do we know this? Because the Apostle teaches us: 'And, because you are his children, God has sent the Spirit of his Son into our hearts, crying, "Abba! Father!"' (Gal 4:6).

"When we call on God the Father, remember that it is the Spirit who, with his motion in your soul, has given you this prayer. If the Holy Spirit were not present, there would be no word of wisdom or knowledge in the Church; for it is written, 'The word of wisdom is given through the Spirit' (1 Cor 12:8).... If the Holy Spirit were not present, the Church would not exist. But if the Church exists, there is no doubt of the presence of the Holy Spirit."[17]

Beyond all human deficiencies and limitations, the Church is the sign and in a certain sense, though not in the strict sense in which the Church has defined the nature of the seven sacraments of the new law, the universal sacrament of the presence of God in the world. To be a Christian is to be reborn of God and sent to men to announce the news of salvation.

---

[17] St John Chrysostom, *Sermones panegyrici in solemnitates D.N. Jesu Christi*, hom. 1, *De Sancta Pentecoste*, n. 3-4 (PG 50, 457).

If we had a strong and living faith, if we were bold in making Christ known to others, we would see with our own eyes miracles such as those that took place in the times of the Apostles.

Today too blind men, who had lost the ability to look up to heaven and contemplate the wonderful works of God, recover their sight. Lame and crippled men, who were bound by their passions and whose hearts had forgotten love, recover their freedom. Deaf men, who did not want to know God, are given back their hearing. Dumb men, whose tongues were bound because they did not want to acknowledge their defeats, begin to talk. And dead men, in whom sin had destroyed life, come to life again. We see once more that "the word of God is living and active, sharper than any two-edged sword."[18] And just as the first Christians did, we rejoice when we contemplate the power of the Holy Spirit and see the results of his action on the mind and will of his creatures.

---

[18] Heb 4:12.

MAKING CHRIST KNOWN

I see all the circumstances of life—those of 132
every individual person's existence as well as,
in some way, those of the great cross-roads of
history—as so many calls that God makes to
men, to bring them face to face with truth, and
as occasions that are offered to us Christians,
so that we may announce, with our deeds and
with our words strengthened by grace, the
Spirit to whom we belong.[19]

Every generation of Christians needs to
redeem, to sanctify its own time. In order to
do this, it must understand and share the
desires of other men—one's equals—in order to
make known to them, with a *gift of tongues*, how
they are to correspond to the action of the Holy
Spirit, to that permanent outflow of rich treasures that comes from our Lord's heart. We
Christians are called upon to announce, in our
own time, to this world to which we belong and
in which we live, the message—old and at the
same time new—of the Gospel.

It is not true that everyone today—in general—is closed or indifferent to what our

---

[19] Cf. Lk 9:55.

Christian faith teaches about man's being and
destiny. It is not true that men in our time are
turned only toward the things of this earth and
have forgotten to look up to heaven. There is
no lack of narrow ideologies, it is true, or of
persons who maintain them. But in our time we
find both great desires and base attitudes,
heroism and cowardice, zeal and disenchant-
ment: men who dream of a new world, more
just and more human, and others who, discour-
aged perhaps by the failure of their youthful
idealism, hide themselves in the selfishness of
seeking only their own security or remaining
immersed in their errors.

To all these men and women, wherever they
may be, in their more exalted moments or in
their crises and defeats, we have to bring the
solemn and unequivocal message of St Peter in
the days that followed Pentecost: Jesus is the
cornerstone, the redeemer, the hope of our
lives. "For there is no other name under heaven
given to men by which we must be saved."[20]

133　　Among the gifts of the Holy Spirit, I would
say that there is one which we all need in a
special way: the gift of wisdom. It makes us

---

[20] Acts 4:12.

know God and rejoice in his presence, thereby placing us in a perspective from which we can judge accurately the situations and events of this life. If we were consistent with our faith when we looked around us and contemplated the world and its history, we would be unable to avoid feeling in our own hearts the same sentiments that filled the heart of our Lord: "Seeing the crowds, he was moved with compassion for them, because they were bewildered and dejected, like sheep without a shepherd."[21]

Not that the Christian should neglect to see all that is good in humanity, appreciate its healthy joys or participate in its enthusiasm and ideals. On the contrary, a true Christian will vibrate in unison with all the good he finds in the world. And he will live in the midst of it with a special concern, since he knows, better than anyone, the depth and the richness of the human spirit.

A Christian's faith does not diminish his spirit or limit the noble impulses of his soul— rather it makes them grow with the realization of their true and authentic meaning. We do not

[21] Mt 9:36.

exist in order to pursue just any happiness. We have been called to penetrate the intimacy of God's own life, to know and love God the Father, God the Son, and God the Holy Spirit, and to love also—in that same love of the one God in three divine Persons—the angels and all men.

This is the great boldness of the Christian faith: to proclaim the value and dignity of human nature and to affirm that we have been created to achieve the dignity of children of God, through the grace that raises us up to a supernatural level. An incredible boldness it would be, were it not founded on the promise of salvation given us by God the Father, confirmed by the blood of Christ, and reaffirmed and made possible by the constant action of the Holy Spirit.

We must live by faith. We must grow in faith—up to the point when it will be possible to describe any one of us, or any Christian, in the terms used by one of the great Doctors of the eastern Church: "In the same way as transparent bodies, upon receiving a ray of light, become resplendent and shine out, so the souls that are borne and illuminated by the Holy Spirit become themselves spiritual and carry to others the light of grace. From the Holy Spirit comes knowledge of future events, understanding of mysteries, comprehension of hidden truths, giving of gifts, heavenly citizenship, conversation with the angels. From him comes never-ending joy, perseverance in God, likeness to God, and the most sublime state that can be conceived, becoming God-like."[22]

Together with humility, the realization of the greatness of man's dignity—and of the overwhelming fact that, by grace, we are made children of God—forms a single attitude. It is not our own forces that save us and give us life; it is the grace of God. This is a truth which can never be forgotten. If it were, the *divinization* of our life would be perverted and would become presumption, pride. And this would lead, sooner or later, to a breakdown of spiritual life, when the soul came face to face with its own weakness and wretchedness.

"And shall I dare to say, 'I am holy'?" asks St Augustine. "If I mean by 'holy' that I bring holiness and that I need no one to make me holy, I would be a liar and full of pride. But if by 'holy' I understand one who is made holy,

[22] St Basil, *De Spiritu Sancto*, 9, 23 (PG 32, 110).

as we read in Leviticus, 'You will be holy,
because I, God, am holy,' then the whole body
of Christ, down to the last man living at the
ends of the earth, may dare to say, together
with its head and under him, 'I am holy'."[23]

Love the Third Person of the most Blessed
Trinity. Listen in the intimacy of your being to
the divine motions of encouragement or reproach you receive from him. Walk through the
earth in the light that is poured out in your soul.
And the God of hope will fill us with all peace,
so that this hope may grow in us more and
more each day, by the power of the Holy
Spirit.[24]

GETTING TO KNOW THE HOLY SPIRIT

134   To live according to the Holy Spirit means
to live by faith and hope and charity—to allow
God to take possession of our lives and to
change our hearts, to make us resemble him
more and more. A mature and profound
Christian life cannot be improvised, because it
is the result of the growth of God's grace in

[23] St Augustine, *Enarrationes in psalmos*, 85, 4 (PL 37, 1084).
[24] Cf. Rom 15:13.

us. In the Acts of the Apostles we find the early Christian community described in a single sentence, brief but full of meaning: "and they continued steadfastly in the teaching of the apostles and in the communion of the breaking of the bread and in prayers."[25]

This is how the early Christians lived, and this how we too should live: meditating the doctrine of our faith until it becomes a part of us; receiving our Lord in the Eucharist; meeting him in the personal dialogue of our prayer, without trying to hide behind an impersonal conduct, but face to face with him. These means should become the very substance of our attitude. If they are lacking we will have, perhaps, the ability to think in an erudite manner, an activity that is more or less intense, some practices and devotions.

But we will not have an authentically Christian way of life, because we will lack that personal relationship with Christ, which is a real and living participation in the divine work of salvation.

This is a teaching that applies to any Christian, because we are all equally called to

---

[25] Acts 2:42.

sanctity. There are no second-class Christians, obliged to practice only a "simplified version" of the Gospel. We have all received the same baptism, and although there is a great variety of spiritual gifts and human situations, there is only one Spirit who distributes God's gifts, only one faith, only one hope, only one love.[26]

And so we can apply to ourselves the question asked by the Apostle: "Do you not know that you are the temple of God, and that the Spirit of God dwells in you?"[27] And we can understand it as an invitation to deal with God in a more personal and direct manner. For some, unfortunately, the Paraclete is the Great Stranger, the Great Unknown. He is merely a name that is mentioned, but not Someone, not one of the three persons in the one God, with whom we can talk and with whose life we can live.

We have to deal with him simply and trustingly, as we are taught by the Church in its liturgy. Then we will come to know our Lord better, and at the same time, we will realize more fully the great favor that has been

[26] Cf. 1 Cor 12:4-6; 13:1-13.
[27] 1 Cor 3:16.

granted us when we became Christians. We will see all the greatness and truth of the *divinization* to which I referred before, which is a sharing in God's own life.

"The Holy Spirit is not an artist who draws the divine substance in us, as though he were alien to it. It is not in this way that he leads us to a resemblance with God—but rather, being God and proceeding from God, he himself marks the hearts of those who receive him as a seal upon wax. In this way, by the communication of his own life and resemblance, he restores nature according to the beauty of the divine model, and returns to man his resemblance with God."[28]

Let us see how this truth applies to our daily lives. Let us describe, at least in general, the way of life which will bring us to deal in a familiar manner with the Holy Spirit, and together with him, the Father and the Son.

We can fix our attention on three fundamental points: docility, life of prayer, and union with the cross.

135

---

[28] St Cyril of Alexandria, *Thesaurus de sancta et consubstantiali Trinitate*, 34 (PG 75, 609).

First of all docility, because it is the Holy Spirit who, with his inspirations, gives a supernatural tone to our thoughts, desires, and actions. It is he who leads us to receive Christ's teaching and to assimilate it in a profound way. It is he who gives us the light by which we perceive our personal calling and the strength to carry out all that God expects of us. If we are docile to the Holy Spirit, the image of Christ will be formed more and more fully in us, and we will be brought closer every day to God the Father. "For whoever are led by the Spirit of God, they are the children of God."[29]

If we let ourselves be guided by this life-giving principle, who is the Holy Spirit in us, our spiritual vitality will grow. We will place ourselves in the hands of our Father God, with the same spontaneity and confidence with which a child abandons himself to his father's care. Our Lord has said: "Unless you become like little children, you will not enter the kingdom of heaven."[30] This is the old and well-known "way of childhood," which is not sentimentality or lack of human maturity. It is

[29] Rom 8:14.
[30] Mt 18:3.

a supernatural maturity, which makes us realize more deeply the wonders of God's love, while leading us to acknowledge our own smallness and identify our will fully with God's will.

In the second place a life of prayer, because 136 the giving of one's self, the obedience and meekness of a Christian, are born of love and lead to love. And love leads to a personal relationship, to conversation and friendship. Christian life requires a constant dialogue with God, one in three persons, and it is to this intimacy that the Holy Spirit leads us. "For who among men knows the things of a man save the spirit of the man which is in him? Even so, the things of God no one knows but the Spirit of God."[31] If we have a constant relationship with the Holy Spirit, we will become spiritual ourselves, we will realize that we are Christ's brothers and children of God, and we will not hesitate to call upon our Father at any time.[32]

Let us acquire the habit of conversation with the Holy Spirit, who is the one who will make us holy. Let us trust in him and ask his help

---

[31] 1 Cor 2:11.
[32] Cf. Gal 4:6; Rom 8:15.

and feel his closeness to us. In this way our poor heart will grow; we will have a greater desire to love God and to love all creatures for God's sake. And our lives will reproduce that final vision of the Apocalypse: the Spirit and the Spouse, the Holy Spirit and the Church— and every Christian—calling on Jesus Christ to come and be with us forever.[33]

137   And finally, union with the cross, because in the life of Christ the resurrection and Pentecost were preceded by Calvary. This is the order that must be followed in the life of any Christian. We are, as St Paul tells us, "heirs indeed of God and joint heirs with Christ, provided, however, we suffer with him, that we may also be glorified with him."[34] The Holy Spirit comes to us as a result of the cross—as a result of our total abandonment to the will of God, of seeking only his glory and renouncing ourselves completely.

Only when a man is faithful to grace and decides to place the cross in the center of his soul, denying himself for the love of God, detaching himself in a real way from all self-

---

[33] Cf. Rev 22:17.
[34] Rom 8:17.

ishness and false human security, only then—
when a man lives by faith in a real way—will
he receive the fullness of the great fire, the great
light, the great comfort of the Holy Spirit.

It is then, too, that the soul begins to
experience the peace and freedom which Christ
has won for us,[35] and which are given to us
with the grace of the Holy Spirit. "But the fruit
of the Spirit is: charity, joy, peace, patience,
kindness, goodness, long-suffering, mildness,
faith, modesty, continency, chastity,"[36] and
"where the Spirit of the Lord is, there is freedom."[37]

In the midst of the limitations that accom- 138
pany our present life, in which sin is still
present in us to some extent at least, we
Christians perceive with a particular clearness
all the wealth of our divine filiation, when we
realize that we are fully free because we are
doing our Father's work, when our joy becomes
constant because no one can take our hope
away. It is then that we can admire at the same
time all the great and beautiful things of this

[35] Cf. Gal 4:31.
[36] Gal 5:22-23.
[37] 2 Cor 3:17.

earth, can appreciate the richness and goodness of creation, and can love with all the strength and purity for which the human heart was made. It is then that sorrow for sin does not degenerate into a bitter gesture of despair or pride, because sorrow and knowledge of human weakness lead us to identify ourselves again with Christ's work of redemption and feel more deeply our solidarity with other men.

It is then, finally, that we Christians experience in our own life the sure strength of the Holy Spirit, in such a way that our own failures do not drag us down. Rather they are an invitation to begin again, and to continue being faithful witnesses of Christ in all the moments of our life—in spite of our own personal weaknesses, which, in such a case, are normally no more than small failings that hardly perturb the soul. And even if they were grave sins, the sacrament of penance, received with true sorrow, enables us to recover our peace with God and to become again a good witness of his mercy.

Such is a brief summary, which can barely be expressed in human language, of the richness of our faith and of our Christian life, if we let ourselves be guided by the Holy Spirit.

That is why I can only end these words in one way: by voicing the prayer, contained in one of the liturgical hymns for the feast of Pentecost, which is like an echo of the unceasing petition of the whole Church: "Come, creating Spirit, to the minds of those who belong to you, and fill the hearts that you have created with grace from above.... Grant that through you we may know the Father and become acquainted with the Son; may we believe in you, the Spirit who proceeds from the Father and Son, forever. Amen."[38]

[38] Hymn *Veni, Creator*, divine office of Whit Sunday.

TO JESUS THROUGH MARY*

If we look at the world, at the People of God,[1] during this month of May, we will see devotion to our Lady taking the form of many old and new customs practiced with great love. It makes me very happy to see that this devotion is always alive, awakening in Christians a supernatural desire to act as "members of God's household."[2]

Seeing how so many Christians express their affection for the Virgin Mary, surely you also feel more a part of the Church, closer to those brothers and sisters of yours. It is like a family reunion. Grown-up children, whom life has separated, come back to their mother for some family anniversary. And even if they have not

---

* A homily given on May 4, 1957.
[1] Cf. 1 Pt 2:10.
[2] Eph 2:19: *domestici Dei*.

always got on well together, today things are different; they feel united, sharing the same affection.

Mary continually builds the Church and keeps it together. It is difficult to have devotion to our Lady and not feel closer to the other members of the mystical body and more united to its visible head, the pope. That's why I like to repeat: *All with Peter to Jesus through Mary!* By seeing ourselves as part of the Church and united to our brothers in the faith, we understand more deeply that we are brothers of all mankind, for the Church has been sent to all the peoples of the earth.[3]

My own experience and yours are proof of the effects of sincere devotion to our Lady. I remember how in 1933 I went to visit a shrine in Spain, the shrine of our Lady of Sonsoles. It wasn't a pilgrimage in the normal sense: nothing noisy or elaborate, just three of us. I respect and love public demonstrations of devotion, but I must admit I prefer to offer Mary the same affection, the same enthusiasm, in private visits or with very few people—a more intimate sort of thing.

[3] Cf. Mt 28:19.

During that visit to Sonsoles I was told the origin of the name of the shrine. The statue had been hidden during the wars between Christians and Moslems in Spain, and after a number of years it was found by shepherds. According to the story, when they saw it they exclaimed: "What beautiful eyes; they are suns!" [Spanish: *son soles*].

MOTHER OF CHRIST, MOTHER OF CHRISTIANS

Since 1933, during many visits to shrines of 140 our Lady, I have often reflected and meditated on the wonderful affection which so many Christians have for the Mother of Jesus. And I have always seen it as a response of love, of filial love and thanksgiving to our Lady, a sign of a child's affection. For Mary is closely tied to the greatest sign of God's love—the Word made flesh who took upon himself our sins and weakness. Faithful to the divine purpose for which she was born, Mary continues to spend herself in the service of men, who are all called to be brothers of her son Jesus. The Mother of God is also truly the mother of men.

Our Lord wanted it to be this way. So that future generations might know it, the Holy Spirit inspired St John to write: "Now there were standing by the cross of Jesus his mother and his mother's sister, Mary of Cleophas, and Mary Magdalene. When Jesus, therefore, saw his mother and the disciple standing by, whom he loved, he said to his mother, 'Woman, behold your son.' Then he said to the disciple, 'Behold your mother.' And from that hour the disciple took her into his home."[4]

John, the disciple whom Jesus loved, brought Mary into his home, into his life. Spiritual writers have seen these words of the Gospel as an invitation to all Christians to bring Mary into their lives. Mary certainly wants us to invoke her, to approach her confidently, to appeal to her as our mother, asking her to "show that you are our mother."[5]

But she is a mother who anticipates our requests. Knowing our needs, she comes quickly to our aid. If we recall that God's mercies come to us through the hands of our Lady, each of us can find many reasons for

[4] Jn 19:25-27.
[5] Hymn *Ave maris stella: Monstra te esse Matrem.*

feeling that Mary is our mother in a very special way.

The Gospel passages about our Lady show 141 her as the Mother of Jesus, following her Son step by step, playing a part in his redemptive mission, rejoicing and suffering with him, loving those whom Jesus loves, looking after all those around her with maternal care.

Just think, for example, of the marriage at Cana. Our Lady was a guest at one of those noisy country weddings attended by crowds of people from many different villages. But she was the only one who noticed the wine was running out.[6] Don't these scenes from Christ's life seem familiar to us? The greatness of God lives at the level of ordinary things. It is natural for a woman, a housewife, to notice something was lacking, to look after the little things which make life pleasant. And that is how Mary acted. Notice also that it is John who tells the story of Cana. He is the only evangelist who has recorded this example of our mother's concern for us. St John wants us to remember that Mary was present at the beginning of the public life of our Lord. He alone has appreciated the

---

[6] Cf. Jn 2:3.

importance of that fact. Jesus knew to whom he was entrusting his Mother—to a disciple who had learned to understand and love her as his own mother.

Let's turn now to the days between the ascension and Pentecost. As a result of the triumph of Christ's resurrection, the disciples are full of faith; they eagerly await the promised Holy Spirit. They want to stay close to one another, and so we find them "with Mary, the mother of Jesus,"[7] praying as a single family.

It was St Luke who related this fact, the evangelist who gave us the longest account of Jesus' childhood. It is as if he wanted us to understand that just as Mary had a major role in the incarnation of the Word, she was intimately involved in the beginning of the Church, Christ's body.

From the first moment of the Church all Christians who have sought the love of God— that love revealed in Jesus Christ—have encountered our Lady and experienced her motherly care. She can truly be called the Mother of Christians. As St Augustine puts it:

[7] Acts 1:14.

"With her charity she cooperates in the birth of the faithful to the Church and they are members of a head, of which she is effectively Mother in the flesh."[8]

It is not surprising then that one of the oldest witnesses to this devotion to Mary is confident prayer: "We gather under your protection, holy Mother of God. Do not reject the prayers we say to you in our need, but save us from all dangers, O glorious and blessed Virgin."[9]

GETTING TO KNOW OUR LADY

In a very natural way we start wanting to   142
speak to the Mother of God, who is also our mother. We want to treat her as someone who is alive. For death has not triumphed over her; she is body and soul in the presence of God the Father, her Son, and the Holy Spirit.

If we want to understand Mary's role in the Christian's life and to feel attracted to her, to be in her company, we don't need to go into

---

[8] *De Sancta virginitate*, 6 (PL 40, 399).
[9] *Sub tuum praesidium confugimus, Sancta Dei Genetrix: nostras deprecationes ne despicias in necessitatibus, sed a periculis cunctis libera nos semper, Virgo gloriosa et benedicta.*

the theological theory, even though it is an inexhaustible mystery that she is the Mother of God.

The catholic faith sees Mary as a sign of God's special love. God calls us his friends; his grace acts in us, winning us from sin, enabling us to reflect in some way the features of Christ, even though we are still wretched dirt. We are not stranded people whom God has promised to save. His salvation is already at work in us. In our relationship to God, we are not blind men yearning for light and crying in anguished darkness. We are children who know our Father loves us.

Mary tells us about this warmth and security. That's why her name goes straight to our heart. Our relationship with our own mother may show us how to deal with Mary the Lady of the Sweet Name. We have to love God with the same heart with which we love our parents, our brothers and sisters, the other members of our family, our friends. And we must love Mary with that same heart, too.

How does a normal son or daughter treat his mother? In different ways, of course, but always affectionately and confidently, never coldly. In an intimate way, through small, commonplace customs. And a mother feels hurt if we omit them: a kiss or an embrace when leaving or coming home, a little extra attention, a few warm words.

In our relationship with our mother in heaven, we should act in very much the same way. Many Christians have the custom of wearing the scapular; or they have acquired the habit of greeting those pictures—a glance is enough—which are found in every Christian home and in many public places; or they recall the central events in Christ's life by saying the rosary, never getting tired of repeating its words, just like people in love; or they mark out a day of the week for her—Saturday, which is today—doing some special little thing for her and thinking particularly about her motherhood.

There are many other marian devotions which I needn't mention here. A Christian doesn't need to live them all. (Growing in supernatural life is not a matter of piling one devotion on top of another.) I would say, however, that anyone who doesn't live some of them, who doesn't express his love for Mary in some way, does not possess the fullness of the faith.

Those who think that devotions to our Lady are a thing of the past seem to have lost sight of the deep Christian meaning they contain. They seem to have forgotten the source from which they spring: faith in God the Father's saving will; love for God the Son who really became man and was born of a woman; trust in God the Holy Spirit who sanctifies us with his grace. It is God who has given us Mary, and we have no right to reject her. We should go to her with a son's love and joy.

BECOMING CHILDREN IN GOD'S LOVE

143   Let's think about this. It can help us to understand some very important things. The mystery of Mary helps us see that in order to approach God we must become little. As Christ said to his disciples: "Believe me, unless you become like little children again, you shall not enter the kingdom of heaven."[10]

To become children we must renounce our pride and self-sufficiency, recognizing that we can do nothing by ourselves. We must realize that we need grace, and the help of God our

[10] Mt 18:3.

Father to find our way and keep to it. To be little, you have to abandon yourself as children do, believe as children believe, beg as children beg.

And we learn all this through contact with Mary. Devotion to our Lady is not something soft and sentimental. It fills the soul with consolation and joy to precisely the extent that it means a deep act of faith making us go outside ourselves and put our hope in the Lord. "The Lord is my shepherd," says one of the psalms, "how can I lack anything? He gives me a resting-place where there is green pasture, leads me out to the cool water's brink, refreshed and content. As in honor pledged, by sure paths he leads me; dark be the valley about my path, hurt I fear none while he is with me."[11]

Because Mary is our mother, devotion to her teaches us to be authentic sons: to love truly, without limit; to be simple, without the complications which come from selfishly thinking only about ourselves; to be happy, knowing that nothing can destroy our hope. "The beginning of the way, at the end of which you will find yourself completely carried away by love

---

[11] Ps 22:1-4.

for Jesus, is a trusting love for Mary."[12] I wrote that many years ago, in the introduction to a short book on the rosary, and since then I have often experienced the truth of those words. I am not going to complete that thought here with all sorts of reasons. I invite you to discover it for yourself, showing your love for Mary, opening your heart to her, confiding to her your joys and sorrows, asking her to help you recognize and follow Jesus.

144   If you seek Mary, you will find Jesus. And you will learn a bit more about what is in the heart of a God who humbles himself, discarding all manifestations of his power and majesty to take the form of a servant.[13] Speaking in human terms, we could say that God outdoes himself, because he goes much further than he needs in order to save us. The only way to measure what he does is to say that it cannot be measured; it comes from a madness of love which leads him to take on our flesh and bear the weight of our sins.

Can we realize that God loves us and not be overcome with love ourselves? We must let

---

[12] *Holy Rosary*, Manila 1977.
[13] Cf. Phil 2:6-7.

these truths of faith fill our soul until they
change our life. God loves us! The Almighty
who made heaven and earth!

God is interested even in the smallest events
in the lives of his creatures—in your affairs
and mine—and he calls each of us by our
name.[14] This certainty which the faith gives
enables us to look at everything in a new light.
And everything, while remaining exactly the
same becomes different, because it is an expression of God's love. Our life is turned into
a continuous prayer, we find ourselves with
good humor and a peace which never ends,
and everything we do is an act of thanksgiving running through all our day. "My soul
magnifies the Lord," Mary sang, "and my spirit
rejoices in God my savior; because he has
regarded the lowliness of his handmaid; for,
behold, henceforth all generations shall call me
blessed; because he who is mighty has done
great things for me."[15]

Our prayer can accompany and imitate
this prayer of Mary. Like her, we feel the
desire to sing, to acclaim the wonders of God,

[14] Cf. Is 43:1.
[15] Lk 1:46-49.

so that all mankind and all creation may share our joy.

MARY MAKES US FEEL LIKE BROTHERS

145   If we have this filial contact with Mary, we won't be able to think just about ourselves and our problems. Selfish personal problems will find no place in our mind. Mary brings us to Jesus, and Jesus is "the firstborn among many brothers."[16] And so, if we know Jesus, we realize that we can live only by giving ourselves to the service of others. A Christian can't be caught up in personal problems; he must be concerned about the universal Church and the salvation of all souls.

Concern for one's own spiritual improvement is not really a personal thing, for sanctification is completely bound up with apostolate. We must, therefore, develop our interior life and the Christian virtues with our eyes upon the good of the whole Church. We cannot do good and make Christ known, if we're not making a sincere effort to live the teachings of the Gospel.

[16] Rom 8:29.

If we are imbued with this spirit, our conversations with God eventually aid other men, even though they may begin on an apparently personal level. And if we take our Lady's hand, she will make us realize more fully that all men are our brothers—because we are all sons of that God whose daughter, spouse, and mother she is.

Our neighbors' problems must be our problems. Christian fraternity should be something very deep in the soul, so that we are indifferent to no one. Mary, who brought up Jesus and accompanied him through his life and is now beside him in heaven, will help us recognize Jesus as he crosses our path and makes himself present to us in the needs of our fellowmen.

On our way to visit the shrine of Sonsoles, 146 which I mentioned earlier, we passed some wheat fields. The wheat shone as it waved in the breeze, and I remembered a part of the Gospel where Jesus said to his disciples: "Do you not say, 'There are yet four months and then comes the harvest'? Well, I say to you: lift up your eyes and behold that the fields are already white for the harvest."[17] And I realized

<hr />

[17] Jn 4:35.

again that our Lord wanted to put the same yearning into our hearts as he had in his own. And I left the road to pluck some ears of grain to keep as souvenirs.

We have to open our eyes; we have to look around us and recognize how God is calling us through the people at our side. We cannot turn our backs on others, ignoring them, because we are caught up in our own little world. That wasn't how Jesus lived. The Gospel often speaks of his mercy, his ability to feel the sorrow and share the needs of others. He consoled the widow of Naim;[18] he wept at the death of Lazarus;[19] he felt compassion for the crowds that followed him with nothing to eat;[20] he also had pity on sinners, on those who go through life without knowing light or truth. "And when he landed, Jesus saw a large crowd, and had compassion on them, because they were like sheep without a shepherd. And he began to teach them many things."[21]

When we are truly sons of Mary, we understand this attitude of our Lord, and our

[18] Cf. Lk 7:11-17.
[19] Cf. Jn 11:35.
[20] Cf. Mt 15:32.
[21] Mk 6:34.

heart expands and becomes tender. We feel the
sufferings, doubts, loneliness, and sorrows of all
other men, our brothers. And we urgently want
to help them and speak to them about God, so
that they can treat him as their Father and
understand the motherly care which Mary is
offering them.

BEING AN APOSTLE OF APOSTLES

Filling the world with light, being the salt 147
and light[22]—that was how our Lord described
the mission of his disciples. To bring to the ends
of the earth the good news of God's love. All
of us Christians should devote our life to doing
this, in one way or another.

I'll go further than that. We have to yearn
not to be alone. We have to encourage others
to help in this divine task of bringing joy and
peace to men's hearts. As St Gregory the Great
says: "Insofar as you progress, attract others to
go along with you, desire to have companions
on the road to the Lord."[23]

[22] Cf. Mt 5:13-14.
[23] *In Evangelia homiliae*, 6, 6 (PL 76, 1098).

But bear in mind that, as our Lord tells us in a parable, the sower of weeds came "while men slept."[24] We so easily allow ourselves to be carried away by the torpor of selfishness and superficiality, getting wrapped up in thousands of passing experiences, that we avoid coming to grips with the real meaning of the world and life. A bad thing that lethargy, which smothers man's dignity and makes him a slave of sadness!

There is one case that we should be especially sorry about: that of Christians who could do more and don't. Christians who could live all the consequences of their vocation as children of God, but refuse to do so through lack of generosity. We are partly to blame, for the grace of faith has not been given us to hide but to share with other men.[25] We cannot forget that the happiness of these people, in this life and in the next, is at stake. The Christian life is a divine wonder with immediate promises of satisfaction and serenity—but on condition that we know how to recognize the gift of God[26] and be generous, not counting the cost.

[24] Mt 13:25: *cum dormirent homines.*
[25] Cf. Mt 5:15-16.
[26] Cf. Jn 4:10.

So we have to awaken the people who have fallen into the dangerous sleep our Lord mentioned. We must remind them that life is not something to play with—it is a divine treasure which must grow. We must also show the way to those who have good will and good desires, but don't know how to put them into practice. Christ urges us. Each one of us has to be not only an apostle, but an apostle of apostles, bringing others along, so that they in turn will encourage others to make Jesus Christ known to everyone.

Perhaps someone will ask how we are to 148 bring this knowledge of Christ to others. And I reply: naturally, simply, living as you live in the middle of the world, devoted to your professional work and to the care of your family, sharing the noble interest of men, respecting the rightful freedom of every man.

For over thirty years God has been putting into my heart the desire to help people of every condition and background to understand that ordinary life can be holy and full of God. Our Lord is calling us to sanctify the ordinary tasks of every day, for the perfection of the Christian is to be found precisely there. Let's consider it once more as we contemplate Mary's life.

We can't forget that Mary spent nearly every day of her life just like millions of other women who look after their family, bring up their children and take care of the house. Mary sanctifies the ordinary everyday things—what some people wrongly regard as unimportant and insignificant: everyday work, looking after those closest to you, visits to friends and relatives. What a blessed ordinariness, that can be so full of love of God!

For that's what explains Mary's life—her love. A complete love, so complete that she forgets herself and is happy just to be there where God wants her, fulfilling with care what God wants her to do. That is why even her slightest action is never routine or vain but, rather, full of meaning. Mary, our mother, is for us both an example and a way. We have to try to be like her, in the ordinary circumstances in which God wants us to live.

If we act in this way, we give those around us the example of a simple and normal life which is consistent, even though it has all the limitations and defects which are part and parcel of the human condition. And when they see that we live the same life as they do, they will ask us: Why are you so happy? How do you manage to overcome selfishness and comfort-seeking? Who has taught you to understand others, to live well and to spend yourself in the service of others? Then we must disclose to them the divine secret of Christian existence. We must speak to them about God, Christ, the Holy Spirit, Mary. The time has come for us to use our poor words to communicate the depth of God's love which grace has poured into our souls.

In his Gospel St John has recorded a 149 wonderful phrase of our Lady. At the wedding of Cana she turned to the waiters and said: "Do whatever he tells you."[27] That's what it's all about—getting people to face Jesus and ask him: "Lord, what do you want me to do?"[28]

The Christian apostolate—and I'm talking about an ordinary Christian living as just one more man or woman among equals—is a great work of teaching. Through real, personal, loyal friendship, you create in others a hunger for God and you help them to discover new horizons—naturally, simply. With the example

[27] Jn 2:5.
[28] Acts 9:6.

of your faith lived to the full, with a loving word which is full of the force of divine truth.

Be daring. Count on the help of Mary, queen of apostles. Without ceasing to be a mother, our Lady is able to get each of her children to face his own responsibilities. Mary always does the immense favor of bringing to the cross, of placing face to face with the example of the Son of God, those who come close to her and contemplate her life. It is in this confrontation that Christian life is decided. And here Mary intercedes for us so that our behavior may lead to a reconciliation of the younger brother—you and me—with the firstborn Son of the Father.

Many conversions, many decisions to give oneself to the service of God have been preceded by an encounter with Mary. Our Lady has encouraged us to look for God, to desire to change, to lead a new life. And so the "Do whatever he tells you" has turned into real self-giving, into a Christian vocation, which from then on enlightens all our personal life.

This conversation in our Lord's presence, in which we have thought about devotion to and affection for his Mother and ours, can really give new vigor to our faith. The month of May is beginning. Our Lord wants us to make good use of this opportunity to increase in his love through dealing with his Mother. Let's try each day to show her, through little things, little attentions, that we, her children, love her, that our holiness and apostolate are becoming something real, that we are making a constant effort to contribute to the salvation which Christ has brought to the world.

Sancta Maria, spes nostra, ancilla Domini, sedes Sapientiae, ora pro nobis! Holy Mary, our hope, handmaid of the Lord, seat of Wisdom, pray for us!

ON THE FEAST
OF CORPUS CHRISTI*

Today, on the feast of Corpus Christi, we 150
come together to consider the depths of our
Lord's love for us, which has led him to stay
with us, hidden under the appearances of the
blessed Sacrament. It almost seems as if we can
physically hear him teaching the multitude: "A
sower went out to sow his seed. And as he
sowed, some seeds fell along the path, and the
birds came and devoured them. Other seeds fell
on rocky ground, where they had not much soil,
and immediately they sprang up, since they
had no depth of soil, but when the sun rose
they were scorched; and since they had no root
they withered away. Other seeds fell among
thorns, and the thorns grew up and choked

* A homily given on May 28, 1964, the feast of Corpus
Christi.

them. Other seeds fell on good soil and brought forth grain, some a hundredfold, some sixty, some thirty."[1]

It is a vivid scene. The divine sower is also sowing his seed today. The work of salvation is still going on, and our Lord wants to share that work. He wants Christians to open to his love all the paths of the earth. He invites us to spread the divine message, by both teaching and example, to the farthest corners of the earth. He asks us, as citizens of both ecclesial and civil society, to be other Christs by fulfilling our duties conscientiously, sanctifying our everyday work and the responsibilities of our particular walk of life.

If we look around, if we take a look at the world, which we love because it is God's handiwork, we will find that the parable holds true. The word of Jesus Christ is fruitful, it stirs many souls to dedication and fidelity. The life and conduct of those who serve God have changed history. Even many of those who do not know our Lord are motivated, perhaps unconsciously, by ideals which derive from Christianity.

[1] Mt 13:3-8.

We can also see that some of the seed falls on barren ground or among thorns and thistles; some hearts close themselves to the light of faith. Ideals of peace, reconciliation, and brotherhood are widely accepted and proclaimed, but all too often the facts belie them. Some people are futilely bent on smothering God's voice. To drown it out they use brute force or a method which is more subtle but perhaps more cruel because it drugs the spirit—indifference.

THE BREAD OF ETERNAL LIFE

When thinking about all this, I should like 151 us to take stock of our mission as Christians. Let's turn our eyes to the holy Eucharist, toward Jesus. He is here with us, he has made us a part of himself: "Now you are the body of Christ and individually members of it."[2] God has decided to stay in the tabernacle to nourish us, strengthen us, make us divine, and give effectiveness to our work and efforts. Jesus is at one and the same time the sower, the seed

[2] 1 Cor 12:27: *Vos estis corpus Christi et membra de membro.*

and the final result of the sowing: the bread of eternal life.

The miracle of the holy Eucharist is being continually renewed and it has all Jesus' personal traits. Perfect God and perfect man, Lord of heaven and earth, he offers himself to us as nourishment in the most natural and ordinary way. Love has been awaiting us for almost two thousand years. That's a long time and yet it's not, for when you are in love time flies.

I remember a lovely poem, one of the songs collected by Alfonso X the Wise. It's a legend about a simple monk who begged our Lady to let him see heaven, even if only for a moment. Our Lady granted him his wish and the good monk found himself in paradise. When he returned, he could not recognize the monastery—his prayer, which he had thought very short, lasted three centuries. Three centuries are nothing to a person in love. That's how I explain Christ's waiting in the Eucharist. It is God waiting for us, God who loves man, who searches us out, who loves us just as we are—limited, selfish, inconstant, but capable of discovering his infinite affection and of giving ourselves fully to him.

Motivated by his own love and by his desire to teach us to love, Jesus came on earth and has stayed with us in the Eucharist. "Having loved his own who were in the world, he loved them to the end"[3]: that's how St John begins his account of what happened on the eve of the pasch when Jesus "took bread and after he had given thanks, broke it, and said, 'This is my body which is given up for you. Do this in remembrance of me.' In the same way also the cup, after supper, saying: 'This is the new covenant in my blood. Do this, as often as you drink it, in remembrance of me'."[4]

A NEW LIFE

It is the simple and solemn moment of the establishment of the new alliance. Jesus dissolves the old economy of the law and reveals to us that he himself will be the content of our prayer and life. Just look at the joy which invades today's liturgy: "Let the anthem be clear and strong and full of joy."[5] It is a great

152

---

[3] Jn 13:1.
[4] 1 Cor 11:23-25.
[5] Sequence *Lauda Sion*.

Christian celebration which sings about a new era: "The old pasch is by the new replaced; the substance hath the shadow chased and rising day dispels the night."[6]

This is a miracle of love. "This is truly the bread for God's children."[7] Jesus, the first son of the eternal Father, offers us himself as food. And the same Jesus is waiting to receive us in heaven as "his guests, his co-heirs and his fellows,"[8] for "those who are nourished by Christ will die the earthly death of time, but they will live eternally because Christ is life everlasting."[9]

Eternal happiness begins now for the Christian who is comforted with the definitive manna of the Eucharist. The old life has gone forever. Let us leave everything behind us so that everything will be new, "our hearts, our words and our actions."[10]

This is the Good News. *News*, because it speaks to us of a deep love which we never could have dreamed of. *Good*, because there is

---

[6] *Ibid.*

[7] *Ibid.*

[8] *Ibid.*

[9] St Augustine, *In Ioannis Evangelium tractatus*, 26, 20 (PL 35, 1616).

[10] Hymn *Sacris solemnis*.

nothing better than uniting ourselves to God, the greatest Good of all. It is *Good News*, because in an inexplicable way it gives us a foretaste of heaven.

Jesus hides in the blessed Sacrament of the altar because he wants us to *dare* to approach him. He wants to nourish us so we become one single thing with him. When he said, "Apart from me you can do nothing,"[11] he was not condemning Christians to ineffectiveness or obliging them to seek him by a difficult and arduous route. On the contrary. He has stayed here with us, he is totally available to us.

When we gather before the altar where the holy sacrifice of the Mass is being celebrated, when we contemplate the sacred host in the monstrance or adore it hidden in the tabernacle, our faith should be strengthened; we should reflect on this new life which we are receiving and be moved by God's affection and tenderness.

"They devoted themselves to the apostles' teaching and fellowship, to the breaking of the bread and the prayers."[12] That is how the

[11] Jn 15:5.
[12] Acts 2:42.

Scriptures describe the life of the early Christians. They were brought together by the faith of the Apostles in perfect unity, to share in the Eucharist and to pray with one mind. Faith, bread, word.

In the Eucharist Jesus gives us a sure pledge of his presence in our souls; of his power, which supports the whole world; of his promises of salvation, which will help the human family to dwell forever in the house in heaven when time comes to an end. There we shall find God the Father, God the Son, God the Holy Spirit: the Blessed Trinity, the one and only God. Our whole faith is brought into play when we believe in Jesus, really present under the appearances of bread and wine.

154   I cannot see how anyone could live as a Christian and not feel the need for the constant friendship of Jesus in the word and in the bread, in prayer and in the Eucharist. And I easily understand the ways in which successive generations of faithful have expressed their love for the Eucharist, both with public devotions making profession of the faith and with silent, simple practices in the peace of a church or the intimacy of their hearts.

The important thing is that we should love the Mass and make it the center of our day. If we attend Mass well, surely we are likely to think about our Lord during the rest of the day, wanting to be always in his presence, ready to work as he worked and love as he loved. And so we learn to thank our Lord for his kindness in not limiting his presence to the time of the sacrifice of the altar. He has decided to stay with us in the host which is reserved in the tabernacle.

For me the tabernacle has always been a Bethany, a quiet and pleasant place where Christ resides. A place where we can tell him about our worries, our sufferings, our desires, our joys, with the same sort of simplicity and naturalness as Martha, Mary, and Lazarus. That is why I rejoice when I come across a church— even if I can only see the silhouette in the distance—as I make my way through the streets of an unfamiliar town or city; it's another tabernacle, another opportunity for the soul to escape and join in intention our Lord in the Sacrament.

THE RICHNESS OF THE EUCHARIST

155   When our Lord instituted the Eucharist during the last supper, night had already fallen. This indicated, according to St John Chrysostom, that "the times had run their course."[13] The world had fallen into darkness, for the old rites, the old signs of God's infinite mercy to mankind, were going to be brought to fulfillment. The way was opening to a new dawn —the new pasch. The Eucharist was instituted during that night, preparing in advance for the morning of the resurrection.

We too have to prepare for this new dawn. Everything harmful, worn out or useless has to be thrown away—discouragement, suspicion, sadness, cowardice. The holy Eucharist gives the sons of God a divine newness and we must respond "in the newness of your mind,"[14] renewing all our feelings and actions. We have been given a new principle of energy, strong new roots grafted onto our Lord. We must not return to the old leaven, for now we have the bread which lasts forever.

---

[13] *In Matthaeum homiliae*, 82, 1 (PG 58, 700).
[14] Rom 12:2: *in novitate sensus*.

On this feast of Corpus Christi in cities and towns throughout the world, Christians accompany our Lord in procession. Hidden in the host he moves through the streets and squares—just as during his earthly life—going to meet those who want to see him, making himself available to those who are not looking for him. And so, once more, he comes among his own people. How are we to respond to this call of his?

The external signs of love should come from the heart and find expression in the testimony of a Christian life. If we have been renewed by receiving our Lord's body, we should *show* it. Let us pray that our thoughts be sincere, full of peace, self-giving, and service. Let us pray that we be true and clear in what we say—the right thing at the right time—so as to console and help and especially bring God's light to others. Let us pray that our actions be consistent and effective and right, so that they give off "the good fragrance of Christ,"[15] evoking his way of doing things.

The Corpus Christi procession makes Christ present in towns and cities throughout the

---

[15] 2 Cor 2:15: *bonus odor Christi*.

352 CHRIST IS PASSING BY

world. But his presence cannot be limited to just
one day, a noise you hear and then forget. It
should remind us that we have to discover our
Lord in our ordinary everyday activity. Side by
side with this solemn procession, there is the
simple, silent procession of the ordinary life of
each Christian. He is a man among men, who
by good fortune has received the faith and the
divine commission to act so that he renews the
message of our Lord on earth. We are not
without defects; we make mistakes and commit
sins. But God is with us and we must make
ourselves ready to be used by him, so that he
can continue to walk among men.

Let us ask our Lord then to make us souls
devoted to the Blessed Eucharist, so that our
relationship with him brings forth joy and
serenity and a desire for justice. In this way we
will make it easier for others to recognize
Christ; we will put Christ at the center of all
human activities. And Jesus' promise will be
fulfilled: "I, when I am lifted up from the earth,
will draw all men to myself."[16]

157   Jesus, as we were saying, is the sower, and
he goes about his task by means of us Chris-

---

[16] Jn 12:32.

tians. Christ presses the grain in his wounded hands, soaks it in his blood, cleans it, purifies it, and throws it into the furrows, into the world. He plants the seeds one by one so that each Christian in his own setting can bear witness to the fruitfulness of the death and resurrection of the Lord.

If we are in Christ's hands, we should absorb his saving blood and let ourselves be cast on the wind. We should accept our life as God wants it. And we should be convinced that the seed must be buried and die[17] if it is to be fruitful. Then the shoots start to appear, and the grain. And from the grain, bread is made which is changed by God into the body of Christ. In this way we once more become united with Jesus, our sower. "Because there is one bread, we who are many are one body, for we all partake of the one bread."[18]

We should always remember that if there is no sowing there is no harvest. That is why we need to sow the word of God generously, to make Christ known to men so that they hunger

[17] Cf. Jn 12:24-25.
[18] 1 Cor 10:17.

for him. Corpus Christi—the feast of the bread of life—is a good opportunity to reflect on the hunger which people suffer: hunger for truth, for justice, for unity, and for peace. To meet the hunger for peace we have to repeat what St Paul said: Christ is our peace, *pax nostra*.[19] The desire for truth should remind us that Jesus is the way, the truth, and the life.[20] Those who aspire to unity should be shown Christ who prays that we will all be *consummati in unum*: "made perfectly one."[21] Hunger for justice should lead us to the original source of harmony among mankind: the fact that we are, and know ourselves to be, sons of the Father, brothers.

Peace, truth, unity, justice. How difficult it often seems to eliminate the barriers to human harmony! And yet we Christians are called to bring about that miracle of brotherhood. We must work so that everyone with God's grace can live in a Christian way, "bearing one another's burdens,"[22] keeping the command-

---

[19] Eph 2:14.
[20] Cf. Jn 14:6.
[21] Jn 17:23.
[22] Gal 6:2.

ment of love which is the bond of perfection and the essence of the law.[23]

We cannot deny that a great deal remains 158 to be done. On one occasion, when he was looking perhaps at the swaying wheatfields, Jesus said to his disciples: "The harvest is plentiful, but the laborers are few; pray therefore the Lord of the harvest to send out laborers into his harvest."[24] Now, as then, laborers are needed to bear "the burden of the day and the scorching heat."[25] And if we, the laborers, are not faithful, there will come to pass what was described by the prophet Joel: "The fields are laid waste, the ground mourns; because the grain is destroyed, the wine fails, the oil languishes. Be confounded, O tillers of the soil, wail, O winedressers, for the wheat and the barley, because the harvest of the field has perished."[26]

There is no harvest if we are not ready for constant, generous work, which can be long and tiring: ploughing the land, sowing the seed,

[23] Cf. Col 3:14; Rom 13:10.
[24] Mt 9:38.
[25] Mt 20:12.
[26] Joel 1:10-11.

weeding the fields, reaping and threshing... The kingdom of God is fashioned in history, in time. Our Lord has entrusted this task to us, and no one can feel exempt. Today, as we adore Christ in the Eucharist, let us remember that the time has not yet come for resting. The day's work must go on.

It is written in the book of Proverbs: "He who tills his land will have plenty of bread."[27] Let us apply this passage to our spiritual life. If we do not work God's land, are not faithful to the divine mission of giving ourselves to others, helping them recognize Christ, we will find it very difficult to understand what the eucharistic bread is. No one values something which does not cost an effort. In order to value and love the holy Eucharist, we must follow Jesus' way. We must be grain; we must die to ourselves and rise full of life and give an abundant yield: a hundredfold![28]

Christ's way can be summed up in one word: love. If we are to love, we must have a big heart and share the concerns of those around us. We must be able to forgive and

[27] Prov 12:11.
[28] Cf. Mk 4:8.

understand; we must sacrifice ourselves, with Jesus Christ, for all souls. If we love Christ's heart, we shall learn to serve others and we shall defend the truth clearly, lovingly. If we are to love in this way, we need to root out of our individual lives everything which is an obstacle to Christ's life in us: attachment to our own comfort, the temptation to selfishness, the tendency to be the center of everything. Only by reproducing in ourselves the word of Christ can we transmit it to others. Only by experiencing the death of the grain of wheat can we work in the heart of the world, transforming it from within, making it fruitful.

CHRISTIAN OPTIMISM

We may sometimes be tempted to think that 159 this is very nice but an impossible dream. I have spoken to you about renewing your faith and your hope. Let us not get used to the miracles which are happening before our eyes, especially the wonderful fact that our Lord comes down each day into the priest's hands. Jesus wants us to remain wide awake, so that we are convinced of his power and can hear once more his promise: "Follow me and I will make you become fishers of men;"[29] you will be effective and attract souls to God. We should therefore trust our Lord's words: get into the boat, take the oars, hoist the sails, and launch out into this sea of the world which Christ gives us as an inheritance. "Put out into the deep and let down your nets for a catch."[30]

The apostolic zeal which Christ has put in our hearts must not be diminished or extinguished by a false humility. Maybe we experience the dead weight of our personal failings, but our Lord takes into account our mistakes. In his merciful gaze he realizes that we are creatures with limitations, weaknesses and imperfections, that we are inclined to sin. But he tells us to fight, to acknowledge our weaknesses, not to be afraid, but to repent and foster a desire to improve.

We must also remember that we are only instruments. "What is Apollo? What is Paul? They are servants who brought the faith to you. Even the different ways in which they brought it were assigned to them by the Lord. I did the

---

[29] Mk 1:17.
[30] Lk 5:4: *Duc in altum et laxate retia vestra in capturam.*

planting, Apollo the watering, but God gave the growth."[31] The teaching, the message which we have to communicate, has in its own right an infinite effectiveness which comes not from us, but from Christ. It is God himself who is bent on bringing about salvation, on redeeming the world.

We must, then, have faith and not be dis- 160 pirited. We must not be stopped by any kind of human calculation. To overcome the obstacles we have to throw ourselves into the task so that the very effort we make will open up new paths. Personal holiness, giving oneself to God, is the one cure which overcomes any difficulty.

Being holy means living exactly as our Father in heaven wants us to live. You will say that it is difficult. It is. The ideal is a very high one. And yet it is also easy. It is within our reach. When a person becomes ill, there may be no appropriate medicine. But in supernatural affairs, it is not like that. The medicine is always at hand. It is Jesus Christ, present in the holy Eucharist, and he also gives us his grace in the other sacraments which he established.

[31] 1 Cor 3:4-6.

Let us say again, in word and in action: "Lord, I trust in you; your ordinary providence, your help each day, is all I need." We do not have to ask God to perform great miracles. Rather, we have to beg him to increase our faith, to enlighten our intellect, and strengthen our will. Jesus always stays by our side and is always himself.

Ever since I began to preach, I have warned people against a certain mistaken sense of holiness. Don't be afraid to know your real self. That's right, you are made of clay. Don't be worried. For you and I are sons of God—and that is the right way of being made divine. We are chosen by a divine calling from all eternity: "The Father chose us in Christ before the foundation of the world, that we should be holy and blameless before him."[32] We belong especially to God, we are his instruments in spite of our great personal shortcomings. And we will be effective if we do not lose this awareness of our own weakness. Our temptations give us the measure of our own weakness.

If you feel depressed when you experience, perhaps in a very vivid way, your own petti-

[32] Eph 1:4.

ness, then is the time to abandon yourself
completely and obediently into God's hands.
There is a story about a beggar meeting Alexander the Great and asking him for alms.
Alexander stopped and instructed that the man
be given the government of five cities. The
beggar, totally confused and taken aback,
exclaimed: "I didn't ask for that much." And
Alexander replied: "You asked like the man you
are: I give like the man I am."

Even in moments when we see our limitations clearly, we can and should look at God
the Father, God the Son, and God the Holy
Spirit, and realize that we share in God's own
life. There is never reason to look back.[33] The
Lord is at our side. We have to be faithful and
loyal; we have to face up to our obligations and
we will find in Jesus the love and the stimulus
we need to understand other people's faults
and overcome our own. In this way even
depression—yours, mine, anyone's—can also
be a pillar for the kingdom of Christ.

Let us recognize our infirmity but confess
the power of God. The Christian life has to be
shot through with optimism, joy and the strong

[33] Cf. Lk 9:62.

conviction that our Lord wishes to make use of us. If we feel part of the Church, if we see ourselves sustained by the rock of Peter and by the action of the Holy Spirit, we will decide to fulfil the little duty of every moment. We will sow a little each day, and the granaries will overflow.

161   We must finish these minutes of prayer. Savoring in the intimacy of your soul the infinite goodness of God, realize that Christ is going to make himself really present in the host, with his body, his blood, his soul, and his divinity. Adore him reverently, devoutly; renew in his presence the sincere offerings of your love. Don't be afraid to tell him that you love him. Thank him for giving you this daily proof of his tender mercy, and encourage yourself to go to communion in a spirit of trust. I am awed by this mystery of Love. Here is the Lord seeking to use my heart as a throne, committed never to leave me, provided I don't run away.

Comforted by Christ's presence and nourished by his body, we will be faithful during our life on earth and then we will be victors with Jesus and his Mother in heaven. "O death, where is your victory? O death, where is your sting?... Thanks be to God, who gives us the victory through our Lord Jesus Christ."[34]

[34] 1 Cor 15:55, 57.

FINDING PEACE IN THE HEART OF CHRIST*

God our Father has seen fit to grant us, in 162 the heart of his Son, "infinite treasures of love,"[1] mercy and affection. If we want to find evidence that God loves us—that he not only listens to our prayers but anticipates them—we need only follow the same line of thought as St Paul: "He who did not spare his own Son but gave him up for us all, will he not also give us all things in him?"[2]

Grace renews a man from within and converts a sinner and rebel into a good and faithful servant.[3] The source of all grace is God's love for us, and he has revealed this not

---

* A homily given on June 17, 1966, the feast of the Sacred Heart of Jesus.

[1] Prayer, Mass of the Sacred Heart.

[2] Rom 8:32.

[3] Cf. Mt 25:21.

just in words but also in deeds. It was divine
love which led the second Person of the holy
Trinity, the Word, the Son of God the Father,
to take on our flesh, our human condition,
everything except sin. And the Word, the Word
of God, is the Word from which Love proceeds.[4]

Love is revealed to us in the incarnation, the
redemptive journey which Jesus Christ made on
our earth, culminating in the supreme sacrifice
of the cross. And on the cross it showed itself
through a new sign: "One of the soldiers
pierced his side with a spear, and at once there
came out blood and water."[5] This water and
blood of Jesus speak to us of a self-sacrifice
brought to the last extreme: "It is finished"[6]—
everything is achieved, for the sake of love.

Today when we consider once more the
central mysteries of our faith, we are surprised
to see how very human gestures are used to
express the deepest truths: the love of God the
Father who gives up his Son, and the Son's love
which calmly leads him to Calvary. God does

---

[4] St Thomas, *S. Th.*, I, q. 43, a. 5 (quoting St Augustine,
De Trinitate, IX, 10).
[5] Jn 19:34.
[6] Jn 19:30.

not approach us in power and authority. No, he "takes the form of a servant, being born in the likeness of man."[7] Jesus is never distant or aloof, although sometimes in his preaching he seems very sad, because he is hurt by the evil men do. However, if we watch him closely, we will note immediately that his anger comes from love. It is a further invitation for us to leave infidelity and sin behind. "'Have I any pleasure in the death of the wicked,' says the Lord God, 'and not rather that he should turn from his way and live?'"[8] These words explain Christ's whole life. They allow us to understand why he has come to us with a heart made of flesh, a heart like ours. This is a convincing proof of his love and a constant witness to the mystery of divine charity.

I must confide to you something which makes me suffer and spurs me on to action: the thought of all those people who do not yet know Christ, who do not even suspect the great good fortune which awaits us in heaven. They live like blind men looking for a joy whose real name they don't know, lost on roads which take

163

[7] Phil 2:7.
[8] Ezek 18:23.

them away from true happiness. How well one understands what Paul the Apostle must have felt that night in Troas when he had a vision in a dream: "A man of Macedonia was standing beseeching him and saying 'Come over to Macedonia and help us.' And when he had seen the vision, immediately we sought to go on to Macedonia, concluding that God had called us to preach the gospel to them."[9]

Don't you also feel that God is calling us? Through the things which happen around us he is urging us to proclaim the good news of the coming of Jesus. Yet sometimes we Christians turn our calling into something very paltry. We become superficial and waste our time in dissension and jealousy. Or, worse still, some people are artificially scandalized by the way others choose to live certain aspects of the faith. Instead of doing all they can to help others, they set out to destroy and criticize. It is true that sometimes you find serious shortcomings in Christians' lives. But the important thing is not ourselves and our shortcomings. The only thing that matters is Jesus. It is Christ we must talk about, not ourselves.

[9] Acts 16:9-10.

These reflections have been provoked by suggestions that there is a crisis in devotion to the sacred heart of Jesus. But there is no crisis. True devotion to the sacred heart has always been and is still truly alive, full of human and supernatural meaning. It has led and still leads to conversion, self-giving, fulfillment of God's will and a loving understanding of the mysteries of the redemption.

However, we must distinguish this genuine devotion from displays of useless sentimentality, a veneer of piety devoid of doctrine. No less than you, I dislike sugary statues, figures of the sacred heart which are incapable of inspiring any trace of devotion in people who have the common sense and supernatural outlook of a Christian. But it is bad logic to turn these particular abuses—which are disappearing anyway—into some sort of doctrinal, theological problem.

If a crisis does exist, it is a crisis in men's hearts. Men are shortsighted, selfish and narrow-minded. They fail to appreciate the great depth of Christ's love for us. Ever since the holy Church instituted today's feast, the liturgy has offered us the nourishment of true piety by including among the readings a text from St

Paul. In it he proposes to us a whole program of contemplative life—knowledge and love, prayer and life—beginning with this devotion to the heart of Jesus. God himself invites us in the Apostle's words to follow this way: "May Christ dwell in your hearts through faith; may you, being rooted and grounded in love, have power to comprehend with all the saints what is the breadth and length and height and depth, and to know the love of Christ which surpasses knowledge, that you may be filled with all the fullness of God."[10]

The fullness of God is revealed and given to us in Christ, in the love of Christ, in Christ's heart. For it is the heart of him in whom "the whole fullness of deity dwells bodily."[11] Were one to lose sight of this great plan of God— the overflow of love in the world through the incarnation, the redemption and Pentecost—he could not understand the refinement with which our Lord deals with us.

---

[10] Eph 3:17-19.
[11] Col 2:9.

TRUE DEVOTION TO THE SACRED HEART

Let us realize all the richness hidden in the 164 words "the sacred heart of Jesus." When we speak of a person's heart, we refer not just to his sentiments, but to the whole person in his loving dealings with others. In order to help us understand divine things, Scripture uses the expression "heart" in its full human meaning, as the summary and source, expression and ultimate basis, of one's thoughts, words, and actions. A man is worth what his heart is worth...

To the heart belongs joy: "let my heart rejoice in your saving help";[12] repentance: "my heart is like wax, it is melted within my breast";[13] praise of God: "my heart overflows with a goodly theme";[14] the decision to listen to the Lord: "my heart is ready, Lord";[15] loving vigilance: "I slept, but my heart was awake";[16] and also doubt and fear: "let not your hearts be troubled, believe in me."[17]

[12] Ps 12:6.
[13] Ps 21:15.
[14] Ps 44:2.
[15] Ps 56:8.
[16] Song 5:2.
[17] Jn 14:1.

The heart not only feels, it knows and understands. God's law is received in the heart[18] and remains written there.[19] Scripture also adds: "Out of the abundance of the heart the mouth speaks."[20] Our Lord reproaches the scribes: "Why do you think evil in your hearts?"[21] And, summing up all the sins man might commit, he says: "Out of the heart come evil thoughts, murder, adultery, fornication, theft, false witness, slander, and blasphemy."[22]

When holy Scripture refers to the heart, it does not refer to some fleeting sentiment of joy or tears. By heart it means the personality which directs its whole being, soul and body, to what it considers its good, as Jesus himself indicated: "For where your treasure is, there will your heart be also."[23]

So when we talk about the heart of Jesus, we stress the certainty of God's love and the truth of his commitment to us. When we recommend devotion to the sacred heart, we are

---

[18] Cf. Ps 39:9.
[19] Cf. Prov 7:3.
[20] Mt 12:34.
[21] Mt 9:4.
[22] Mt 15:19.
[23] Mt 6:21.

recommending that we should give our whole self to Jesus, to the whole Jesus—our soul, our feelings and thoughts, our words and actions, our joys.

That is what true devotion to the heart of Jesus means. It is knowing God and ourselves. It is looking at Jesus and turning to him, letting him encourage and teach and guide us. The only superficiality that could beset this devotion would be due to man's own failure to understand the reality of an incarnate God.

Jesus on the cross, with his heart overflowing with love for men, is such an eloquent commentary on the value of people and things that words only get in the way. Men, their happiness and their life, are so important that the very Son of God gave himself to redeem and cleanse and raise them up. "Who will not love this heart so wounded?" a contemplative asks in this connection. "Who will not return love for love? Who will not embrace a heart so pure? We, who are made of flesh, will repay love with love. We will embrace our wounded one, whose hands and feet ungodly men have nailed; we will cling to his side and to his heart. Let us pray that we be worthy of linking our heart with his love and of wounding it with a lance, for it is still hard and impenitent."[24]

These are thoughts, affections, and conversations which souls in love with Jesus have offered him from the beginning. But if we are to understand this language, if we are really to know the heart of man, Christ's heart and the love of God, we need both faith and humility. We need the faith and humility that prompted St Augustine to write: "You have made us for you, O Lord, and restless will our heart be until it rests in you."[25]

If a man is not humble, he will try to make God his own, but not in the divine way which Christ made possible when he said: "Take, eat; this is my body."[26] The proud man tries to confine the grandeur of God within human limits. Then reason, the cold, blind reason that is so different from the mind imbued with faith and even from the well-directed mind of someone capable of enjoying and loving things, becomes irrational in a person's attempt to reduce everything to his cramped human

[24] St Bonaventure, *Vitis mystica*, 3, 11 (PL 184, 643).
[25] *Confessiones*, 1, 1, 1 (PL 32, 661).
[26] 1 Cor 11:24.

experience. Thus is superhuman truth impoverished, and man's heart develops a crust that makes it insensitive to the action of the Holy Spirit. Our limited intelligence would be completely at a loss then if the merciful power of God did not break down the barriers of our wretchedness. "A new heart I will give you, and a new spirit I will put within you; and I will take out of your flesh your heart of stone and give you a heart of flesh."[27] Only with God's help will the soul see again and be filled with joy on hearing the promises of sacred Scripture.

"I know the plans I have for you, plans for peace and not affliction"[28] was God's promise through Jeremiah. The liturgy applies these words to Jesus, for in him we are clearly shown that God does love us in this way. He did not come to condemn us, to accuse us of meanness and smallness. He came to save us, pardon us, excuse us, bring us peace and joy. If only we realize the wonderful way in which God deals with his children, our hearts *must* change. We will see opening up before us an absolutely new panorama, full of relief, depth, and light.

[27] Ezek 36:26.
[28] Jer 29:11.

BRINGING OTHERS TO CHRIST'S LOVE

166   But note that God does not say: "In exchange
         for your own heart, I will give you a will of
         pure spirit." No, he gives us a heart, a human
         heart, like Christ's. I don't have one heart for
         loving God and another for loving people. I
         love Christ and the Father and the Holy Spirit
         and our Lady with the same heart with which
         I love my parents and my friends. I shall never
         tire of repeating this. We must be very human,
         for otherwise we cannot be divine.

         Human love, the love we experience on
         earth when it is really genuine, helps us to
         savor divine love. That is how we grasp the
         love by which we rejoice in God and which we
         will share in heaven when the Lord is "every-
         thing to everyone."[29] If we begin to understand
         God's love, we will feel impelled to become
         increasingly more compassionate, more gener-
         ous, more dedicated.

         We must give what we receive, we must
         teach what we learn. Very simply, without any
         kind of conceit, we must help others to share
         in the knowledge of God's love. As you go

---

[29] 1 Cor 15:28.

about your work, doing your job in society, each of you can and should turn your occupation into a real service. Your work should be done well, mindful of others' needs, taking advantage of all advances in technology and culture. Such work fulfills a very important function and is useful to the whole of humanity, if it is motivated by generosity, not selfishness, and directed to the welfare of all, not our own advantage, if it is filled with the Christian sense of life.

Through your work, through the whole network of human relations, you ought to show the charity of Christ and its concrete expression in friendship, understanding, human affection, and peace. Just as Christ "went about doing good"[30] throughout Palestine, so must you also spread peace in your family circle, in civil society, in your work, and in your cultural and leisure activities. This will be the best proof that the kingdom of God has reached your heart. As St John wrote: "We know that we have passed out of death into life, because we love the brethren."[31]

[30] Acts 10:38.
[31] 1 Jn 3:14.

But no one can live out this love unless he is taught in the school of the heart of Jesus. Only if we watch and contemplate the heart of Jesus will we ensure that our heart is freed from hatred and indifference. Only in this way will we know how to react as Christians to the pain and sufferings of others.

Do you remember the scene St Luke depicts when Jesus is approaching Naim?[32] Jesus crosses paths again with a crowd of people. He could have passed by or waited until they called him. But he didn't. He took the initiative, because he was moved by a widow's sorrow. She had just lost all she had, her son.

The evangelist explains that Jesus was moved. Perhaps he even showed signs of it, as when Lazarus died. Jesus Christ was not, and is not, insensitive to the suffering that stems from love. He is pained at seeing children separated from their parents. He overcomes death so as to give life, to reunite those who love one another. But at the same time, he requires that we first admit the pre-eminence of divine love, which alone can inspire genuine Christian living.

[32] Lk 7:11-17.

Christ knows he is surrounded by a crowd which will be awed by the miracle and will tell the story all over the countryside. But he does not act artificially, merely to make an effect. Quite simply he is touched by that woman's suffering and cannot keep from consoling her. So he goes up to her and says, "Do not weep."[33] It is like saying: "I don't want to see you crying; I have come on earth to bring joy and peace." And then comes the miracle, the sign of the power of Christ who is God. But first came his compassion, an evident sign of the tenderness of the heart of Christ the man.

If we don't learn from Jesus, we will never 167 love. If, like some people, we were to think that to keep a clean heart, a heart worthy of God, means "not mixing it up, not contaminating it" with human affection, we would become insensitive to other people's pain and sorrow. We would be capable only of an "official charity," something dry and soulless. But ours would not be the true charity of Jesus Christ, which involves affection and human warmth. In saying this, I am not supporting the mistaken

---

[33] Lk 7:13.

theories—pitiful excuses—which misdirect
hearts away from God and lead them into
occasions of sin and perdition.

On today's feast we should ask our Lord to
give us a good heart, capable of having
compassion for other people's pain. Only with
such a heart can we realize that the true balm
for the suffering and anguish in this world is
love, charity. All other consolations hardly even
have a temporary effect and leave behind them
bitterness and despair.

If we want to help others, we must love
them—I insist—with a love clothed in understanding, dedication, affection, and voluntary
humility. Then we will understand why our
Lord summed up the whole law in that double
commandment, which is really just one: love of
God, and love of one's neighbor, with all our
heart.[34]

Maybe you are thinking that sometimes
Christians—not just other people, you and I—
forget the most elementary applications of this
duty. Perhaps you bring to mind all the injustices which cry for redress, all the abuses which
go uncorrected, the discrimination passed on

[34] Cf. Mt 22:40.

from one generation to the next with no attempt to find permanent solutions.

I cannot propose to you a particular way to solve problems of this kind, there is no reason why I should. But, as a priest of Jesus Christ, it is my duty to remind you of what sacred Scripture says. Meditate on the scene of the judgment which Jesus himself has described: "Depart from me, you cursed, into the eternal fire prepared for the devil and his angels; for I was hungry and you gave me no food; I was thirsty and you gave me no drink; naked and you did not clothe me; sick and in prison and you did not visit me."[35]

A man or a society that does not react to suffering and injustice and makes no effort to alleviate them is still distant from the love of Christ's heart. While Christians enjoy the fullest freedom in finding and applying various solutions to these problems, they should be united in having one and the same desire to serve mankind. Otherwise their Christianity will not be the word and life of Jesus; it will be a fraud, a deception of God and man.

[35] Mt 25:41-43.

THE PEACE CHRIST BRINGS

168   But I have still a further consideration to put before you. We have to fight vigorously to do good, precisely because it is difficult for us men to resolve seriously to be just, and there is a long way to go before human relations are inspired by love and not hatred or indifference. We should also be aware that even if we achieve a reasonable distribution of wealth and a harmonious organization of society, there will still be the suffering of illness, of misunderstanding, of loneliness, of the death of loved ones, of the experience of our own limitations.

Faced with the weight of all this, a Christian can find only one genuine answer, a definitive answer: Christ on the cross, a God who suffers and dies, a God who gives us his heart opened by a lance for the love of us all. Our Lord abominates injustice and condemns those who commit it. But he respects the freedom of each individual. He permits injustice to happen because, as a result of original sin, it is part and parcel of the human condition. Yet his heart is full of love for men. Our suffering, our sadness, our anguish, our hunger and thirst for justice...

he took all these tortures on himself by means of the cross.

Christian teaching on pain is not a series of facile considerations. It is, in the first place, a call to accept the suffering inseparable from all human life. I cannot hide from you the fact that there has often been pain in my life and more than once I have wanted to cry. I tell you this joyfully, because I have always preached and tried to live the truth that Christ, who is love, is to be found on the cross. At other times, I have felt a great revulsion to injustice and evil, and I have fought against the frustration of not being able to do anything—despite my desire and my effort—to remedy those unjust situations.

When I speak to you about suffering, I am not just talking theory. Nor do I limit myself to other people's experience when I tell you that the remedy is to look at Christ, if when faced with suffering, you at some time feel that your soul is wavering. The scene of Calvary proclaims to everyone that afflictions have to be sanctified, that we are to live united to the cross.

If we bear our difficulties as Christians, they are turned into reparation and atonement. They give us a share in Jesus' destiny and in his life.

Out of love for men he volunteered to experience the whole gamut of pain and torment. He was born, lived and died poor. He was attacked, insulted, defamed, slandered, and unjustly condemned. He knew treachery and abandonment by his disciples. He experienced isolation and the bitterness of punishment and death. And now the same Christ is suffering in his members, in all of humanity spread throughout the earth, whose head and firstborn and redeemer he is.

Suffering is part of God's plans. This is the truth, however difficult it may be for us to understand it. It was difficult for Jesus Christ the man to undergo his passion: "Father, if you are willing, remove this cup from me; nevertheless not my will, but yours be done."[36] In this tension of pleading and acceptance of the Father's will, Jesus goes calmly to his death, pardoning those who crucify him.

This supernatural acceptance of suffering was, precisely, the greatest of all conquests. By dying on the cross Jesus overcame death. God brings life from death. The attitude of a child of God is not one of resignation to a possibly

---

[36] Lk 22:42.

tragic fate; it is the sense of achievement of someone who has a foretaste of victory. In the name of this victorious love of Christ, we Christians should go out into the world to be sowers of peace and joy through everything we say and do. We have to fight—a fight of peace—against evil, against injustice, against sin. Thus do we serve notice that the present condition of mankind is not definitive. Only the love of God, shown in the heart of Christ, will attain the glorious spiritual triumph of men.

Previously we referred to what happened at 169 Naim. We could recall other examples, for the Gospel is full of such scenes. Each incident reveals not only the sincere gesture of a man who suffers when his friends suffer, but above all the immense charity of our Lord. Jesus' heart is the heart of God made flesh, the heart of Emmanuel, God with us.

"The Church, united to Christ, is born of a wounded heart."[37] From this heart, opened wide, life is transmitted to us. Here we must, even if only in passing, recall the sacraments through which God works in us and makes us sharers in the redeeming strength of Christ.

[37] Hymn, vigil of the feast of the Sacred Heart.

glory. Mary is present at the mysteries surrounding the infancy of her son, but these are
"normal" mysteries, so to speak. When the
great miracles take place and the crowds
acclaim them in amazement, she is nowhere to
be found. In Jerusalem when Christ, riding a
little donkey, is proclaimed king, we don't catch
a glimpse of Mary. But after all have fled, she
reappears next to the cross. This way of acting
bespeaks personal greatness and depth, the
sanctity of her soul.

Following her example of obedience to God,
we can learn to serve delicately without being
slavish. In Mary, we don't find the slightest
trace of the attitude of the foolish virgins, who
obey, but thoughtlessly. Our Lady listens attentively to what God wants, ponders what she
doesn't fully understand and asks about what
she doesn't know. Then she gives herself
completely to doing the divine will: "Behold the
handmaid of the Lord, be it done unto me
according to your word."[14] Isn't that marvelous? The blessed Virgin, our teacher in all
we do, shows us here that obedience to God
is not servile, does not bypass our conscience.

[14] Lk 1:38.

We should be inwardly moved to discover the "freedom of the children of God."[15]

THE SCHOOL OF PRAYER

The Lord will grant you the ability to 174 discover many other aspects of the faithful response to grace of the blessed Virgin. And to know these facets of her life is to want to imitate them: her purity, her humility, her fortitude, her generosity, her fidelity.... But now I want to speak to you of an aspect that in a way encompasses all the others because it is a condition for spiritual growth. I'm speaking of her life of prayer.

To take advantage of the grace which our mother offers us today and to second at any time the inspirations of the Holy Spirit, the shepherd of our souls, we ought to be seriously committed to dealing with God. We cannot take refuge in the anonymous crowd. If interior life doesn't involve personal encounter with God, it doesn't exist—it's as simple as that. There are few things more at odds

[15] Cf. Rom 8:21.

with Christianity than superficiality. To settle down to routine in our Christian life is to dismiss the possibility of becoming a contemplative soul. God seeks us out, one by one. And we ought to answer him, one by one: "Here I am, Lord, because you have called me."[16]

We all know that prayer is to talk to God. But someone may ask, "What should I talk about?" What else could you talk about but his interests and the things that fill your day? About the birth of Jesus, his years among us, his hidden life, his preaching, his miracles, his redemptive passion and death, his resurrection. And in the presence of the Triune God, invoking Mary as our mediatrix and beseeching St Joseph, our father and lord, to be our advocate, we will speak of our everyday work, of our family, of our friendships, of our big plans and little shortcomings.

The theme of my prayer is the theme of my life. That's the way I speak to God. As I consider my situation, there comes to mind a specific and firm resolution to change, to improve, to be more docile to the love of God.

[16] 1 Kings 3:5.

It should be a sincere and concrete resolution. And we cannot forget to ask the Holy Spirit, with as much urgency as confidence, not to abandon us, because "you, Lord, are my strength."[17]

We are ordinary Christians. We work at the most varied professions. All our activity takes place amid everyday circumstances. Everything follows a customary rhythm in our lives. The days seem the same, even monotonous. But don't forget that our condition which is apparently so common has a divine value. God is interested in everything we do, because Christ wishes to become incarnate in our things, to vivify from within even our most insignificant actions.

This thought is a clear, objective, supernatural reality. It is not a pious consideration to comfort those of us who will never get our names inscribed in the annals of history. Christ is interested in the work we do—whether once or thousands of times—in the office, in the factory, in the shop, in the classroom, in the fields, in the exercise of any manual or intellectual occupation. He is likewise interested in

[17] Ps 42:2.

the hidden sacrifices we make to keep our bad
humor or temper to ourselves.

Review in your prayer these thoughts. Take
occasion of them to tell Jesus that you adore
him. And thus you have a formula to become
contemplatives in the middle of the world,
amid the noises of the street, at all times and
in all places. This is the first lesson we should
learn in the school of intimacy with Christ. And
in this school, Mary is the best teacher, because
the Virgin always kept this attitude of faith, of
supernatural vision, regardless of what happened around her: "and his mother kept all
these words in her heart."[18]

Let us ask the blessed Virgin to make us
contemplatives, to teach us to recognize the
constant calls from God at the door of our heart.
Let us ask her now: Our mother, you brought
to earth Jesus, who reveals the love of our
Father God. Help us to recognize him in the
midst of the cares of each day. Stir up our mind
and will so that we may listen to the voice of
God, to the calls of grace.

[18] Lk 2:51.

TEACHER OF APOSTLES

But let's not think only of ourselves. Ex- 175
pand your heart until it takes in all mankind.
Above all, think of those near you—relatives,
friends, colleagues—and see how you can get
them to appreciate a deeper friendship with
our Lord. If they are upright and noble, capable of being habitually close to God, commend
them specifically to our Lady. And ask also
for all those souls you don't know, because
we have embarked together on a single voy-
age.

Be loyal, generous. We form part of a single
body, the mystical body of Christ, the holy
Church, to which are called those who seek the
whole truth. Consequently, we are strictly
obliged to manifest to others the quality and
depth of the love of Christ. A Christian cannot
be selfish. If he were, he would betray his
vocation. Far from Christ are those content with
keeping their soul in peace—and a false peace
at that—while ignoring the good of others.

If we have accepted the authentic meaning
of human life, which is revealed to us in faith,
we cannot remain peacefully on the sidelines.
If in a practical and concrete way we aren't

serve all men, is none other than the fullness of faith, hope, and love. In a word: sanctity. I can find no other prescription than personal sanctity.

Today, in union with the whole Church, we celebrate the triumph of the Mother, Daughter, and Spouse of God. And just as we rejoiced at the resurrection of our Lord three days after his death, we are now happy that Mary, after accompanying Jesus from Bethlehem to the cross, is next to her Son in body and soul, glorious forever.

Behold the mystery of the divine economy. Our Lady, a full participant in the work of our salvation, follows in the footsteps of her Son: the poverty of Bethlehem, the everyday work of a hidden life in Nazareth, the manifestation of his divinity in Cana of Galilee, the tortures of his passion, the divine sacrifice on the cross, the eternal blessedness of paradise.

All of this affects us directly, because this supernatural itinerary is the way we are to follow. Mary shows us that we can walk this path with confidence. She has preceded us on the way of imitating Christ; her glorification is the firm hope of our own salvation. For these reasons we call her "our hope, cause of our joy."

We can never lose hope of becoming holy, of accepting the invitations of God, of persevering until the very end. God, who has begun in us the work of our sanctification, will bring it to completion.[23] Because if the Lord "is with us, who can be against us? After having not spared his very own Son, but rather turned him over to death for us, after having thus given us his Son, can he fail to give us every good thing?"[24]

On this feast, everything points to joy. The firm hope of our personal sanctification is a gift from God, but man cannot remain passive. Remember the words of Christ: "If anyone would come after me, let him deny himself, take up his daily cross and follow me."[25] Do you see? The *daily* cross. No day without a cross; not a single day in which we are not to carry the cross of the Lord, in which we are not to accept his yoke. Let this opportunity serve to remind us again that the joy of the

[23] Cf. Phil 1:6.
[24] Rom 8:31-32.
[25] Lk 9:23.

resurrection is a consequence of the suffering of the cross.

But don't fear. Our Lord himself has told us, "Come unto me all you who are burdened and labor, for I will give you rest. Take my yoke upon you and learn from me, for I am meek and humble of heart, and you will find rest for your souls. For my yoke is sweet and my burden light."[26] And St John Chrysostom comments: "Come, not to give an account but to be freed of your sins. Come, because I don't need the glory you can give me: I need your salvation.... Don't fear if you hear me talk of a yoke, it is sweet; don't fear if I speak about a burden, it is light."[27]

The way to our personal sanctification should daily lead us to the cross. This way is not a sorrowful one, because Christ himself comes to our aid, and in his company there is no room for sadness. I like to repeat with my soul filled with joy, there is not a single day without a cross—the Cross.

[26] Mt 11:28-30.
[27] In Matthaeum homiliae, 37, 2 (PG 57, 414).

CHRISTIAN JOY

Let us pick up again the subject proposed 177
to us by the Church: Mary has gone to heaven
in both body and soul, and the angels rejoice.
I can imagine, too, the delight of St Joseph,
her most chaste spouse, who awaited her in
paradise. Yet what of us who remain on earth?
Our faith tells us that here below, in our
present life, we are pilgrims, wayfarers. Our
lot is one of sacrifices, suffering, and priva-
tions. Nonetheless, joy must mark the rhythm
of our steps.

"Serve the Lord with joy"[28]—there is no
other way to serve him. "God loves a cheerful
giver,"[29] the man who gives himself entirely
with wholehearted sacrifice, because there is
absolutely no reason to be disheartened.

We could think perhaps that this optimism
is excessive. Are we not well acquainted with
our shortcomings and failures? We are no
strangers to suffering, tiredness, ingratitude,
even hate. If we Christians are made of the
same stuff as other men, how can we shake off

[28] Ps 99:2.
[29] 2 Cor 9:7.

the retinue of misery that constantly accompanies our human nature?

It would be naive to ignore the suffering and discouragement, the sadness and loneliness that meet us relentlessly as we go through life. But our faith has taught us with absolute certainty to see that life's disagreeable side is not due to blind fate, that the destiny of the creature is not to rid himself of his desires for happiness. Faith teaches us that everything around and in us is impregnated with divine purpose, that all things echo the call beckoning us to the house of our Father.

This supernatural understanding of earthly existence does not oversimplify the complexity of human life. Rather, it assures us that this complexity can be shot through with the love of God, that beyond the disagreeable surface can be discovered the strong and indestructible link that binds our life on earth to our definitive life in heaven.

The feast of the assumption of our Lady prompts us to acknowledge the basis for this joyful hope. Yes, we are still pilgrims, but our mother has gone on ahead, where she points to the reward of our efforts. She tells us that we can make it. And, if we are faithful, we will reach home. The blessed Virgin is not only our model, she is the help of Christians. And as we besiege her with our petitions—"Show that you are our Mother"[30]—she cannot help but watch over her children with motherly care.

For a Christian, joy is a treasure. Only by offending God do we lose it, because sin is the fruit of selfishness, and selfishness is the root of sadness. Even then, a bit of joy survives under the debris of our soul: the knowledge that neither God nor his Mother can ever forget us. If we repent, if an act of sorrow springs from our heart, if we purify ourselves in the holy sacrament of penance, God comes out to meet and forgive us. Then there can be no sadness whatsoever. Then there is every right "to rejoice, because your brother was dead and has come back to life, was lost and has been found."[31]

These words are taken from the marvelous ending of the parable of the prodigal son, which we shall never tire of meditating. "Behold [the Father] comes out to meet you. He will bend down to greet you. He will give you a kiss as

[30] Hymn Ave Maris Stella: Monstra te esse Matrem.
[31] Lk 15:32.

a sign of love and tenderness. He will order the servants to bring you new clothing, a ring, shoes for your feet. You still fear reproach and he returns your dignity. You fear punishment and he gives you a kiss. You dread a harsh word and he prepares for you a banquet."[32]

The love of God is unfathomable. If he is so generous with those who have offended him, what won't he do to honor his immaculate Mother, the most holy Virgin, faithful always?

If the love of God can achieve such great results when the response from our human heart, which is frequently a traitor, is so small, how much more will it accomplish in the heart of Mary, who never resisted in the slightest the will of God?

See how the liturgy of today's feast reveals the impossibility of understanding divine mercy by human reasons alone. More than explaining, the liturgy sings. It arouses the imagination, so that each of us can add enthusiasm to praise. Yet, when all is said and done, we will fall short. "A great marvel appeared in the heaven: a woman, dressed with the sun,

[32] St Ambrose, *Expositio Evangelii secundum Lucam*, 7 (PL 15, 1540).

with the moon at her feet, and on her head a crown of twelve stars."[33] "The king has fallen in love with your beauty. How resplendent is the daughter of the king, with her robe spun from gold!"[34]

The liturgy draws to a close with some words of Mary, in which the greatest humility is combined with the greatest glory: "All generations shall call me blessed, because he who is mighty has done great things in me."[35]

Cor Mariae Dulcissimum, iter para tutum: Most Sweet Heart of Mary, prepare a safe way. Guide our steps on earth with strength and security. Become for us the path we are to follow, since you in your love know the way, a sure short-cut, to the love of Jesus Christ.

[33] Rev 12:1.
[34] Ps 44:12-14.
[35] Lk 1:48-49.

CHRIST THE KING*

The liturgical year is coming to a close and in the holy sacrifice of the altar we renew the offering of the victim to the Father—the offering of Christ, the king of justice, love, and peace, as we shall read shortly in the preface.[1] You all experience a great joy in your souls as you consider the sacred humanity of our Lord. He is a king with a heart of flesh, like yours; he is the author of the universe and of every creature, but he does not lord it over us. He begs us to give him a little love, as he silently shows us his wounds.

Why then do so many people not know him? Why do we still hear that cruel protest: "We do not want this man to reign over us"?[2] There

---

* A homily given on November 22, 1970, the feast of Christ the King.

[1] ...*regnum sanctitatis et gratiae, regnum iustitiae, amoris et pacis*, preface of the Mass.

[2] Lk 19:14: *Nolumus hunc regnare super nos.*

are millions of people in the world who reject Jesus Christ in this way; or rather they reject his shadow, for they do not know Christ. They have not seen the beauty of his face, they do not realize how wonderful his teaching is. This sad state of affairs makes me want to atone to our Lord. When I hear that endless clamor—expressed more in ignoble actions than in words—I feel the need to cry out, "He must reign!"[3]

OPPOSITION TO CHRIST

Many people will not accept that Christ should reign. They oppose him in thousands of ways: in their attitude toward their circumstances, in their approach to human society, in morality, in science and the arts. Even in the Church itself! "I am not referring," says St Augustine, "to those scoundrels who blaspheme against Christ with their tongues. There are very many who blaspheme against him through their own conduct."[4]

[3] 1 Cor 15:25: *Oportet illum regnare.*
[4] *In Ioannis Evangelium tractatus,* 27, II (PL 35, 1621).

Some people are even annoyed by the expression "Christ the king." They take naïve objection to the word, as if Christ's kingship could be thought of in political terms. Or they refuse to admit that Christ is king, because that would involve accepting his law. And law they will not accept, not even the wonderful precept of charity, for they do not want to reach out to God's love. Their ambition is to serve their own selfishness.

For many years now, our Lord has urged me to repeat a silent cry, *Serviam:* "I will serve!" Let us ask him to strengthen our desire to give ourselves, to be faithful to his calling—with naturalness, without fuss or noise—in the middle of everyday life. Let us thank him from the depth of our heart. We will pray to him as his subjects, as his sons! And our mouth will be filled with milk and honey. We will find great pleasure in speaking of the kingdom of God, a kingdom of freedom, a freedom he has won for us.[5]

[5] Cf. Gal 4:31.

THE LORD OF THE WORLD

180   This Christ, whose birth we witnessed at Bethlehem, this adorable child, is the Lord of the universe. Let us meditate upon this fact. Everything in heaven and on earth was created by him. He has reconciled all things to the Father. He has re-established peace between heaven and earth through the blood he shed on the cross.[6] Today Christ is king, at the right hand of the Father. As the two angels in white robes said to the disciples who were gazing into heaven after our Lord's ascension: "Men of Galilee, why do you stand looking into heaven? This Jesus, who was taken up from you into heaven, will come in the same way as you saw him go into heaven."[7] Through him kings hold power,[8] although kings—that is, human political authority—do not last. Yet the kingdom of Christ "will remain forever."[9] "His is an ever-lasting dominion and his kingdom endures from generation to generation."[10]

[6] Cf. Col 1:11-16.
[7] Acts 1:11.
[8] Cf. Prov 8:15.
[9] Ex 15:18.
[10] Dan 4:34.

Christ's kingdom is not just a figure of speech. Christ is alive; he lives as a man, with the same body he took when he became man, when he rose after his death, the glorified body which subsists in the person of the Word together with his human heart. Christ, true God and true man, lives and reigns. He is the Lord of the universe. Everything that lives is kept in existence only through him. Why, then, does he not appear to us in all his glory? Because his kingdom is "not of this world"[11] though it is *in* this world. Jesus replied to Pilate: "I am a king. For this I was born and for this I have come into the world, to bear witness to the truth. Everyone who is of the truth hears my voice."[12] Those who expected the Messiah to have visible temporal power were mistaken. "The kingdom of God does not mean food and drink but righteousness and peace and joy in the Holy Spirit."[13] Truth and justice, peace and joy in the Holy Spirit. That is the kingdom of Christ: the divine activity which saves men and which will reach its culmination when history

[11] Jn 18:36.
[12] Jn 18:37.
[13] Rom 14:17.

ends and the Lord comes from the heights of paradise finally to judge men.

When Christ began to preach on earth he did not put forward a political program. He said: "Repent, for the kingdom of God is at hand."[14] He commissioned his disciples to proclaim this good news[15] and he taught them to pray for the coming of the kingdom.[16] The kingdom of God and his justice—a holy life: that is what we must first seek,[17] that is the only thing really necessary.[18]

The salvation which our Lord Jesus Christ preaches is an invitation which he addresses to every person: "A king gave a marriage feast for his son, and he sent his servants to call those who were invited to the marriage feast."[19] Therefore, our Lord shows that "the kingdom of God is in the midst of you."[20] No one is excluded from salvation, if he responds freely to the loving demands of Christ: to be born again;[21] to become like children, in simplicity of spirit;[22] to avoid everything which separates

---

[14] Mt 3:2; 4:17.
[15] Cf. Lk 10:9.
[16] Cf. Mt 6:10.
[17] Cf. Mt 6:33.
[18] Cf. Lk 10:42.

[19] Mt 22:2-3.
[20] Lk 17:21.
[21] Cf. Jn 3:5.
[22] Cf. Mk 10:15;
    Mt 18:3; 5:3.

us from God.[23] Jesus wants deeds, not just words.[24] And he wants us to make a determined effort, because only those who fight will merit the eternal inheritance.[25]

His kingdom will not achieve its perfection on earth. The definitive judgment of salvation or condemnation will not be made here. It is rather like sowing seed,[26] like the growth of the grain of mustard seed.[27] At its finish it will be like the net full of fish—they are all thrown out on the sand and sorted into those who led a just life and those who did evil.[28] But as long as we live here the kingdom can be compared to yeast which a woman took and mixed with three measures of flour so that the whole batch was leavened.[29]

Anyone who understands the kingdom Christ proposes realizes that it is worth staking everything to obtain it. It is the pearl the

[23] "Truly I say to you, it will be hard for a rich man to enter the kingdom of heaven" (Mt 19:23).

[24] Cf. Mt 7:21.

[25] "The kingdom of heaven has suffered violence, and men of violence take it by force" (Mt 11:12).

[26] Cf. Mt 13:24.

[27] Cf. Mt 13:31-32.

[28] Cf. Mt 13:47.

[29] Cf. Mt 13:33.

merchant gets by selling all his property; it is the treasure found in the field.[30] The kingdom of heaven is difficult to win. No one can be sure of achieving it,[31] but the humble cry of a repentant man can open wide its doors. One of the thieves who was crucified with Jesus pleaded with him: "Lord, remember me when you come into your kingdom." And Jesus said to him, "Truly, I say to you, today you will be with me in paradise."[32]

HIS REIGN IN OUR SOUL

181 Our Lord and our God: how great you are! It is you who give our life supernatural meaning and divine vitality. For love of your Son, you cause us to say with all our being, with our body and soul: "He must reign!" And this we do against the background of our weakness, for you know that we are creatures made of clay[33]—and what creatures! Not just feet of clay,

---

[30] Cf. Mt 13:44-46.
[31] Cf. Mt 21:43; 8:12.
[32] Lk 23:42-43.
[33] Cf. Dan 2:33.

but heart and head too. Only through you can we live a divine life.

Christ should reign first and foremost in our soul. But how would we reply if he asked us: "How do you go about letting me reign in you?" I would reply that I need lots of his grace. Only that way can my every heartbeat and breath, my least intense look, my most ordinary word, my most basic feeling be transformed into a hosanna to Christ my king.

If we are trying to have Christ as our king we must be consistent. We must start by giving him our heart. Not to do that and still talk about the kingdom of Christ would be completely hollow. There would be no real Christian substance in our behavior. We would be making an outward show of a faith which simply did not exist. We would be misusing God's name to human advantage.

If Jesus' reign in my soul, in your soul, meant that he should find it a perfect dwelling place, then indeed would we have reason to despair. But "fear not, daughter of Sion; behold, your king is coming, sitting on an ass' colt."[34] Don't you see? Jesus makes do with a poor

[34] Jn 12:15.

animal for a throne. I don't know about you; but I am not humiliated to acknowledge that in the Lord's eyes I am a beast of burden: "I am like a donkey in your presence, but I am continually with you. You hold my right hand,"[35] you take me by the bridle.

Try to remember what a donkey is like— now that so few of them are left. Not an old, stubborn, vicious one that would give you a kick when you least expected, but a young one with his ears up like antennae. He lives on a meager diet, is hardworking and has a quick, cheerful trot. There are hundreds of animals more beautiful, more deft and strong. But it was a donkey Christ chose when he presented himself to the people as king in response to their acclamation. For Jesus has no time for calculations, for astuteness, for the cruelty of cold hearts, for attractive but empty beauty. What he likes is the cheerfulness of a young heart, a simple step, a natural voice, clean eyes, attention to his affectionate word of advice. That is how he reigns in the soul.

[35] Ps 72:23-24.

TO REIGN BY SERVING

If we let Christ reign in our soul, we will 182
not become authoritarian. Rather we will serve
everyone. How I like that word: service! To
serve my king and, through him, all those who
have been redeemed by his blood. I really wish
we Christians knew how to serve, for only by
serving can we know and love Christ and make
him known and loved. And how will we show
him to souls? By our example. Through our
voluntary service of Jesus Christ, we should be
witnesses to him in all our activities, for he is
the Lord of our entire lives, the only and
ultimate reason for our existence. Then, once we
have given this witness of service, we will be
able to give instruction by our word. That was
how Christ acted. "He began to do and to
teach";[36] he first taught by his action, and then
by his divine preaching.

If we are to serve others, for Christ's sake,
we need to be very human. If our life is less
than human, God will not build anything on
it, for he normally does not build on disorder,
selfishness or emptiness. We have to under-

---

[36] Acts 1:1: *Coepit facere et docere.*

stand everyone; we must live peaceably with everyone; we must forgive everyone. We shall not call injustice justice; we shall not say that an offense against God is not an offense against God, or that evil is good. When confronted by evil we shall not reply with another evil, but rather with sound doctrine and good actions: drowning evil in an abundance of good.[37] That's how Christ will reign in our souls and in the souls of the people around us.

Some people try to build peace in the world without putting love of God into their own hearts. How could they possibly achieve peace in that way? The peace of Christ is the peace of the kingdom of Christ; and our Lord's kingdom has to be based on a desire for holiness, a humble readiness to receive grace, an effort to establish justice, a divine outpouring of love.

CHRIST AT THE CENTER OF HUMAN ACTIVITIES

183   This can be done; it is not an empty dream. If only we men would decide to receive the love

[37] Cf. Rom 12:21.

of God into our hearts! Christ our Lord was crucified; from the height of the cross he redeemed the world, thereby restoring peace between God and men. Jesus reminds all of us: "And I, if I be lifted up from the earth, I will draw all things to myself."[38] If you put me at the center of all earthly activities, he is saying, by fulfilling the duty of each moment, in what appears important and what appears unimportant, I will draw everything to myself. My kingdom among you will be a reality!

Christ our Lord still wants to save men and the whole of creation—this world of ours which is good, for so it came from God's hands. It was Adam's offense, the sin of human pride, which broke the divine harmony of creation. But God the Father, in the fullness of time, sent his only-begotten Son to take flesh in Mary ever Virgin, through the Holy Spirit, and re-establish peace. In this way, by redeeming man from sin, "we receive adoption as sons."[39] We become capable of sharing the intimacy of God. In this way the new man, the new line of the children of God,[40]

---

[38] Jn 12:32: *Et ego, si exaltatus fuero a terra, omnia traham ad meipsum.*

[39] Gal 4:5: *Adoptionem filiorum reciperemus.*

[40] Cf. Rom 6:4-5.

is enabled to free the whole universe from disorder, restoring all things in Christ, [41] as they have been reconciled with God.[42]

That is the calling of Christians, that is our apostolic task, the desire which should consume our soul: to make this kingdom of Christ a reality, to eliminate hatred and cruelty, to spread throughout the earth the strong and soothing balm of love. Let us ask our king today to make us collaborate, humbly and fervently, in the divine task of mending what is broken, of saving what is lost, of fixing what man has put out of order, of bringing to his destination whoever has gone off the right road, of reconstructing the harmony of all created things.

Embracing the Christian faith means committing oneself to continuing Jesus Christ's mission among men. We must, each of us, be *alter Christus, ipse Christus*: another Christ, Christ himself. Only in this way can we set about this great undertaking, this immense, unending task of sanctifying all temporal structures from within, bringing to them the leaven of redemption.

[41] Cf. Eph 1:9-10.
[42] Cf. Col 1:20.

I never talk politics. I do not approve of committed Christians in the world forming a political-religious movement. That would be madness, even if it were motivated by a desire to spread the spirit of Christ in all the activities of men. What we have to do is put God in the heart of every single person, no matter who he is. Let us try to speak then in such a way that every Christian is able to bear witness to the faith he professes by example and word in his own circumstances, which are determined alike by his place in the Church and in civil life, as well as by ongoing events.

By the very fact of being a man, a Christian has a full right to live in the world. If he lets Christ live and reign in his heart, he will feel— quite noticeably—the saving effectiveness of our Lord in everything he does. It does not matter what his occupation is, whether his social status is "high" or "low"; for what appears to us to be an important achievement can be very low in God's sight; and what we call low or modest can in Christian terms be a summit of holiness and service.

PERSONAL FREEDOM

184   When he does his work, a Christian is
obliged not to side-step or play down the values
that earthly things have in themselves. If the
expression "bless all human activities" meant
abusing or neglecting their intrinsic qualities I
would never use such a phrase. Personally I
have never been convinced that the ordinary
activities of men should carry a placard or
confessional label. Although I respect the
opposite opinion, I feel that using such a label
involves a risk of using the holy name of our
faith in vain. And there is evidence of the label
"catholic" being used to justify activities and
behavior which sometimes are not even de-
cently human.

The world and all that it contains, except for
sin, is good because it is made by God our Lord.
Therefore, a Christian who fights continuously
to avoid offending God—fighting in a positive
way, out of love—has to devote himself to all
earthly tasks, shoulder to shoulder with other
citizens. He must defend all the values which
derive from human dignity.

But there is one value which he must
particularly cherish: personal freedom. Only if

he defends the individual freedom of others—
with the personal responsibility that must go
with it—only then can he defend his own with
human and Christian integrity. I will keep on
repeating that our Lord has gratuitously given
us a great supernatural gift, divine grace, and
another wonderful human gift, personal freedom. To avoid this degenerating into license,
we must develop integrity, we must make a real
effort to conform our behavior to divine law,
for where the Spirit is, there you find freedom.[43]

The kingdom of Christ is a kingdom of
freedom. In it the only slaves are those who
freely bind themselves, out of love of God.
What a blessed slavery of love, that sets us free!
Without freedom, we cannot respond to grace.
Without freedom, we cannot give ourselves
freely to our Lord, for the most supernatural
of reasons, *because we want to.*

Some of you listening to me have known me
for a long time. You can bear out that I have
spent my whole life preaching personal freedom, with personal responsibility. I have
sought freedom throughout the world and I'm
still looking for it, just like Diogenes trying to

[43] 2 Cor 3:17.

find an honest man. And every day I love it more. Of all the things on earth, I love it most. It is a treasure which we do not appreciate nearly enough.

When I talk about personal freedom, I am not using it as an excuse to discuss other very legitimate questions which are not of my competence as a priest. I know that it is not proper for me to discuss secular and current topics which belong to the temporal and civil sphere—subjects which our Lord has left to the free and calm discussion of men. I also know that a priest's lips must avoid all human, partisan controversy. He has to open them only to lead souls to God, to his saving doctrine and to the sacraments which Jesus Christ established, to the interior life which brings us closer to God, so that we see we are his children and therefore brothers to all men without exception.

We are celebrating today the feast of Christ the king. And I do not go outside my role as a priest when I say that if anyone saw Christ's kingdom in terms of a political program he would not have understood the supernatural purpose of the faith, and he would risk burdening consciences with weights which have nothing to do with Jesus, for his yoke is easy and his burden is light.[44] Let us really love all men; let us love Christ above all; and then we cannot avoid loving the rightful freedom of others, living in harmony with them.

SERENE AS CHILDREN OF GOD

But perhaps you will say: "People do not 185 want to hear this, much less put it into practice." I realize that. Freedom is a strong and healthy plant which does not grow well among stones and brambles or on the roadway, trodden under foot.[45] We learned that long before Christ came to the earth.

Do you remember the second psalm? "Why do the nations conspire, and the people plot in vain? The kings of the earth set themselves up and the rulers take council together, against the Lord and his anointed."[46] You see: nothing new. People opposed Christ, the anointed, even before he was born. They opposed him as he went his peaceable way along the roads of

---

[44] Mt 11:30.
[45] Cf. Lk 8:5-7.
[46] Ps 2:1-2.

Palestine; they persecuted him and continue to do so by attacking the members of his real and mystical body. Why so much hatred, why are people so easily taken in, why this universal smothering of the freedom of every conscience?

"Let us burst their bonds asunder and cast their yokes from us."[47] They break the mild yoke, they throw off their burden, a wonderful burden of holiness and justice, of grace and love and peace. Love makes them angry; they laugh at the gentle goodness of a God who will not call his legions of angels to his help.[48] If our Lord would only make a deal, if only he would sacrifice a few innocent people to satisfy a majority of blame-worthy people, there might be a chance of arriving at some understanding with him. But that's not the way God thinks. Our Father is a real father, he's ready to forgive thousands of evildoers if there are even ten just men.[49] People motivated by hatred cannot understand this mercy; they get more and more settled in their apparent earthly immunity, feeding on injustice.

[47] Ps 2:3.
[48] Cf. Jn 18:36; Mt 26:52-54.
[49] Cf. Gen 18:32.

"He who sits in the heavens laughs; the Lord holds them in derision. Then he will speak to them in his wrath, and terrify them in his fury."[50] How righteous is God's anger, how just his ire, and how great his clemency!

"I have been set as a king by him on Sion, his holy mountain, to tell of his decrees. The Lord said to me, 'You are my son, today I have begotten you'."[51] The kindness of God our Father has given us his Son for a king. When he threatens he becomes tender, when he says he is angry he gives us his love. "You are my son": this is addressed to Christ—and to you and me if we decide to become another Christ, Christ himself.

Words cannot go so far as the heart, which is moved by God's goodness. He says to us: "You are my son." Not a stranger, not a well-treated servant, not a friend—that would be a lot already. A son! He gives us free access to treat him as sons, with a son's piety and I would even say with the boldness and daring of a son whose Father cannot deny him anything.

[50] Ps 2:4-5.
[51] Ps 2:6-7.

186   True, many people are bent on injustice. But
the Lord insists: "Ask of me, and I will make
the nations your heritage, and the ends of the
earth your possession. You shall break them
with a rod of iron, and dash them in pieces like
a potter's vessel."[52] That is a strong promise,
and it's God who makes it. We cannot tone it
down. Not for nothing is Christ the redeemer
of the world; he rules as sovereign, at the right
hand of the Father. It is a terrifying announcement of what awaits each man when life is
over—for over it will be. When history comes
to an end, it will be the lot of all those whose
hearts have been hardened by evil and despair.

    But God, although he can conquer, prefers
to convince people: "Now therefore, O kings,
be wise; be warned, O rulers of the earth. Serve
the Lord with fear, with trembling kiss his feet,
lest he be angry, and you perish in the way;
for his wrath is quickly kindled."[53] Christ is the
Lord, the king. "And this is the message we
preach to you; there was a promise made to our
forefathers, and this promise God has redeemed
for our posterity, by raising Jesus to life. Thus,

[52] Ps 2:8-9.
[53] Ps 2:10-13.

it is written in the second psalm, 'You are my son, I have begotten you this day.'... Here is news for you, then, brethren; remission of your sins is offered to you through him. There are claims from which you could not be acquitted by the law of Moses, and whoever believes in Jesus is quit of all these. Beware, then, of incurring the prophets' rebuke: 'Look upon this, you scornful souls, and lose yourselves in astonishment. Such wonders I am doing in your days, that if a man told you the story you would not believe him'."[54]

This deed is the working of salvation, the kingdom of Christ in souls, the manifestation of the mercy of God. "Blessed are they who take refuge in him."[55] We Christians have the right to proclaim the royalty of Christ. Although injustice abounds, although many do not desire the kingdom of love, the work of salvation is taking place in the same human history that harbors evil.

[54] Acts 13:32-33; 38-41.
[55] Ps 2:13.

GOD'S ANGELS

187   "I know the thoughts that I think toward you, says the Lord, thoughts of peace and not of affliction."[56] Let us be men of peace, men of justice, doers of good, and our Lord will not be our judge, but our friend, our brother, our love.

On our happy way through the world we enjoy the company of the angels of God. "Before the birth of our redeemer," St Gregory the Great writes, "we had lost the friendship of the angels. Original sin and our daily sins had kept us away from their bright purity... But ever since the moment we acknowledged our king, the angels have recognized us as their fellow citizens.

"And seeing that the king of heaven wished to take on our earthly flesh, the angels no longer shun our misery. They do not dare consider as inferior to their own this nature which they adore in the person of the king of heaven; there it is, raised up above them; they have now no difficulty in regarding man as companion."[57]

---

[56] Jer 29:11.
[57] *In Evangelia homiliae*, 8, 2 (PL 76, 1104).

Mary, the holy Mother of our king, the queen of our heart, looks after us as only she knows how. Mother of mercy, throne of grace: we ask you to help us compose, verse by verse, the simple poem of charity in our own life and the lives of the people around us; it is "like a river of peace."[58] For you are a sea of inexhaustible mercy: "All streams run to the sea, but the sea is never full."[59]

---

[58] Is 66:12: *Quasi fluvium pacis.*
[59] Eccles 1:7.

INDEX TO QUOTATIONS FROM SCRIPTURE

(References are to the numbered sections of the text.)

INDEX TO QUOTATIONS
FROM FATHERS AND DOCTORS
OF THE CHURCH, DOCUMENTS
OF THE MAGISTERIUM,
LITURGICAL TEXTS ETC.

(References are to the numbered sections of the text.)

SUBJECT INDEX

(References are to the numbered sections of the text.)